THE RESOURCEFUL SELF

The Resourceful Self

And a Little Child Shall Lead Them

Donald Capps

CASCADE *Books* · Eugene, Oregon

THE RESOURCEFUL SELF
And a Little Child Shall Lead Them

Cascade Books
An Imprint of Wipf and Stock Publishers
199 W. 8th Ave., Suite 3
Eugene, OR 97401

www.wipfandstock.com

ISBN 13: 978-1-62564-741-2

Cataloguing-in-Publication data:

Capps, Donald.

The resourceful self : and a little child shall lead them / Donald Capps.

xiv + 204 p. ; 23 cm. Includes bibliographical references and index.

ISBN 13: 978-1-62564-741-2

1. Erikson, Erik H. (Erik Homberger), 1902–1994. 2. Freud, Sigmund, 1856–1939.
3. Melancholy. 4. Mothers and sons. 5. Psychology—Religious. 6. Pastoral Care. I. Title.

BL53 C267 2014

Manufactured in the U.S.A.   09/25/2014

Contents

Preface

Some years ago, I taught a course on men and their psychological issues and challenges. The class was predominantly made of men. One week the topic was fathers and we had a very spirited discussion. The following week the topic was mothers and no one had much to say. There was some shuffling of feet, heads were down, and no one volunteered to talk until one of the women in the class offered a few thoughts about mothers. After class, a few of the male students apologized to me for the class's lethargy, and after they left the classroom another male student told me that he didn't speak up because there were women in the class and he didn't think they would like what he had to say about his own mother.

When Erik Erikson's writings were becoming popular in the 1950s and 1960s, students would often be informed by their professors that a major difference between Erikson and Freud was that Freud didn't have much to say about mothers and their role in the developmental process, but that Erikson did. Professors pointed out that Erikson devoted a great deal of attention to the relationship between the infant and the mother and emphasized how important this relationship was to the child's ongoing development. What these professors did not tell their students in the 1950s and '60s is that what Erikson had to say about mothers was not always complimentary. In fact, because they focused almost exclusively on the relationship between the infant and the mother, they gave the impression that Erikson's view of mothers was idealized (and often commended him for this).

This book is an attempt to set the record straight. It shows that Erikson's view of mothers was far more complex than it has been popularly represented to be. In setting the record straight, this book treads on rather dangerous ground because, as the ominous silence in my class that day suggests, there is a cultural taboo against talking about mothers except in highly idealized ways (especially on Mother's Day). I believe, however, that Erikson's writings about the relationship between the small child and the mother are as relevant today as they were when they were written, and that a major reason for their relevance is that they show how children develop into resourceful individuals precisely because their relationships with their mothers are not without their difficulties.

As I note in chapter 1, this is not a book about blaming mothers. In fact, as we will see, the difficulties that begin to emerge in the relationship between small children and their mothers is due to a large extent to the fact that the children are becoming more independent as a direct consequence of their physical, mental, and emotional development. I talk a lot about the emergence of the melancholy self in this book as I believe that the word *melancholy* expresses how the child feels about these emerging difficulties. I think that this word also captures the mood of the class the day we were supposed to be discussing mothers. I realize that the word *melancholy* has a certain heaviness about it that may for some readers be immediately off-putting. But I find the word useful because it has several connotations—sadness, gloominess, pensiveness, irritability, anger—and for this very reason invites the reader to reflect on which of them may be more relevant to his or her experience than others. Also, the word *melancholy* has a history within the psychoanalytic tradition itself, and, as the introduction shows, provides an important link between Sigmund Freud and Erik Erikson.

However, this book is not primarily about melancholy. As the formal structure of Erikson's life-cycle schema indicates, he viewed the ongoing development of the individual as a continuing struggle between life-enhancing and life-diminishing qualities, and contended that there should be a certain ratio favoring the former over the latter. If we assume that *melancholy* is essentially a life-diminishing quality, then we need to identify the quality that stands over against it, and a word that seems especially appropriate is *resourcefulness*.

Erikson used the word *resourceful* in the Preface to *Young Man Luther*. Here he notes that he had originally intended that his study of Luther would be a chapter in a book on emotional crises in late adolescence and early adulthood, but "Luther proved too bulky a man to be merely a chapter."[1] The other chapters would have focused on young persons who were his patients at Austen Riggs Center, where he had been a member of the staff since 1952. He goes on to note in the preface that "any comparison made between young man Luther and our patients is, for their sake as well as his, not restricted to psychiatric diagnosis and the analysis of pathological dynamics, but is oriented toward those moments when young patients, like young beings anywhere, prove resourceful and insightful beyond all professional and

1. Erikson, *Young Man Luther*, 7.

personal expectation."[2] Thus, his book on Luther "will concentrate on the powers of recovery in the young ego."[3] It is reasonable to assume, therefore, that Erikson would have no objections to the emphasis that I am placing here on the *resourceful self*.

The dictionary defines *resourcefulness* as the ability to deal effectively and creatively with problems, difficulties, etc.[4] In light of Erikson's insistence that his life-cycle schema is a *psychosocial* one, it is noteworthy that *resource* applies both to a source of strength or ability within oneself (an *inner* resource) and to anything or any one person to which one can turn for aid in time of need or emergency (an *external* resource). My purpose here is not to suggest that this polarity between *melancholy* and *resourcefulness* might replace any of the polarities that comprise Erikson's life-cycle model, nor would I be so bold as to claim that the polarity between melancholy and resourcefulness underlies these other polarities. It is sufficient to claim that the polarity between melancholy and resourcefulness is an enduring life-theme with origins in early childhood and that it plays a central role in the realization of one's potentialities and aspirations.

Finally, since the dictionary defines *resourcefulness* as not only the ability to deal *effectively* but also *creatively* with problems, difficulties, and the like, this book reflects the fact that Erikson aspired to become an artist before he became a psychoanalyst. Several months after his death on May 12, 1994, I wrote Joan M. Erikson, his wife, asking her what she felt to be the most significant aspects of his work. She replied on February 20, 1995: "About Erik's way of looking at things, it is important to stress—always— that he was an artist." The phrase "way of looking at things" is from the concluding chapter of *Childhood and Society*, where Erikson concedes "that whatever message has not been conveyed by my description and discourse has but a slim chance of being furthered by a formal conclusion. I have nothing to offer except a way of looking at things."[5] His way of looking at things was the artist's way: with imagination, a feeling for form and a sense that there is usually more—but sometimes less—than meets the eye.

Now, for a few words about the structure of the book: In chapters 1 and 2 I discuss the melancholy self. Chapter 1 draws on Freud's understanding of melancholia, and then moves to Erikson's thoughts on melancholia as he presents them in *Young Man Luther*. It concludes with a brief account of Erikson's personal life, noting that the circumstances of his early childhood

2. Ibid., 8.

3. Ibid.

4. Agnes, *New World College Dictionary*, 121.

5. Erikson, *Childhood and Society* (original version), 359.

would make him especially vulnerable to the formation of a melancholy self. Chapter 2 focuses on Freud's psychobiographical study of Leonardo da Vinci and suggests that two of the themes that Freud highlights in this study—dual mothers and artistic inhibition—are applicable to Erikson as well. This chapter supports the view presented in chapter 1 that Erikson was especially vulnerable to the formation of a melancholy self, but it also suggests that the very makings of a resourceful self were the consequence of da Vinci's struggles with the effects of the melancholy self. Chapter 3 focuses on Erikson's essay in *Insight and Responsibility* titled "Human Strength and the Cycle of Generations"[6] and suggests that the virtues or human strengths whose development he assigns to the infancy and to early and late childhood stages of the life cycle are the foundation for the resourceful self and its development.

Chapters 4–7 focus on resources that Erikson discusses in his writings. I call them "primordial" because they exist at or from the beginning of life. These chapters will take us on a journey, as it were, through selected writings of Erikson's from 1931 to 1977. Chapter 4 on humor and chapter 5 on play focus especially on children and the positive use that they make of these two resources. Chapter 6 on dreams deals with adolescents and young adults and the role that dreams play in helping them to find their way in life. Chapter 7 centers on hope, the first of the virtues or human strengths in Erikson's life-cycle model, and suggests that the paternal voice may play a critical role in sustaining the hopefulness that develops in the mother-infant relationship.

The epilogue draws upon Erikson's late essay about Jesus and suggests that Jesus addressed the melancholy of the men who became his disciples by assuming the role of the reassuring mother. The epilogue also suggests that Jesus exemplified the self-reconciliation that we all desire, one form of which is the reconciliation of our melancholy and resourceful selves. Most important, the epilogue centers on Jesus's admonition to adults that they become like children. The central argument of this book is that the resourceful self has its origins in childhood: hence the subtitle—"And a Little Child Shall Lead Them."

Finally, I would like to note that this book is a sequel to my *At Home in the World.*[7] In the earlier book I discussed the fact that although the emotional separation of boys from their mothers in early childhood enables them to connect with their father and their father's world, this separation also produces a melancholic reaction of sadness and sense of loss.

6. Erikson, *Insight and Responsibility,* 109–57.

7. Capps, *At Home in the World.*

Realizing that they cannot return to their original maternal environment, men, whether knowingly or not, embark on a lifelong search for a sense of being at home in the world. Thus, the earlier book focused on the ways men engage in this search, and centered especially on the work of artists. *The Resourceful Self* is also concerned with the melancholy self that develops in early childhood, but rather than elaborating the ways men seek to alleviate its negative effects, it argues that another self develops at the same time: a self that I call the resourceful self. Thus, this book addresses the same issue as the earlier one, but it has a different focus. Whereas *At Home in the World* centered on the world beyond the maternal environment, this book focuses on the inherent strengths that children possess and develop. Also, while it is concerned with the emotional separation that occurs in early childhood between the mother and her son, it also considers ways in which this separation is overcome or reversed, and ways in which the father and other paternal figures are a helpful resource. I view these two ways of coping with the emotional separation of mother and child as complementary. Thus, in offering two ways of looking at the issue, the books hopefully support the popular adage that two eyes are better than one.

Acknowledgments

I want to thank the editorial team at Cascade Books for their support, including K. C. Hanson, editor-in-chief; Jim Tedrick, managing editor; Matthew Wimer, assistant managing editor; Jeremy Funk, copy editor; and Ian Creeger, typesetter. I would also like to express my appreciation to James Stock, marketing director; and Amanda Wehner, marketing coordinator.

This book reflects my continuing indebtedness to Erik H. Erikson, to whom I was introduced as a divinity-school student in the early 1960s. Now, some fifty years later, it is difficult to imagine what my life and work would have been like had I not become acquainted with his writings. Later, I also became acquainted with Erik Erikson and his wife, Joan Erikson. Readers of books often wonder what their authors are really like, and, most important, whether there is a congruence or consistency between the person and the author. My several encounters with Erik Erikson were deeply confirmatory in this regard. In fact, his ability to put me at ease in his presence and his openness to what I wanted to say enabled me to understand, in a new way, what it must have been like for young men and women to meet and talk with Jesus. It is my hope that this book conveys not only the ideas but also the living spirit of Erik Erikson.

I

Reconciling Selves

1

The Melancholy Self

In my book *Men, Religion, and Melancholia* I focused on four authors—all men—who wrote texts that have been central to the course I teach on the psychology of religion.[1] These men and their texts are William James, author of *The Varieties of Religious Experience*; Rudolf Otto, author of *The Idea of the Holy*; C. G. Jung, who wrote *Answer to Job*; and Erik H. Erikson, who authored *Young Man Luther*.[2] I use these texts in my course on psychology of religion because viewed together they provide students with a sense of what counts as important work in the psychology of religion, of what its major preoccupations have been, and of how the psychology of religion has been shaped by modern Western religion, reflecting its preoccupations.

I also suggest to students that they read these four books as, in a sense, autobiographical, because the four authors appear to be writing about issues that concern them personally. Unlike most texts—and certainly textbooks—in the psychology of religion, these four seem to have been written with considerable self-investment. Their authors were not simply writing *about* religion but struggling to articulate their own stake in religion, its personal meaning and significance for them. While these books are not overtly autobiographical, I suggest nonetheless that we look for what Erikson calls "the sense of 'I'" in them,[3] to discern the ways each author locates himself in the text. What makes this proposal natural is that I always start the class

1. Capps, *Men, Religion, and Melancholia*.

2. James, *The Varieties of Religious Experience*; Otto, *The Idea of the Holy*; Jung, *Answer to Job*; Erikson, *Young Man Luther*.

3. Erikson, "The Galilean Sayings and the Sense of 'I.'"

with James's *Varieties* and point out that James included autobiographical material in his chapter "The Sick Soul" but concealed his identity, so that his original readers may not have known that the account was his own.[4] This serves to illustrate my point that the authors are *in* their texts, but often surreptitiously or in disguise.

This illustration, however, enables me to make another, related point. James begins his autobiographical account with the claim that "the worst kind of melancholy is that which takes the form of panic fear," and suggests that the case he is about to relate is "an excellent example."[5] Over the years leading up to the writing of *Men, Religion, and Melancholia*, I had been slowly evolving an argument that I presented in the book alongside the four authors' own arguments regarding religion, one that derived from the view that these texts reflected the personal interests and struggles of their authors. This argument consisted of two interrelated points. The first is that each author was struggling with the relationship between religion and psychopathology, but, more specifically, the psychopathology they knew as *melancholy*. For reasons that I made clear in the course of the book, I indicated my preference for the word *melancholy* over the more contemporary term *depression*. I also suggested that when one discovers the "sense of 'I'" in these texts, one finds that this is a melancholic I, one that is acquainted not only with sadness and a sense of loss but also with feelings of abandonment, despair, rage, fury, and perhaps even hate.

The second interrelated point of my argument was that the melancholy may be traced, ultimately, to the author's relationship with his own mother. The sadness, despair, and rage characteristic of melancholy have an object, and in these four cases this object is the author's mother. This point is more difficult to establish, as none of the authors writes about his relationship to his mother. But this, I suggest to students, is precisely where their own capacities as psychologists of religion come in. It becomes their task to try to understand how religion serves as a stand-in for the mother, or for the son's relationship to his mother, and how, within his mature views on religion, there is a personal prehistory, as it were, that has to do with this relationship. Thus, a book in the psychology of religion needs to be read psychologically, and one way to do this is to read it as a text in which the author is searching in religion for the lost object who is his natural mother as he experienced her in infancy and the earliest years of childhood. An assumption that lies behind this argument is that one would not have become so personally

---

4. James, *The Varieties of Religious Experience*, 149–51.
5. Ibid., 149.

invested in religion had one not experienced as a child the emotional loss of one's intimate relationship with one's mother.

I also argued that for these four authors this emotional loss of their intimate relationship with their mothers when they were small boys had complications that, while not unique, are not necessarily the experience of all children. There were traumas associated with the loss that were perhaps more severe, or more deeply felt, than is usually the case. A commonplace of the developmental literature is talk about the boy's separation from his mother in early childhood, and it is typically noted that the boy's separation may be more decisive or thoroughgoing than the girl's, as he needs to achieve gender differentiation from his mother and to identify with his father instead. Thus, separation is assumed, and it is considered normal, therefore, that all boys will feel a sense of loss. But I believe that this natural separation process was more traumatic for these four boys than is normally the case (for example, Jung's mother was hospitalized for several months when he was three years old), and that the trauma of separation disposed these four boys to melancholia, on the one hand, and toward a certain receptivity to religion, on the other.

In *Men, Religion, and Melancholia*, I suggested that the boy experiences in fact two losses in this regard. One is that the boy experiences a loss of his mother: even though she is still present, and the two of them continue to relate to each other, he has in a sense lost the mother he had previously experienced, the mother who held him close and made no effort to help him achieve the separation. The other loss concerns himself as the boy who has lived in the aura of his mother's unmitigated love and has experienced himself as her beloved son. In the process of separation, this self-image proves untenable and altogether too simplistic. The boy finds it necessary to separate from the original boy so as to become a different boy, a boy who will not take his mother's unmitigated love for granted. The new boy feels—and rightly so—that his mother's love now needs to be earned, that her love is no longer an unconditional love. If the separation is fraught with unusual anxiety, the loss both of his original mother and of his original self will create a disposition toward melancholia.

I believe that Erik Erikson is correct when he observes that young adulthood allows for a return to one's origins, and especially for a revisiting of the separation process, in search of grounds for trust and reassurance. At this time, the fact of the young man's disposition to melancholia may become evident to himself, whether or not he uses the actual word *melancholia*. He discovers within himself an unexplainable sadness, exacerbated, but not fully accounted for, by broken relationships, difficulties in finding what he wants to do with his life, and so on. He also discovers within himself a silent anger, even rage, he did not know was there, and he has great difficulty understanding its source, because the frustrations he encounters in his struggle to come into his own do not seem to warrant such depth of feeling, such negative affect. However, the way he now relates to his mother, if she is still living, is a clue to its source, as he has feelings toward her that are disproportionate to her actual provocations. Such feelings are rooted, I suggest, in the early separation process, when he lost her unconditional love, and experienced the unbridgeable gulf that separated him from the child he was before the separation.

The argument that I am making here raises an issue that needs to be addressed with the utmost sensitivity. At the time I was writing *Men, Religion, and Melancholia*, various authors were cautioning us against the tendency of an earlier generation of psychologists to blame mothers for whatever may have gone wrong in a child's formation. While her role in such formation is certainly formidable, the tendency to blame mothers for "poor outcomes" (however defined) was being challenged—and appropriately so, for we know so little about what makes a child turn out well or badly. This explicit or implicit attack on mothers was being recognized for what it was: a social and cultural prejudice against women and against the social involvements and responsibilities typically associated with women. Also, as all four of the male authors discussed in the book had succeeded in life, the issue of where to place the blame was, in a sense, beside the point.

Yet, the issue of blame could not be so easily dismissed, because it had importance *within* the mother-son relationship itself. Whether mothers are to blame for how their boys turn out was, in my view, a nonissue, a fallacy I did not wish to perpetuate. But the issue of blame was a very important one in terms of the relationship between *this* mother and *this* son, as there *is* explicit or implicit blame in the very ways these four authors wrote about their mothers or in the ways they related to their mothers in later years. Moreover, the issue of who is to blame is at the very core of the melancholic condition, for, as Freud makes clear in his famous essay "Mourning and Melancholia," the core issue in melancholia is that the sufferer has a "plaint" against another, that is, the lost object.[6] Rightly or wrongly, legitimately or not, the sufferer blames his mother for his plight or, if he finds it too threatening to cast blame on her, he internalizes the blame in the form of *self*-reproach.

Melancholia, then, is a condition in which the sons cannot bring themselves to blame directly the one against whom they have a grievance but instead internalize the object of blame and punish that aspect of the self with which the object is now identified. In a sense, this is a very reasonable

6. Freud, "Mourning and Melancholia," 169.

thing to do. In *Young Man Luther*, Erik Erikson discusses William James's portrayal of melancholy in *The Varieties of Religious Experience*. Here Erikson notes that the growing child feels guilty over the fact that he employs his gradually maturing organs and his muscular growth in the service of his autonomous strivings.[7] Thus, if his mother is devoting herself to the project of helping her boy become independent in order that her son will identify with persons of his own gender, the boy is also initiating his own bid for autonomy. Attributing the loss of his original relationship with his mother to his own actions instead of his mother's enables him to repress his feelings of having been ill treated by the mother he thought he knew and whose unconditional love he enjoyed prior to the separation.

FREUD'S "MOURNING AND MELANCHOLIA"

In *Men, Religion, and Melancholia*, I devoted several pages to a discussion of Freud's essay "Mourning and Melancholia." A reprisal of this discussion is necessary here because it provides the basis for the argument of this book : that melancholia is the condition out of which the resourceful self emerges. In "Mourning and Melancholia," Freud explores the similarities and differences between the normal grieving process ("mourning") and the psychopathology known to the psychiatric community of his day as "melancholia." He warns that this exploration may not bear much fruit, in part because the psychiatric definition of *melancholia* is so uncertain. Yet he believes that a correlation between mourning and melancholia is justified because they have the same cause: Both are reactions to the loss of someone or something that was deeply loved. We assume that mourning will end and that the loss will be overcome in the normal course of time, whereas melancholia is a pathological condition that may require medical treatment. How to account for these very different outcomes?

In Freud's view, the distinguishing features of melancholia are a profoundly painful dejection, diminished interest in the outside world, loss of the capacity to love, inhibition of all activity, and a lowering of one's self-regarding feelings to such a degree that one engages in self-reproach and self-reviling, often culminating in a delusional expectation of punishment. Many of these characteristics also occur in mourning. But in the mourning process, there is little if any of the self-reproach invariably present in melancholia. Nor is there the anticipation of impending punishment. In mourning, the loss is deeply painful, yet it is experienced not as punishment but as integral to life itself.

7. Erikson, *Young Man Luther*, 120–22.

Why this loss of self-esteem in melancholia? Why this self-abasement? Why this "delusional belittling" of self? Why this expectation of punishment and chastisement? That some of this self-criticism is justified cannot be doubted. After all, the patient is as lacking in interest and as incapable of love and of any achievement as he says he is. Moreover, in his self-criticisms, he has a keener eye for truth than do those who are not given to melancholia; for others cling to views of themselves and human nature that are much too positive and sanguine. The issue, however, is not whether the melancholy person's distressing self-abasement is justified in the opinion of others but whether he is in fact correctly describing not only his experience of himself but also the underlying reasons for it. If he has lost his self-respect, which seems to be the case, is there some good reason for this, as he seems to believe there is? This, and not others' objective assessment of him, is the issue, and the more he protests that he has lost his self-respect for good and unassailable reasons, the emptier these self-assessments seem to be.

Given his loss of self-esteem, it might seem as though melancholia is the very antithesis of grief: for grief involves the loss of an object in the external world, whereas melancholia involves the loss of self. But, says Freud, this difference is only apparent, and further probing reveals why. Like the griever, the melancholy person has experienced the painful loss of a loved object. But while the griever mourns the loss of the loved object who has been taken from him, the melancholy person experiences the loss of the object with considerable ambivalence, as he feels that the loss he is now having to endure is the object's own fault; he feels that the object has abandoned him. This, however, is not a feeling that he can openly acknowledge, because the feeling of abandonment is more painful than the feeling, in grief, of bereavement, where the loved one has been taken away against her will. So, the reproachful feelings he has toward the lost object are turned against himself. The lost object is not relinquished and released, as in grief, but is internalized, becoming an aspect of the ego, so that the ego itself becomes the focus of reproach, the focus of delusions of future punishment.

Freud suggests that this is how conscience comes to be created. Reproaches against the external object are redirected against the self. Thus, in the clinical picture of melancholia, dissatisfaction with the self on moral grounds is by far its most outstanding feature, and the self-criticism much less frequently involves bodily infirmity, physical appearance, or feelings of social inferiority. By viewing the self-reproaches of melancholy persons as the reproach of the lost object turned against the self, Freud suggests that another puzzling feature of melancholia becomes more understandable. This feature centers on the fact that the melancholy person exhibits little if any signs of shame before others. We would assume that anyone who genuinely feels himself to be worthless would shrink from the gaze of others. But this is not the case with melancholy persons. On the contrary, they perpetually take offense and behave as if they have been treated with great injustice. These reactions and behaviors are indicative of the fact that the melancholy person's underlying attitude is one of revolt expressed through vengeful feelings toward the lost object. His revenge, Freud suggests, is the pathology itself. His illness is the means by which he torments the one who has forsaken him. Such tormenting of the other is possible because, unlike a person being mourned (who is dead), the person who occasioned the injury to the melancholy person's feelings—the person against whom his illness is aimed—is usually nearby, in the neighborhood, so to speak, and, most likely, a family member. Thus, the melancholy person's relationship to the lost object has a twofold fate: the internalization of the object, which then takes the form of self-reproach, and the punishment inflicted on the actual object by means of the pathology itself.

As a therapist, Freud takes great interest in the question of whether or not melancholia is curable. He notes that melancholia is more complicated than mourning because the lost object evokes such highly ambivalent feelings. Therefore, the melancholy person experiences many single conflicts in which love and hate wrestle together. Also, unlike in mourning, where the object is finally relinquished, in melancholia the release of the object is greatly complicated because the object has become so self-identified, which means that the melancholy person is unconscious of the causes of his pathology. On the other hand, just as the work of grief enables the ego to give up the object in time, so in melancholia each single conflict in which ambivalent feelings wrestle together loosens the fixation to the object. Thus, it is possible for the process in the unconscious to come to an end, either because the fury has spent itself, or because the object is abandoned as no longer having value. Which of these two possibilities is the more typical one in bringing the melancholia to an end is impossible to determine. What seems indisputable, however, is that the melancholia ends as the sufferer experiences the sense that he is superior to the object, thus indicating that reproach of the other was in some sense justified.

It is important to keep in mind that the object in the case of melancholia is the internalized other, who bears only a partial resemblance to the other in real life. The struggle is an internalized one, in which the ego (or *I*) wrestles ambivalently, experiencing both love and hate, with the internalized other. That the struggle is internal helps to explain why the melancholy person typically experiences symptoms both of mania and of depletion. The mania is usually associated with the sense of triumph over the internalized other while the depletion is the sense that the ego is weak and unable to hold its own against the superior power of the internalized other. When the ego feels strong, it has the ability to "slay" the object, bringing the melancholia itself to an end. Therapeutically speaking, the goal is to strengthen the ego so that it may defeat the internalized object, thus achieving, in an admittedly violent manner, what grief accomplishes without the need for violence.

Although Freud does not identify the lost object as the mother, the very intensity of the melancholic reaction suggests that she, the boy's first love object, is the object who has been lost. This would explain, for example, why one important feature of melancholia is its role in the formation of a conscience and in the fear of punishment for wrongdoing. The melancholia has roots in the boy's belief that he has done something to warrant the loss of his mother's unconditional love: that if he makes certain reparations and promises to amend his ways, he might then win her back. Because, for reasons of gender differentiation, the son's separation from his mother is more decisive than the daughter's, he is also more likely to form a false conscience, one more delusional as to his own personal culpability for the initial separation and the failure to restore the original relationship.

If the mother is the original lost object, all subsequent experiences of loss for reasons other than death (where grieving is possible) will be reminiscent of the loss of the boy's original relationship with his mother and will evoke similar feelings of shame and rage, guilt, and remorse. These subsequent losses may involve other persons (for example, women with whom he falls in love) or desires symbolically linked to his mother (for example, the desire to pursue a career in art, music, or caregiving). To assert that the lost object is the mother—that is, the mother who had nothing but love for her son—is therefore consistent with Freud's analysis of melancholia. Melancholia is a reaction to the palpable fact that this object has been taken away, replaced by a mother whose love is perceived *not* to be unconditional but dependent on the son's capacity and willingness to be a certain kind of boy, one whom only she is in the position to declare acceptable to her. To regain the lost object, he will do whatever is in his power to make himself acceptable in her eyes. He promises to be good, and tries valiantly to keep this solemn promise.

While all this is going on at the conscious or preconscious level, something else entirely is occurring unconsciously, outside his conscious awareness. The lost object—the mother who has nothing but love for her son—is internalized, and this object now becomes the focus of his ambivalent feelings of love and hate. He loves the perfect mother, the mother of his fondest and most beautiful visions, but he also detests her, because she has betrayed and forsaken him, and in so doing, has caused the demise of his image of himself as inherently good and admirable. His struggle with her may continue indefinitely, even long after the mother of real flesh and blood is dead and mourned.

Given the role that conscience and fear of future punishment play in melancholia, the paradigmatic experience that triggers this plunge into melancholia is the mother's punishment of her son for misbehavior. But although this punishment scenario may be paradigmatic, other experiences may serve as catalysts for the shattering of the perfect image of his mother. In fact, where melancholy seems especially pronounced or intractable, we should look for other experiential causes besides the punishment scenario, or some combination of punishment and other factors, such as his mother's prolonged physical absence, her preferential treatment of a sibling, or a situation where she appears to her son to place her own self-interests ahead of his, as when she accedes to his father's beating him lest she be beaten herself.

ERIKSON'S REFLECTIONS ON MELANCHOLIA

Unlike Freud, Erikson did not write an article on melancholia. But, as I noted above, he devoted a few pages of *Young Man Luther* to the topic. His study of Martin Luther focuses especially on Luther's relationship to his father. But he also considers Luther's relationship to his mother and relates melancholia to the mother-child relationship. Erikson acknowledges that relatively little is known about Luther's mother. What *is* known, however, indicates that in contrast to his father, who "seems to have been standoffish and suspicious toward the universe," his mother "was more interested in the imaginative aspects of superstition."[8] This fact leads Erikson to surmise that Luther may have received from his mother "a more pleasurable and more sensual attitude toward nature, and a more simply integrated kind of mysticism, such as he later found described by certain mystics." Erikson also notes that historians have guessed that she "suffered under the father's personality, and gradually became embittered," and that "a certain sad isolation which characterized young Luther was to be found also in his mother, who is said to have sung to him a ditty: 'For me and you nobody cares. That is our common fault.'"[9]

Aware if the paucity of information about Luther's mother, Erikson acknowledges that "a big gap exists here, which only conjecture could fill," but

> Instead of conjecturing half-heartedly, I will state, as a clinician's judgment, that nobody could speak and sing as Luther did if his

8. Erikson, *Young Man Luther,* 72.
9. Ibid., 72.

mother's voice did not sing to him of some heaven; that nobody
could be as torn between his masculine and his feminine sides,
nor have such a range of both, who did not at one time feel that
he was like his mother; but also, that nobody would discuss
women and marriage in the way he often did who had not been
deeply disappointed by his mother.[10]

He cites in this connection Luther's comment that when he was a boy his
mother whipped him "for stealing a nut until the blood came," then added
that such "strict discipline drove me to a monastery although she meant it
well."[11] Erikson wonders if she was acting on his father's behalf or acting
on her own initiative. As for Luther's related comment that he entered the
monastery against the will of his father, his mother, God and the devil, did
she object to his decision on her own or in deference to one or more of the
other objectors? It is impossible to know, but what is clear, in Erikson's view,
is that something went awry in Luther's relations with his mother, and this
happened at an early age.

Erikson suggests that Luther later found in the Bible, especially the
Psalms, a resource to compensate for this loss of intimacy with his mother.
He suggests that "in the Bible Luther at last found a mother whom he could
acknowledge: he could attribute to the Bible a generosity to which he could
open himself, and which he could pass on to others, at last a mother's son."[12]
Erikson also notes in the epilogue that religions help to awaken "dim nostalgias," and that one of these is

> the simple and fervent wish for a hallucinatory sense of unity
> with a maternal matrix, and a supply of benevolently powerful
> substances; it is symbolized by the affirmative face of charity,
> graciously inclined, reassuring the faithful of the unconditional
> acceptance of those who will return to the bosom.[13]

Suggesting that the maternal estrangement evoking this wish for unity occurred in the second stage of life—that of "autonomy vs. shame and doubt,"[14]
Erikson adds that in this symbol of the affirmative face of charity "the split
of autonomy is forever repaired: shame is healed by unconditional approval,
doubt by the eternal presence of generous provision."[15] Clearly, in his view,

10. Ibid., 72–73.

11. Ibid., 64.

12. Ibid., 208.

13. Ibid., 263–64.

14. Erikson, *Childhood and Society*, rev. ed., 251–54.

15. Erikson, *Young Man Luther*, 264.

something went wrong for Luther in the second stage of life, the stage corresponding to the child's second and third year.[16]

How did this estrangement between mother and child occur? What precipitated it? Erikson poses this very question about halfway through *Young Man Luther*, in his chapter titled "Allness or Nothingness." Here he asks: "But what destroyed our infantile past, and what destroys in the depth of our adult present, the original unity which provides the imagery of our supreme hopes?" The answer, according to "all religions and most philosophers," is the human will—"the mere will to live, thoughtless and cruel self-will."[17] In support of this view, he quotes two full paragraphs on melancholia from William James's chapter on the sick soul in *The Varieties of Religious Experience*.[18] I will not quote these paragraphs here but simply note Erikson's observation that the mood they evoke is that of "severe melancholy"; Erikson adds that James "is clinically and genetically correct, when he connects the horror of the *devouring* will to live with the content and disposition of melancholia," for, in melancholia, "it is the human being's horror of his own avaricious and sadistic morality which he tires of, withdraws from, wishes often to end even by putting an end to himself."[19]

Then, Erikson relates this devouring will to live to the developmental stages of life. He points out that the devouring will for life does not surface in "the orality of the first, the toothless and dependent stage," but in "the tooth-stage and all that develops within it, especially the pre-stages of what later becomes 'biting' human conscience."[20] In effect, this is the second stage of the life cycle, of autonomy vs. shame and doubt. Continuing his reflections on the tooth stage, Erikson suggests that, on the face of it, there would seem to be "no intrinsic reason for man's feeling more guilty or more evil because he employs, enjoys, and learns to adapt his gradually maturing organs, were it not for the basic division of good and bad which, in some dark way, establishes itself very early."[21]

Thus, even as the image of a paradise of perfect innocence is part of the past of the human species, so too is this sense of the division of good and evil a part of the past of each and every individual. In fact, the individual's loss of this paradise of innocence is analogous to the loss of paradise for the species. In the case of the species, "paradise was lost when man, not satisfied

16. Erikson, *Identity and the Life Cycle*, rev. ed., 67–77.

17. Erikson, *Young Man Luther*, 120.

18. James, *The Varieties of Religious Experience*, 163–65.

19. Erikson, *Young Man Luther*, 121.

20. Ibid.

21. Ibid.

with an arrangement in which he could pluck from the trees all he needed for upkeep, wanted more, wanted to have and to know the forbidden—and bit into it," and thus "came to know good and evil." After that, he was condemned to work by the sweat of his brow, but "he also began to invent tools in order to wrest from nature what it would not just give." In other words, "he became autonomous at the price of shame and gained independent initiative at the price of guilt."[22] Note, here, that Erikson introduces the psychodynamic conflict of the third stage of the life cycle (initiative vs. guilt).

However, because the nurturing mother is the initial victim of the growing child's ability and urgent need to bite, the greatest price one pays for this expression of autonomy is the loss of the original unity with the nurturing mother—the person whom the child had earlier experienced as "the affirmative face of charity, graciously inclined," the person who represented to the child the very reassurance of "unconditional acceptance."[23] Now, the child knows that there are strings attached to that acceptance, and in addition to the emergence of gradually maturing organs one experiences the emergence of a conscience—an accusatory voice—deep inside oneself.

Perhaps it is not surprising therefore that Luther recalls having been whipped by his mother for stealing a single nut. To be sure, he wanted what was forbidden—the word *stole* suggests as much—but he feels that the punishment by a severe whipping resulting in bleeding was excessive. He does not deny that he did wrong. At the same time, he questions the adults' moral code, and, no doubt, begins to notice their own violations of this moral code and the fact that many such violations go unpunished.

Consistent with his suggestion in *Young Man Luther* that it is "the *devouring* will to live" that destroys the original unity with the nurturing mother of one's infantile past, Erikson later, in *Insight and Responsibility*, identified *will* as the human strength that develops in the second stage of the life cycle. He defines *will* as "the unbroken determination to exercise free choice as well as self-restraint, in spite of the unavoidable experiences of shame and doubt in infancy," and suggests that the challenge the *will* poses for parents is how to help the child acquire "a measure of self-control" while learning "to control willfulness, to offer willingness, and to exchange good will."[24] But, he adds, no matter how successful the parents may be in this regard,

> In the end the self-image of the child will prove to have been
> split in the way in which man is apt to remain split for the rest of
> his life. For even as the ideal ("pre-ambivalent," as we say) image

22. Ibid.
23. Ibid., 264.
24. Erikson, *Insight and Responsibility*, 119.

of the loving mother brought with it the child's self-image as reflecting that mother's true recognition of the child as hers and as good, so does the ambivalently loved image of the controlling parent correspond to an ambivalently loved self, or rather selves. From here on, the able and the impotent, the loving and the angry, the unified and the self-contradictory selves will be a part of man's equipment: truly a psychic fall from grace.[25]

Thus, with the emergence of the *will* in early childhood, the threat of maternal estrangement becomes a reality. But so does the sense of *self*-estrangement, of being at odds with—or within—oneself.

ERIKSON'S "SENSE OF 'I'"

To this point, I have painted a rather dark if not hopeless picture of the human condition as reflected in the writings of Freud and Erikson on melancholia. Now, however, I want to draw on a very important point that Erikson makes in *Identity, Youth, and Crisis* in the section headed "I, My Self, and My Ego"[26] in his chapter titled "Theoretical Interlude." He is concerned here with the "sense of 'I'" to which I alluded earlier. He notes that the very idea of the *I* and what it means or entails has been discussed at length by philosophers and psychologists, and that these discussions reveal how obscure this subject can be. He also notes that persons who work with autistic children know how desperately these children struggle to grasp the meaning of saying "I," because "language presupposes the experience of a coherent 'I.'"[27] He also notes that persons who work, as he does, with deeply disturbed young people are often confronted with the awful awareness that the patient is unable to *feel* the *I* that is cognitively present but evokes little if any emotional reaction or response. Freud's description of the symptoms of the melancholic patient in "Mourning and Melancholia" reflects this very inability to feel that one is, in fact, an *I*.

However, Erikson goes on to note that if one is able to reflect on one's sense of *I*, one cannot escape the impression that one consists, as it were, of various selves that make up one's composite Self. Some are more associated with one's sense of having a body or being embodied. Others are more related to one's sense of having a personality that in turn has identifiable characteristics or traits. Still others derive from the fact that one has ascribed or self-chosen social roles. He adds that there are constant and often shock-like

25. Ibid., 119–20.
26. Erikson, *Identity, Youth, and Crisis*, 216–21.
27. Ibid., 217.

transitions between these selves, and notes the difference between the nude and the clothed body, between the excited and the enraged person, and between the patient in the dentist's chair and the rider on horseback.

An especially significant contrast in light of our concern here with melancholia is a contrast Erikson also draws between what he calls "the impotent self" and "the competent self." If we consider the symptoms of the melancholic patient that Freud describes—dejection, diminished interest in the world, loss of the capacity to love, inhibition of all activity, loss of self-esteem, expectation of punishment—we cannot avoid the conclusion that the melancholic patient is an impotent self. One also senses that the melancholic patient provokes a sense of impotence in the therapist, as his situation seems so utterly hopeless. On the other hand, as we have also seen, one of the reasons—perhaps the major one—for why the boy has become susceptible to or the victim of melancholy is that he has begun to exercise his maturing organs and muscular development toward the realization of greater autonomy from parental influence and control. And these autonomous strivings, as Erikson notes, are responsible in part for the very fact that he feels—and is made to feel—guilty. In other words, there is a profound connection between his melancholia on the one hand and his autonomous strivings on the other.

Erikson concludes his paragraph on the various selves that make up our composite self with the observation that it takes "a healthy personality for the 'I' to be able to speak out of all these conditions in such a way that at any given moment it can testify to a reasonably coherent Self."[28] Thus, he does not suggest that the healthy personality is composed only of selves that we would consider positive, strong, effective, and so forth. Rather, the healthy personality is simply one that can testify to "a reasonably coherent Self." Therefore, in terms of his own distinction between the impotent and the competent self, we would not expect that the impotent self would need to be entirely eradicated in order for a person to be able to testify to a reasonably coherent Self. On the other hand, we *would* expect that the impotent self would not be so predominant that the competent self is largely dysfunctional—as is clearly the case with Freud's melancholic patients. We may even consider the very real possibility that the impotent self might play a positive role in the development of the competent self, especially if the experience of impotence is so painful or distressing that one finds within oneself the resolve or will to empower the competent self.

I suggest that the melancholic situation in which the young boy finds himself may be the catalyst toward the development of a *resourceful self.*

28. Ibid., 217.

The four authors discussed in *Men, Religion, and Melancholia* proved to be unusually resourceful in their adult lives, and this resourcefulness was due, to a significant degree, to the fact that they experienced unusual difficulties in their emotional separation from their mothers. These very difficulties could have left them feeling paralyzed and unable to cope with the challenges of life, but, in fact, this was not the case. To be sure, they experienced the resurgence of their melancholia in their young-adult years, but this very resurgence reawakened their resourceful selves, with the result that they were able to deal creatively and effectively with the inevitable problems, difficulties, and challenges of life.

This book, then, is about the resourceful self, which is, as it were, the mirror image of the melancholy self. I use the term *resourceful self* rather than *competent self* because the word *resourceful* has a double meaning, one that, in effect, picks up on Erikson's observation that autistic children who struggle to grasp the meaning of *I* also struggle to grasp the meaning of *you*, and that deeply disturbed young people who are incapable of feeling the *I* have similar difficulties in feeling the *you*, both of which are cognitively present but not emotionally so.

The term *resourceful self* emphasizes, in a way that the term *competent self* does not, that the resources available to the self are personal qualities—capacities and strengths on which one may draw; but they are also persons and other sources of assistance to whom one may turn. An indication that one is truly resourceful is that one does not rely only on one's own personal or inner resources but also reaches out to others for help. The resourceful self is reflected in the life of personal fulfillment, in the realization of one's potentialities and aspirations.

The chapters in this book focus on cases—mostly of males but not exclusively so—that Erikson presents in his writings over the span of some fifty years. They illustrate the fact that he was especially aware of the effects of the emotional separation from one's mother in early childhood on one's subsequent life, and they also illustrate the role of one's inner and outer resources, and their interactions, in the development of a capacity to counter these effects and to develop a healthy personality, one that is reflected in a reasonably coherent Self.

ERIKSON'S PERSONAL STRUGGLE WITH MELANCHOLIA

I have suggested that in the cases of the four men considered in my *Men, Religion, and Melancholia* there were circumstances that exacerbated the normal effects of the emotional separation between the mother and her young three-to-five-year-old son. A brief account of these circumstances in Erikson's own case will enable us to see that he had a personal investment in the issues we have been discussing here, that he would have had a natural proclivity toward melancholia himself, but that for this very reason he was sensitive to its presence not only in young children but also in young adults, because his own melancholia resurfaced for an extended period in his late teens and early twenties. This account will also indicate that he was a resourceful person, both in the sense that he had personal capacities, many of which were the direct result of his melancholia, and in the sense that he was the beneficiary of resources from others at the very time that he was greatly in need of them. Because he was resourceful, he was especially attuned to the resourcefulness of others, especially to the children and adolescents who were the primary focus of his work as a psychoanalytically oriented psychotherapist.

Erikson was born near Frankfurt, Germany, on June 15, 1902. His mother, Karla Abrahamsen, a Danish Jew, had traveled from Copenhagen to Germany several months earlier, after she discovered that she was pregnant. Her marriage at age twenty-one in 1898 to a twenty-seven-year-old Danish Jewish stockbroker, Valdemar Salomonsen, had ended on their honeymoon, apparently because he had disclosed to her that he was involved in some financial irregularities that required him to flee to either Mexico or the United States. His name was listed on Erikson's birth certificate as the father, but he could not have been Erik's biological father because his mother had had no direct contact with her estranged husband for several years.

Throughout his life, Erikson was convinced that his biological father was not Jewish. His own physical characteristics supported this belief. But the identity of his biological father remained a mystery. His mother never took him into her confidence on the matter, and conceivably she herself did not know his father's identity. There were persistent family rumors that his biological father was named Erik, and that he was artistic, either a painter or a photographer. Through painstaking research into family records, documents, and memories, Erikson's biographer Lawrence J. Friedman narrowed the field to two candidates, both named Erik and both involved in artistic endeavors. He presented the material to Erikson in June 1993, a year prior to Erikson's death in May 1994, in hopes that Erikson could settle the question with the aid of these new research findings. But Erikson merely glanced at the material, taking little interest in it. However, he did take note of a photograph of his young mother, and as a smile crossed his face, he remarked, "What a beauty!" At that moment Friedman realized that

Erikson's own "lifelong quest to discover the identity of his father would remain unfulfilled."[29]

Four months after Erik's birth, his mother learned that her husband had died and that she, now a widow, would be free to marry. She settled in Karlsruhe, Germany, and she and her son lived alone. Her friends were artists working in the folk style of Hans Thoma of the Black Forest. In his autobiographical essay, Erikson notes that he received his "first male imprinting" from these artists.[30] When Erik was three years old, his mother married the local pediatrician to whom she had taken her son for medical examinations and treatments. His name was Theodor Homburger, and when he formally adopted her son as his stepson, Erik became Erik Homburger. When Erik became a naturalized United States citizen in 1939, he took the name Erik H. Erikson, the middle initial standing for his former surname.

In his autobiographical essay, Erikson notes that his mother, at her new husband's insistence, told him that Dr. Homburger was his real father. She did so, he believes, "so that I would feel thoroughly at home in their home." As he and his mother had moved into his stepfather's home together, the phrase "their home" seems to suggest that young Erik felt like an outsider and that the fact that he and his mother had lived together for three years made little difference in this regard. In any event, Erikson says that he "played in" with the idea that his mother's new husband was his biological father and "more or less forgot" the period before the age of three when he and his mother lived alone.[31]

On the other hand, he notes that it was incumbent on him, as a young boy, "to come to terms with that intruder, the bearded doctor, with his healing love and mysterious instruments," and that knowing that he himself was "different" from his stepfather, he took refuge "in fantasies of how I, the son of much better parents, had been altogether a foundling." Since he and his mother had moved into Dr. Homburger's home, Erikson's use of the word "intruder" is revealing. In this case the word's use could only mean that Dr. Homburger disrupted the relationship that Erik had with his mother. Later, he notes, he "enjoyed going back and forth between the painters' studios and our house, the first floor of which, in the afternoons, was filled with tense and trusting mothers and children."[32] He is referring here to the fact that his pediatrician stepfather's office was on the first floor of the house where he

29. Friedman, *Identity's Architect,* 19.

30. Erikson, "'Identity Crisis' in Autobiographic Perspective," 27.

31. Ibid.

32. Ibid.

and his mother were now living. In contrast, the painters' studios offered a
calm and quiet atmosphere where he could truly be at home.

As Erikson grew older, he "became intensely alienated from everything
my bourgeois family stood for" and "*set out* to be different."[33] His reference
to his bourgeois family suggests that his mother had adopted the lifestyle of
the wife of a respected physician and a leader in the local synagogue. Erikson also observes that "identity problems sharpen with that turn in puberty
when images of future roles become inescapable," and indicates that in his
case he was confronted with the discord between his stepfather's expectation that Erikson would become a doctor like himself and his own desire to
become an artist. But what also contributed to his sense of alienation from
his family was the fact that his mother never revealed the truth concerning
the identity of his biological father. Friedman points out that when, years
later, Erikson recalled his unsuccessful search for his father,

> He sometimes charged that "MOTHER DECEIVED" him. This
> was an obvious reference to her failure to nurture and sustain
> him with a sense of himself and his past. At times, he under-
> scored "how many discordant signals she must have given me
> as to my origins!"[34]

Friedman also notes that when his mother died in Haifa, Israel, in 1980,
Erikson "had never found a way to open up to Karla concerning his sense
of disability because he had not come to grips with his paternity"; nor had
he "broached with Karla his memories of how she had seemed to shunt him
aside when she met his stepfather."[35]

Clearly, the emotional separation that typically occurs between a
three-year-old boy and his mother was exacerbated by the fact that Erikson's
mother remarried, that she misrepresented her new husband as his biological father, and that she thought that this deception would work despite the
fact that he was "blond and blue-eyed, and grew flagrantly tall." He adds,
"Before long, then, I was referred to as 'goy' in my stepfather's temple; while
to my schoolmates I was a 'Jew.'"[36]

Later, when Erikson graduated from *gymnasium* at the age of eighteen, he briefly attended a local art school but then took to wandering. The
traditional year of wandering after graduation was extended for several
years, during which he viewed himself as an aspiring artist. He enjoyed

33. Ibid., 28 (italics original).
34. Ibid., 39.
35. Friedman, *Identity's Architect*, 299.
36. Erikson, "'Identity Crisis' in Autobiographic Perspective," 27.

making woodcut prints (pictorial sketches drawn and engraved on wood), and through this medium, he was connecting emotionally with the artists he had known as a small boy, as they worked in the folk style popular in the region at the time. He spent a little less than two years in Munich to study artistic technique at the famous Kunst-Akademie, but then left for Italy. In Italy, he felt that his woodcuts of large fields with rocks, hills and other objects resembled at least thematically Vincent van Gogh's scenes of nature. But he also knew that daring use of paint and color had been central to van Gogh's work, and he bemoaned the fact that he had great difficulty in developing a facility for the use of color and paint, adding that this "was where the inhibition was."[37]

Thus, by the time Erikson eventually settled in Florence, he had already forsaken a career as an artist. As he notes in his autobiographical essay, this was a time of severe "identity confusion" whose "pathological" features he chooses not to describe; rather he says that they "assumed at times what some of us today would call a 'borderline' character—that is, the border-line between neurosis and adolescent psychosis."[38] He carried a sketchbook around with him, but instead of drawings and sketches, it mostly contained jottings that were abstract, philosophic, and random, with no perceptible thematic unity. He wrote a four-line poem in which he celebrated the bal-anced life—"Content dies, balanced form lives on / Body dies, beauty lives on / Actuality dies, truth lives on / The person dies, the I lives on"—and in his related jottings he noted that one of the most important balances was that between the masculine and feminine qualities of the self, a balance that he recognized in Goethe's writings and Leonardo da Vinci's art.[39] Here in this poem we can discern intimations of his later formulation of the life-cycle schema with its various polarities.

Erikson's inaction and despondency continued after he returned home to Karlsruhe in 1925 at the age of twenty-three. A photograph taken that year of Erik sitting on a bench with his half sisters suggests that he was quite downcast. According to Friedman, he appears "gaunt, tired, tense, and unable to summon a smile." Later, Erikson observed that he was "in many ways a nonfunctioning artist," suffering from a serious "work disturbance," and he admitted that "there were simply months when I couldn't work at all and didn't feel like putting anything on paper." In fact, he "did not feel like doing anything at all."[40]

---

37. Friedman, *Identity's Architect*, 46–47.

38. Erikson, "'Identity Crisis' in Autobiographic Perspective," 26.

39. Friedman, *Identity's Architect*, 53.

40. Ibid., 56.

In early 1927 Erikson was considering but not acting on the possibility of becoming a local arts-and-crafts teacher when Peter Blos, an old Karlsruhe friend, wrote to invite him to Vienna to sketch portraits of Dorothy Burlingham's children. Burlingham, with the encouragement of Anna Freud, Sigmund Freud's daughter, had offered to help Blos, who had been her children's tutor, establish his own school. This was to be a school for children who were psychoanalytic patients, children of psychoanalytic patients, and children of Viennese psychoanalysts. The invitation extended to Erikson to sketch Burlingham's children would enable her to decide whether to accept Blos's recommendation that his friend Erik might join him as a teacher at the newly established Hietzing School. Erikson later wrote of Blos's invitation, "Nietzsche once said that a friend is the life saver who holds you above water when your divided selves threaten to drag you to the bottom."[41]

Erikson went to Vienna, sketched the portraits, and was offered the position. Thus began his association with Freud's circle. Anna Freud encouraged him to consider a career as a psychoanalyst, and in 1929 at the age of twenty-seven he began his training analysis with her. He remained her protégé until 1933, when he and his young Canadian-born wife Joan, whom he had met in Vienna, immigrated to the United States with their two small sons. In his autobiographical essay, Erikson notes that he experienced Anna Freud as "a liberating agent and as a potential indoctrinator, as an identity model and yet also as a powerful personality from whom one must learn to differentiate oneself."[42] He observed at the conclusion of his analysis that he had repeated the "childhood which I spent with my mother alone."[43]

One of the tensions in Erikson's relationship with Anna Freud was related to the fact that his wife, Joan, whom he had married in 1930, did not think that his psychoanalytic sessions with Anna Freud were doing him much good. She was upset by Anna Freud's disapproval of Erik's "permissive" approach to teaching. Joan also became angry when Anna Freud dismissed his belief that his biological father was from an aristocratic family as "a family romance," the title of a brief essay by Anna's father.[44] In the essay, Freud suggested that the primary motivation behind a family romance is the desire to free oneself as one is growing up from parental authority. He noted that a child who is both neurotic and highly gifted will employ his imagination in "getting free from the parents of whom he now has such a low opinion and of replacing them by others, occupying, as a rule, a higher

41. Ibid.
42. Erikson, "'Identity Crisis' in Autobiographic Perspective," 25.
43. Friedman, *Identity's Architect*, 77.
44. Freud, "The Family Romance."

social station." He added that, although the family romance is typically the work of very young children, it is not uncommon for it to persist far beyond puberty. Freud also pointed out that a child may create such a fantasy in order to place himself in a more privileged position in relation to his siblings or to eliminate a prohibition if he is sexually attracted to one of his sisters.

So when Erikson would mention to Anna Freud what he had pieced together about his biological father, she would dismiss it, pointing out that adopted children tend to fantasize about their real parents. She also warned him that he was transforming his father's betrayal into a life myth. He later recalled his hurt and anger when he brought to an analytic session a photograph supposedly of a Danish aristocrat, claiming that he had found it among his mother's possessions, only to have Anna dismiss the claim. Quite possibly she believed that Erikson's view that his father was a Danish aristocrat was an implicit repudiation of his Jewish identity. Perhaps she felt that Erikson needed instead to place greater value on his stepfather's adoption of him and on his stepfather's desire that Erik would be viewed and treated as his very own son.[45]

Joan Erikson also felt that her husband needed a male analyst to help him work through the issue of his missing father. Conceivably, an equally strong case could have been made for his need to be psychoanalyzed by a woman who was considerably older than Anna Freud, only seven years his senior. A woman closer in age to his mother (who would have been in her early-fifties when he was in psychoanalysis) may well have been able to help Erikson work through his feelings about his mother relating to the fact that the two of them had lived alone together the first three years of his life and that all of this changed when she remarried. On the other hand, at thirty-four years of age when she became his psychoanalyst, Anna Freud would have been just a few years older than his mother had been when he experienced the emotional separation from her, and this may well have made it possible for him to work through some of the unresolved feelings the separation had evoked in him as a young boy.

In any event, Erikson viewed the fact that he was accepted by the Freudian circle as a "truly astounding adoption" and as offering him "a kind of positive stepson identity." He felt that in becoming a disciple of Sigmund Freud, "a mythical figure and, above all, a great doctor who had rebelled

45. In *Identity and the Life Cycle* Erikson mentions his own case of a high-school girl of Middle-European descent who created a Scottish identity for herself. He notes that the bit of reality on which this identity was based was her attachment, in early childhood, to a neighbor woman who was from the British Isles. When he asked her how she had managed to marshal all the details of Scottish life to make her story credible, she responded in a Scottish brogue, "Bless you, sir, I needed a past" (rev. ed.), 141.

against the medical profession, he was being accorded "the kind of training that came as close to the role of children's doctor as one could possibly come without going to medical school." Moreover, something within himself that "responded to this situation was, I think, some strong identification with my stepfather, the pediatrician, mixed with a search for my own mythical father."[46] Prior to this adoption by the Freudian circle, however, it was evident to Erikson that he was paralyzed by his "divided selves," thus experiencing the inner split whose origins were traceable to the period in his life when his mother remarried and he was forced to leave the artists' colony and move into the home of the bearded doctor.

Although brief, this account of Erikson's early years provides sufficient evidence to suggest that if he had been a psychoanalytic patient when he was in his early twenties, a diagnosis of melancholia would have been entirely appropriate. The symptoms that Freud identifies in his "Mourning and Melancholia" apply to Erikson. Although he was the primary victim of his melancholia, the pathology may also have been, in part at least, an indirect way of punishing his mother (who sent him money to support his artistic career without informing her husband that she was doing so) for what had happened to him in his early childhood.

But, in any event, Erikson's situation began to change. Through the intervention of his friend Peter Blos he became a teacher of young children, a member of the Freudian circle, and a husband and father. External resources joined with his personal resources, and he became a new person. It is not surprising, therefore, that when he became a child analyst he did what he could to evoke the child's own inner resources to address the difficulties and challenges of life. He knew what it was like to be paralyzed and immobilized by feelings of frustration, self-reproach, inhibition, anger, and fury, but he also knew what it was like to become reactivated and responsive to the world around him. The resources identified in the various chapters in this book reflect the fact that, as Erikson discovered, it is possible to prevail over the melancholia resulting from the loss of unity with the person that one knows as mother, and that, in fact, there is a sense in which she, in at least one of her various guises, sponsors the determination to prevail. However, Erikson also discovered that one is unlikely to prevail if one relies wholly on one's own inner resources. Against all odds, this struggling but ineffectual artist was adopted into the Freudian circle, and even he—or, rather, *especially* he—found such adoption to be "truly astounding."

---

46. Erikson, "'Identity Crisis' in Autobiographic Perspective," 29.

2

Dual Mothers and Artistic Inhibition

In the preceding chapter I suggested the usefulness of Freud's article on mourning and melancholia for understanding Erikson's own life experiences in early childhood and their bearing on what he called his "identity confusion" in his late teens and early twenties. Although Erikson could have viewed his identity confusion as atypical, he instead proposed that identity confusion is the experience of most if not all young persons. In this chapter, I would like to focus on another of Freud's writings to support my proposal that the melancholy self and the resourceful self are dynamically related, that they are, as it were, mirror images of one another. Here, again, I will make connections between this writing by Freud and Erikson's own identity struggles.

The writing to which I am referring is Freud's monograph titled *Leonardo da Vinci and a Memory of His Childhood*.[1] This is a writing of Freud's that Erikson does not mention in any of his own works. Given the fact that Erikson's *Young Man Luther* and *Gandhi's Truth* are psychobiographical,[2] we might have expected that he would at least make reference to Freud's study of Leonardo da Vinci, which is considered by the psychoanalytic community to be the first psychobiography. On the other hand, Erikson does mention Leonardo da Vinci several times in *Young Man Luther*, and this fact alone suggests that he not only was aware of Freud's book but also knew that many of his readers would have been aware of it too.

1. Freud, *Leonardo da Vinci and a Memory of His Childhood*.
2. Erikson, *Young Man Luther*; Erikson, *Gandhi's Truth*.

Whatever the explanation for his *not* having made any references to Freud's book in his own writings may be, far more significant is the fact that there are notable parallels between the personal themes that Freud writes about in his psychobiography of Leonardo and Erikson's own life. Two such themes that will concern us in this chapter are their illegitimate births and how this affected their relationships with their mothers in early childhood; and the fact that both experienced severe inhibition as artists. Exploration of these two themes will enable us to reflect on the fact that both men overcame these disabilities by transmuting inhibition into initiative. Or, in other words, their resourceful selves developed out of the conditions that instigated the formation of their melancholy selves. I will begin with Freud's discussion of Leonardo's maternal relationships.

LEONARDO'S ILLEGITIMACY AND MOTHER RELATIONSHIPS

Freud indicates that we know very little about Leonardo's youth. However, we do know that he

> was born in 1452 in the little town of Vinci between Florence and Empoli; he was an illegitimate child, which in those days was certainly not considered a grave social stigma; his father was Ser Piero da Vinci, a notary and descended from a family of notaries and farmers who took their name from the locality of Vinci; his mother was a certain Caterina, probably a peasant girl, who later married another native of Vinci.[3]

His father married Donna Albiera, a sixteen-year-old girl of higher social standing than Caterina, the year that Leonardo was born.

Since taxation records of the year 1457 mention Leonardo among the members of the Vinci household as the five-year-old illegitimate son of Ser Piero, Freud surmises that Leonardo was taken into his paternal home sometime after his birth and before the age of five. However, Freud doubts that this would have happened immediately after Leonardo's birth. Furthermore, he guesses it might not have happened at all were it not for the fact that his father's wife was childless:

> Now it is not usual at the start of a marriage to put an illegitimate offspring into the care of the young bride who still expects to be blessed with children of her own. Years of disappointment must surely first have elapsed before it was decided to adopt the

3. Freud, *Leonardo da Vinci and a Memory of His Childhood*, 31.

illegitimate child—who had probably grown up an attractive young boy—as a compensation for the absence of the legitimate children that had been hoped for.[4]

On the basis of his psychoanalytic interpretation of a childhood memory of Leonardo's, Freud suggests that Leonardo "spent the critical years of his life not by the side of his father and stepmother, but with his poor, forsaken, real mother, so that he had time to feel the absence of his father."[5] At least three years of Leonardo's life, and perhaps five, had elapsed before he could exchange the solitary person of his mother for a parental couple: "And by then it is too late," for "in the first three or five years of life certain impressions become fixed and ways of reacting to the outside world are established which can never be deprived of their importance by later experience."[6] That "Leonardo spent the first years of his life alone with his mother will have been of decisive influence on the formation of his inner life."[7]

Leonardo's painting *Saint Anne with Madonna and Child* especially interests Freud because it presents two mothers—the Virgin Mary and her own mother—and represents them as being close in age. Saint Anne is "portrayed as being perhaps a little more mature and serious than the Virgin Mary," but she is still "a young woman of unfaded beauty."[8] Freud suggests that Leonardo has recapitulated his own childhood in this painting because he "had had two mothers; first, his true mother Caterina, from whom he was torn away when he was between three and five, and then a young and tender stepmother, his father's wife, Donna Albiera."[9] Furthermore, the

> maternal figure that is further away from the boy—the grandmother—corresponds to the earlier and true mother, Caterina, in its appearance and in its special relation to the boy. The artist seems to have used the blissful smile of St. Anne to disavow and to cloak the envy which the unfortunate woman left when she was forced to give up her son to her better-born rival, as she had once given up his father as well.[10]

In *Leonardo, Psychoanalysis, and Art History,* Bradley I. Collins notes that Freud's suggestion that Saint Anne corresponds to Leonardo's birth

4. Ibid., 41.
5. Ibid.
6. Ibid., 41–42.
7. Ibid., 42.
8. Ibid., 63.
9. Ibid.
10. Ibid., 63–64.

mother while the Virgin Mary relates to his stepmother is supported by the fact that in the year of Leonardo's birth, Donna Albiera was only sixteen, while Caterina was twenty-five years old.[11] Collins also points out that Leonardo omitted Joseph from nearly all of his Holy Family paintings, an omission that may be related to Leonardo's exclusion from his father's will, presumably on the grounds that, among Ser Piero's ten sons, only Leonardo was illegitimate. The others were progeny from his father's second marriage following the death of Donna Albiera. Ser Piero's death and Leonardo's contestation of his father's will occurred in the middle of the period in which Leonardo was engaged in his paintings of the Holy Family.[12]

Leonardo's exclusion from his father's will may also be reflected in his fresco *The Last Supper,* which focuses on Jesus's shattering announcement of betrayal instead of on the more traditional eucharistic theme of other paintings of the Last Supper. Like Jesus, Leonardo had been betrayed, and Jesus's announcement of betrayal occurs in the company of a group of men, his disciples, who would represent Leonardo's brothers. The fact that Leonardo does not depict Judas slinking guiltily to the door, his moneybag in hand, which would have been appropriate in a painting focusing on the announcement of the betrayal, leaves open the possibility that Leonardo means to suggest that the betrayer is not among those to whom Jesus makes the announcement, but is the Father himself. This, after all, is implied in the statement attributed to Jesus on the cross, "Father, why have you abandoned me?"[13]

Collins concludes that Leonardo's painting *Saint Anne with Virgin and Child* (as well as his sketch *Virgin, Child, Saint Anne and Saint John*) enabled Leonardo to both re-create his past and transform it:

> On the one hand, he could return to a world dominated by multiple maternal figures and marked by unusual and unexpected births. On the other, he could take the actual, humiliating reality of his childhood—an illegitimate birth by a peasant mother—and transfigure it. By identifying with the Christ Child, he could become the divine, not the shameful, product of an unusual pregnancy, and by identifying Caterina with the Virgin, he could undo her degradation. That the theme of an untainted pregnancy leading to a miraculous birth applies to Anne's and

11. Collins, *Leonardo, Psychoanalysis & Art History,* 151.

12. Ibid., 150.

13. I have taken the liberty of giving a paternal referent to the cry "My God, my God, why have you forsaken me?" (Matt. 27:46; Mark 15:24) because Jesus is also said to have called out to the Father as he died, "Father, into your hands I commit my spirit" (Luke 23:46).

> Mary's pregnancies as well as to the Virgin's and the Christ
> Child's births would only have strengthened the subject's un-
> conscious appeal for Leonardo.[14]

Thus, the trauma that Leonardo experienced is transfigured, not only for himself, but also for his biological mother. To put it in the terms that I am proposing, the melancholy self has engendered the resourceful self.

LEONARDO'S ARTISTIC INHIBITION

The second theme that Freud addresses in his psychobiography of Leonardo concerns the "inhibition" that plagued Leonardo's career as an artist. In Freud's view, this inhibition had much to do with the fact that, as he got older, Leonardo's interests in art were being superseded by his interests in science. Although Freud views this shift from art to science as a positive move, he notes that the science in which Leonardo engaged was considered rather questionable at the time because it was not based on established scientific principles derived from Aristotle. His dissection of the dead bodies of humans and horses, his construction of flying machines, and his studies of the nutrition of plants and their reactions to poisons anticipated the empirical methods of Nicolaus Copernicus, who was twenty-one years his junior, and Francis Bacon, who was born more than a century later. Thus, as a scientist, he "was necessarily isolated."[15] The effect of this scientific interest was that Leonardo "took up his brush with reluctance, painted less and less, left what he had begun for the most part unfinished and cared little about the ultimate fate of his works."[16]

Freud observes that Leonardo's attitude toward his art was a riddle to his contemporaries, and his admirers "have made attempts to acquit his character of the flaw of instability."[17] They suggest that this is a feature of great artists, and that even the energetic Michelangelo, who devoted his whole life to his art, left many of his works incomplete. Furthermore, they note that in some instances the paintings were in fact finished despite the fact that Leonardo claimed that they were not. The *Mona Lisa* is cited as a classic example.

As valid as these arguments may be, however, they do not, in Freud's view, fully account for the fact that Leonardo is a special case of an artist

---

14. Collins, *Leonardo, Psychoanalysis & Art History*, 167.

15. Freud, *Leonardo da Vinci and a Memory of His Childhood*. 15.

16. Ibid.

17. Ibid.

who worked very slowly and seemed to have a singular aversion toward the completion of his works:

> The slowness with which Leonardo worked was proverbial. . . . Sometimes he would remain for hours in front of the painting, merely examining it in his mind. At other times he would come straight to the convent from the court in the castle at Milan in order to add a few strokes of the brush to a figure, and then immediately break it off.[18]

Freud concludes that Leonardo suffered from an "inhibition" in the actual execution of his work, which was much deeper than the inhibition that may be explained as "the artist inevitably falling short of his ideal."[19]

In Freud's view, Leonardo's inhibition was due to the fact that his desire or need to experiment would sabotage the completion of a painting: "Here it seems as if an alien interest—in experimentation—at first reinforced the artistic one, only to damage the work later on."[20] In effect, Leonardo took a scientific interest in his art: "When he made the attempt to return from [scientific] investigation to his starting point, the exercise of his art, he found himself disturbed by the new direction of his interests and the changed nature of his mental activity."[21] What interested Leonardo in a

> painting was above all a problem; and behind the first one he saw countless other problems arising, just as he used to in his endless and inexhaustible investigation of nature. He was no longer able to limit his demands, to see the work of art in isolation and to tear it from the wide context to which he knew it belonged. After the most exhausting efforts to bring to expression in it everything which was connected with it in his thoughts, he was forced to abandon it in an unfinished state or to declare that it was incomplete.[22]

Previously, "the artist had once taken the investigator into his service to assist him," but now "the servant had become the stronger and suppressed his master."[23]

Freud suggests that this replacement of artistry with a passion for experimentation was prefigured in Leonardo's early childhood, when loving

18. Ibid., 17.
19. Ibid., 18.
20. Ibid., 18.
21. Ibid., 27.
22. Ibid.
23. Ibid.

devotion to his mother, which was abruptly undermined when he was taken into his father's home, was supplanted by a sexual curiosity, which, in turn, led to an inhibition of the original devotion. A similar process occurs when Leonardo's artistic work (which has deep maternal associations) is inhibited by his scientific curiosity.

ERIKSON'S REFERENCES TO LEONARDO IN *YOUNG MAN LUTHER*

Before we take up the relationship between Freud's consideration of the two themes in Leonardo's life and career to Erikson's life and career, a brief discussion of Erikson's references to Leonardo in *Young Man Luther* will enable us to see that Erikson had much in common with the Renaissance and, more specifically, with Leonardo's understanding of the artistic task. Also, because he referred to Leonardo in *Young Man Luther*, his first major psychobiography, and only there, it seems likely that Erikson was conscious of the fact that he was following, however indirectly, in Freud's footsteps.

In selecting Luther for his first major psychobiography, Erikson chose a contemporary of Leonardo and of Michelangelo. Leonardo was born in 1452 and died in 1519. Michelangelo was born in 1475 and died in 1564. Luther was born in 1483 and died in 1546. Thus, Leonardo was thirty-one years older than Luther, and died when Luther, in his midthirties, was rising to prominence as a religious reformer. In Erikson's view, Luther had more in common with the artists and writers of the Renaissance than we tend to recognize. If Luther "concluded his life in an obese provinciality," he had, nonetheless, occupied the stage of history "with some of the exhibitionistic grandeur of a Renaissance man."[24] Moreover, he did "the dirty work of the Renaissance by applying some of the individualistic principles immanent in the Renaissance to the Church's still highly fortified home-ground—the conscience of ordinary man."[25] Finally, "the tools he used were those of the Renaissance: fervent return to the original texts; determined anthropocentricism (if in Christocentric form); and the affirmation of his own organ of genius and craftsmanship, namely, the voice of the vernacular."[26]

Erikson's first reference to Leonardo occurs in the chapter on "Allness or Nothingness," the chapter in which he argues that Luther was a seriously endangered young man, a candidate for severe mental pathology or social deviance on a grand scale. At the risk of prejudicing the case against Luther,

24. Erikson, *Young Man Luther*, 194.
25. Ibid.
26. Ibid., 195.

Erikson compares him to patients of his who experienced schizophrenic episodes, and uses these comparisons to enable us "to know Martin Luther and marvel the more at his self-transcendence."[27] Then he introduces Adolf Hitler, who, as a young man, aspired to be an artist but was not accepted into either art or architectural schools. Suggesting that "maybe, maybe, if [Hitler] had been permitted to build, he would not have destroyed," Erikson cites Leonardo, "the creator of the immortal da Vincian smile," who "was also an inveterate tinkerer with war machines; on occasion he caught himself, and relegated a design to the bottom of a deep drawer."[28] Erikson continues with a brief discussion of Hitler's childhood and adolescence, noting that Hitler's father, "himself the illegitimate son of a poor servant girl," was intent on "making a civil servant out of the son."[29] (We may recall in this connection that Leonardo's father was a public notary.) After discussing Hitler's urge to destroy and rebuild, Erikson says that he "will not go into the symbolism of Hitler's urge to build except to say that his shiftless and brutal father had consistently denied the mother a permanent residence; one must read how Hitler took care of his mother when she wasted away from lung cancer to get an inkling of this young man's desperate urge to cure."[30]

Erikson's rather unanticipated association between Leonardo da Vinci and Adolf Hitler may have been inspired, at least superficially, by the fact that Hitler's father, like Leonardo, was the illegitimate son of a woman of low social status. But the deeper connection between Leonardo and Hitler is that both struggled with the demonstrable fact that there is a fine line between the urge to build and the urge to destroy. In his discussion of children's expression of their urge to build and to destroy in play in *Childhood and Society* Erikson suggests that a small child's insistence on being the one who destroys what he has created is his way of experiencing "active mastery over a previously passive event."[31]

Erikson's second reference to Leonardo in *Young Man Luther* occurs in a discussion of the contrasting worldviews of medievalism and the Renaissance. The Renaissance, he notes, emphasized the power of a "specific endowment" that contributes to an individual's "gift of workmanship." For Luther, this specific endowment was the voice, for Michelangelo the hand, and for Leonardo, "it was the trained, intent eye, the 'knowing how to see,'

27. Ibid., 104.
28. Ibid., 108–9.
29. Ibid., 105.
30. Ibid., 108.
31. Erikson, *Childhood and Society,* rev. ed., 219–20.

which was 'the natural point' in which 'the images of our own hemisphere are united with those of all the heavenly bodies.'"[32]

Despite the fact that Erikson made large woodcuts that required the use of his hand, his greater inner affinity with Leonardo's "trained, intent eye" was evident in his understanding of himself. He mentions in his autobiographical essay that when he declared to Anna Freud that "he could not see a place for my artistic inclinations in such high intellectual endeavors" as psychoanalysis required, she responded quietly, "You might help to make them see."[33] In a subsequent videotaped commentary, however, he reported that she delayed replying to him until she was able to talk to her father; the next day she came back and said to him, "'I told my father what you said, and he said tell him that he can help us to make them see,' which is such a wonderful way of saying things."[34] He later recalled, "That kind of thing can decide your identity."[35]

Erikson's third reference to Leonardo in *Young Man Luther* also occurs in his discussion of differences between medievalism and the Renaissance. He notes that the Renaissance "anchors the human identity in the hierarchy of organs and functions of the human body," and, unlike medievalism, which permits "the body to be sickened with sinfulness" and "the mind to be chained to a dogma," the Renaissance insists "on a full interplay between man's senses and intuitions and the world of appearances, facts, and laws."[36] This Renaissance ideal is supported by Leonardo's statement: "Mental things which have not gone through the senses are vain and bring forth no truth except detrimental." Erikson endorses this reliance on the senses but adds that such reliance requires "disciplined sensuality, '*exact fantasy*,' and makes the verification of our functioning essence dependent on the meeting between our God-given mental machinery and the world into which God has put us."[37]

This cautionary note about the senses appears to have been derived from Erikson's primary source for his discussion of the Renaissance, Giorgio de Santillana's *The Age of Adventure*, which cites Leonardo's observation that the senses can also be detrimental. For as the artist knows only too well, he is the magician who can arouse passions at will. De Santillana notes:

32. Erikson, *Young Man Luther*, 192. The quoted material is from Giorgio de Santillana's *The Age of Adventure*, 83–84.

33. Erikson, "'Identity Crisis' in Autobiographic Perspective," 30.

34. Friedman, *Identity's Architect*, 69.

35. Ibid., 70.

36. Erikson, *Young Man Luther*, 192.

37. Ibid. (italics original).

"Leonardo tells with a shade of irony of the owner of one of his Madonnas who had to sell it again in haste, because 'in spite of the reverence owed it, he had fallen desperately in love with the image.'"[38] In effect, the painting had awakened feelings in the owner toward his mother that he had repressed or sublimated. By reporting the incident, Leonardo has revealed his own awareness of the artist's power to create the illusion of the living presence of the mother despite the fact that she is no longer there.

Erikson's fourth reference to Leonardo in *Young Man Luther* occurs in a discussion of the fact that, for all its progress in pictorialization, verbalization, and material construction, the Renaissance left "something undone on the inner frontier," the frontier of a guilty, negative, or tragic conscience.[39] Some conscience-stricken men, those who "had loved women, or at any rate their own maleness, too much," turned to monastic asceticism in their middle years, while others, "altogether womanless men, like Leonardo and Michelangelo, found and recognized the defeat of the male self in grandiose ways." Erikson suggests that we find this defeated male self in Michelangelo's *Pietà*—an "unrealistic and unhistorical sculpture" that portrays "an eternally young mother holding on her lap the sacrificial corpse of her grown and aged son"—and contrasts it with "the other Madonnas of the Renaissance (della Robbia's, del Sarto's, Raphael's) who are shown with the boy Jesus making a gay and determined effort to stand on his own feet and to reach out for the world."[40]

Except for his association of Leonardo with Michelangelo as a "womanless man," Erikson says nothing further about Leonardo in this passage. But if he had discussed the Christ Child in Leonardo's painting of *Saint Anne with the Virgin and Child*, in which the Child is reaching out to a lamb, he would have identified a rather different boy Jesus from those of other Renaissance painters, one less "gay and determined," and one more conflicted because he realizes that he is destined to suffer the fate that Michelangelo's *Pietà* portrays. As Bradley I. Collins observes, "Mary tries to lift her son away from the lamb yet smiles as if she accepts his crucifixion," and her gesture of concern "is further contradicted by St. Anne's wider smile."[41] At the same time, the "Christ Child also displays contradictory impulses: On the one hand, he wishes to defy his mother and play with the lamb. Yet on the other hand, by doing so he symbolically embraces his own death."[42]

38. De Santillana, *The Age of Adventure*, 69.
39. Erikson, *Young Man Luther*, 194.
40. Ibid.
41. Collins, *Leonardo, Psychoanalysis & Art History*, 155.
42. Ibid.

Collins's further reflections on the autobiographical significance of the painting for Leonardo lend further support to Erikson's view that Leonardo, like Michelangelo, portrayed the defeated male self in grandiose ways. Collins asks, "What is the relationship between these manifest ambivalences and Leonardo's infantile ambivalence toward his maternal figures?" To what extent did Leonardo "project his own murderous rage onto maternal figures" that "smilingly accede to a crucifixion?"[43] Collins suggests that this issue must be confronted "even if it is difficult to distinguish between the replication of a past reality and its transformation by a defensive maneuver."[44] To confront the issue, Collins turns to Leonardo's *The Madonna of the Yarnwinder*. The extant studio versions of this lost or substantially altered painting depict the Christ Child holding the yarnwinder (which is symbolic of the cross). The appearance of the child's mother is one of deep concern but she does not attempt to take the yarnwinder away from him. Collins acknowledges that the unconscious impulses behind the Christ Child's embrace of the yarnwinder are obscure: "What unconscious desire motivates his eager clutching at his own destruction?"[45] But he cites in this connection Jean-Pierre Maïdani-Gerard's suggestion that the Christ Child is enacting a sort of *fort-da* game with the yarnwinder.[46]

Maïdani-Gerard is referring here to Freud's account in *Beyond the Pleasure Principle* of a game played by Freud's grandson Ernest (which I will discuss in chapter 5). Ernest would throw a wooden reel (which would have been somewhat similar to a yarnwinder) with a piece of string tied around it, and say, "Fort!" ("Gone!"). When the reel disappeared, Ernest would utter a long, drawn out *o*, the vowel in the word *fort*. At times, this was the whole game. But Freud also observed that, on occasion, Ernest would throw the reel behind his cot, and, by holding the reel by the string, he could pull the reel back and, as he did so, he hailed its return with a joyful "Da!" ("There!") So the complete game was one of disappearance and return. Freud notes: "At the outset he was in a *passive* situation—he was overpowered by the experience; but by repeating it, unpleasurable though it was, he took on an *active* part."[47] Maïdani-Gerard suggests that something similar is happening in the painting of the Christ Child and the yarnwinder. He writes:

43. Ibid.

44. Ibid.

45. Ibid., 156.

46. Maïdani-Gérard, "Léonard de Vinci, Sigmund Freud . . . L'application de la psychoanalyse à une oeuvre du passé."

47. Freud, *Beyond the Pleasure Principle*, 35.

Like the infant in Freud's *Beyond the Pleasure Principle*, who
masters the trauma of his mother's leave-takings by throwing
and recovering a reel, Leonardo's Christ Child grabs the winder
in order to play with his fate. Instead of passively submitting
to God's will, he toys actively with the symbol of his supreme
exaltation and bloody mortification.[48]

How does this depiction of the Christ Child connect with Leonardo's
own experience? Collins suggests that the most obvious parallel "would be
the narcissistic defeat of Caterina's abandonment [of him] combined with
a compensatory grandiosity reinforced by Leonardo's actual accomplish-
ments as an artist."[49] In short, Leonardo's Christ Child is anything but the
"gay and determined" boy depicted in other Renaissance paintings. He reflects, instead, the accuracy of Erikson's judgment that both Leonardo and
Michelangelo "found and recognized the defeat of the male self in grandiose
ways."[50]

If, however, Collins is correct, this defeat is less owing to the Christ
Child's obedience to the will of the Father and more owing to his reluctant
acceptance of the fate of separation from his mother. If the Christ Child
pulls away from his mother and reaches for the yarnwinder, Leonardo,
pulled away from his mother by others, will reach for the artist's brush. He
may have suffered irreparable defeat, but, through the artist's version of the
"gone-there" game, he will at least be able to depict the story from his own
point of view, for such are the powers of artistic projection. Leonardo writes
in a notebook entry, "If the painter wishes to see beauties that would enrap-
ture him, he is master of their production, and if he wishes to see monstrous
things which might terrify or which would be buffoonish and laughable or
truly pitiable, he is their lord and god."[51] As Freud pointed out in reference
to his grandson's game of disappearance and return, "At the outset [the boy]
was in a *passive* situation—he was overpowered by the experience; but by
repeating it, unpleasurable as it was, as a game, he took on an *active* part."[52]
The mother can relinquish or even abandon her boy, but her artist son can
make her reappear—in whatever guise he chooses.

---

48. Collins, *Leonardo, Psychoanalysis & Art Theory,* 156.
49. Ibid.
50. Erikson, *Young Man Luther,* 195.
51. Leonardo da Vinci, *Leonardo on Painting,* 32.
52. Freud, *Beyond the Pleasure Principle,* 35.

THE PROBLEM OF THE DUAL MOTHERS

Having discussed Erikson's references to Leonardo in *Young Man Luther*, I would now like to focus on the ways the two themes in Freud's psychobiography—the mother relationship and artistic inhibition—relate to Erikson's own life and career. As we have seen, Erikson and Leonardo had in common that both were illegitimate, and that both lived alone with their mothers for the first several years of their lives. Leonardo's father may have been present from time to time, but he married another woman the very year that Leonardo was born, so it seems unlikely that Leonardo's father spent very much time with his illegitimate son. The differences between early childhood for Erikson and for Leonardo revolve around the fact that whereas young Leonardo lost his mother when he was taken into his father's home, young Erik did not lose his mother when she married another man and the two of them moved into his home. Also, unlike Leonardo, whose father never took steps to legitimate him, Erik was adopted by his stepfather, though apparently not immediately, but three years later.[53]

Although it might be argued that Leonardo's situation was more traumatic because he lost his mother, Erik felt himself "shunted aside" by his mother when her affections turned toward her new husband, and he implies that she became a different woman when she left her artist friends and became the wife of a respected doctor who was an elder of the local synagogue. In his autobiographical essay, for example, Erikson notes that he remembers "the mother of my early years as pervasively sad."[54] He also makes this observation about Luther's mother.[55] Erikson visualizes his own mother "as deeply involved in reading what I later found to have been such authors as Brandes, Kierkegaard, and Emerson," and this prompted him to believe "that her ambitions for me transcended the conventions which she, nevertheless, faithfully served."[56] Erikson seems to identify the ambitions that she had for him with the mother he knew before her marriage to Theodor Homburger, and identifies the mother who faithfully served the "conventions" with the mother he knew following her marriage. After all, a woman raising her son by herself, and among artists, could hardly be said to be living a conventional life.

In a sense, then, just as Leonardo did, young Erik also experienced *two* mothers, and the fact that *she* was one and the same individual may

53. Friedman, *Identity's Architect*, 34.
54. Erikson, "'Identity Crisis' in Autobiographic Perspective," 31.
55. Erikson, *Young Man Luther*, 72.
56. Erikson, "'Identity Crisis' in Autobiographic Perspective," 31.

well have been as bewildering and emotionally difficult for Erikson as Leonardo's experience of two separate and clearly distinguishable mothers had been. Thus, Erikson's experience would be no less conducive to a melancholic reaction than Leonardo's, for, in both cases, the "lost object" was still "to be found among those in his near neighborhood."[57] We do not know if Leonardo returned to visit his mother, who subsequently married another man, but Erikson tells us that he himself "enjoyed going back and forth between the painters' studios and our house, the first floor of which, in the afternoons, was filled with tense and trusting mothers and children."[58] These visits to the painters' studios were, it would seem, a form of escape, and the place to which he escaped would remind him of the fact that the mother he knew there no longer existed for him, while the mother with whom he now shared a home with "that intruder, the bearded doctor, with his healing love and mysterious instruments"[59] had taken on a very different demeanor from that of the mother he had known before her marriage.

This conclusion is supported by Erikson's discussion of Michelangelo in his 1972 essay, "Play and Actuality."[60] When Erikson was teaching a seminar called "Life History and History" at Harvard University, he invited Helmut Wohl to come to his seminar and present his work on Michelangelo's autobiographical notes.[61] Drawing on Wohl's presentation, Erikson notes that Michelangelo was given a wet nurse immediately after birth because his mother was too sick to take care of him. While a wet nurse was not unusual at the time, the "other woman" in this case was the daughter and wife of stonemasons and lived near a stone quarry: "Michelangelo acknowledged that while his mother had given him life itself, the wet nurse gave him 'delight in the chisel.'"[62] Erikson suggests that his chisel eventually "became for him the executive tool of his very identity," for "when he created young David, Michelangelo equated 'David with the sling' and 'I with the chisel.'" Erikson also notes that "if Michelangelo had two mothers, he, alas, lost both early" for "he was separated from the wet nurse when he returned to his mother and then his mother died when he was six years old."[63]

Implying a connection between these early-childhood experiences and Michelangelo's later work as an artist, Erikson cites Wohl's presentation of

57. Freud, "Mourning and Melancholia," 173.
58. Erikson, "'Identity Crisis' in Autobiographic perspective., 27.
59. Ibid.
60. Erikson, *A Way of Looking at Things*, 311–38.
61. Ibid., 316–17.
62. Ibid., 317.
63. Ibid.

the sequence of the Madonna images that Michelangelo sketched, painted, or sculptured (the first in his late teens and the last in his late eighties), and observes that Michelangelo's Madonnas "always show a marked distance between mother and child, beyond the Renaissance theme of the willful boy Jesus straining away from his mother's arms; here the Madonna herself is looking away from her child, her eyes remaining inward, distant and almost sightless."[64] Yet, "the very last of Michelangelo's preserved sketches of the Madonna portrays, in Wohl's word, a nearly 'conflict-less' image of mother and child" as she "holds the child close to her face and he turns to her fully, attempting to embrace her with his small arms." Erikson concludes, "So it took the closeness of death for Michelangelo to recover what he had lost early in life, and we cannot help connecting this, the old man's refound hope, with St. Paul's saying, 'For now we see through a glass darkly; but then face to face; now I know in part; but then I shall know even as I am known.'"[65] Thus, Erikson suggests that as Michelangelo contemplated his own approaching death, the distance between the mother and her son was transcended, and the aging man regained the small boy's hope that he would never again be separated from the one who gave him life.

The relevance of this discussion of Michelangelo for Erikson himself is in the fact that, like Leonardo, Michelangelo had not one, but two mothers, and this was true, in a sense, for Erikson himself, though, as I have noted, in his case they were one and the same mother at different stages in his formative years: the mother in whose unrivaled company he spent the first several years of his life and the mother with whom he lived together with his stepfather from the age of three. Writing his essay on playing and actuality in 1972, at the age of seventy, Erikson longed for the first of these two mothers, hoping that he might meet *this* mother again.

The very fact that the two mothers would be indistinguishable to the untrained eye, however, recalls Freud's discussion of Leonardo's painting of *Saint Anne with Virgin and Child*. In a footnote added nine years later to his claim that Saint Anne is modeled after Leonardo's birth mother, Freud acknowledges that the painting could be read another way, that it is *Mary*, not Saint Anne, who is modeled after Leonardo's birth mother, Caterina. But this ambiguity does not trouble him, for

> if an attempt is made to separate the figures of Anne and Mary in this picture and to trace the outline of each, it will not be found altogether easy. One is inclined to say that they are fused with each other like badly condensed dream-figures, so that in

64. Ibid.
65. Ibid. Erikson is quoting here from 1 Cor 13:12 (KJV).

some places it is hard to say where Anne ends and where Mary begins. But what appears to a critic's eye as a fault, as a defect in composition, is vindicated in the eyes of analysis by reference to its secret meaning. It seems that for the artist the two mothers of his childhood were melted into a single form.[66]

Perhaps, then, the painting is merely registering the ambiguity universally inherent in the mother-infant relationship, that the infant inevitably experiences the mother as a dual figure. This being the case, it was Leonardo's genius (owing to the traumatic circumstances of his infancy) to have portrayed this ambiguity in the painting of *Saint Anne with Virgin and Child*.

As Collins's detailed analysis of the composition of the two maternal figures indicates, Leonardo struggled with the problem of how to represent multiple maternal figures in a single painting, especially how to portray them as both similar and dissimilar to each other. The Virgin is seated on Saint Anne's lap, their legs are intertwined. Saint Anne, the mother of Mary, is portrayed as a young woman, and the two women's faces bear a striking resemblance: Thus, Collins notes, "he re-created in his art a puzzling fusion of maternal identities that corresponded to the bewildering and traumatic appearance and disappearance of maternal figures during his infancy."[67] This, then, was Leonardo's pictorial representation of the traumatic experience that led Freud's grandson to create the "gone-there" game.

On the other hand, Erikson suggests that Michelangelo's last painting of the mother and child expresses "the old man's refound hope."[68] Thus, the painting takes the old man back to the period in his life before the inevitable loss of his mother, whatever the circumstances may have been, to the period when mother and infant gazed upon one another—face-to-face—and neither turned away.

In the concluding paragraph of his psychobiography of Leonardo, Freud asks whether one has the right to object to an inquiry, the one in which he has just engaged, "which ascribes to accidental circumstances of his parental constellation so decisive an influence on a person's fate—which, for example, makes Leonardo's fate depend on his illegitimate birth and on the barrenness of his first stepmother Donna Albiera?"[69] He answers his own question with an unequivocal no:

> If one considers chance to be unworthy of determining our fate,
> [this] is simply a relapse into the pious view of the Universe

66. Freud, *Leonardo da Vinci and a Memory of His Childhood*, 64.

67. Collins, *Leonardo, Psychoanalysis & Art Theory*, 102.

68. Erikson, *A Way of Looking at Things*, 317.

69. Freud, *Leonardo da Vinci and a Memory of His Childhood*, 86–87.

which Leonardo himself was on the way to overcoming when he wrote that the sun does not move. We naturally feel hurt that a just God and a kindly providence do not protect us better from such influences during the most defenseless period of our lives. At the same time we are all too ready to forget that in fact everything to do with our life is chance, from our origin out of the meeting of spermatozoon and ovum onwards—chance which nevertheless has a share in the law and necessity of nature, and which merely lacks any connection with our wishes and illusions.[70]

Erikson wrote what amounts to a coda to Freud's concluding paragraph in his elegiac description of the eighth stage of the life cycle in *Childhood and Society*. The problem he set for himself was how to communicate what he meant by the "ego integrity" that stands over against "despair." Calling this ego integrity "a state of mind," he noted that one of its constituents is "the acceptance of one's one and only life cycle as something that had to be and that, by necessity, permitted of no substitutions: it thus means a new, a different love of one's parents."[71] Thus, ego integrity entails the acceptance of one's fate, and through such acceptance, a "different" love of one's parents emerges, a love based on the recognition that although one is the progeny of chance, such chance has its own inevitability, allowing for no substitutions. This love arises out of the ashes of fantasies, beginning in childhood, of a different fate from the one into which one was born. Erikson's own childhood fantasy was that he, "the son of much better parents, had been altogether a foundling."[72] In place of this fantasy, he suggests, in effect, that the key to the old man's refound hope is *acceptance* of one's one-and-only life cycle as something that had to be, and had to be as it was.

ERIKSON'S INHIBITION AS AN ARTIST

The second theme in Freud's psychobiography of Leonardo that bears on Erikson's own life and career concerns Leonardo's inhibition as an artist as reflected in his slowness and in his difficulty in completing paintings. According to biographer Lawrence Friedman, Erikson viewed himself as decidedly "impressionistic," and "focused on themes of being 'alone w[ith] nature like Van Gogh.'"[73] His woodcuts of large fields with rocks, hills, and

70. Ibid., 87.
71. Erikson, *Childhood and Society,* rev. ed., 268.
72. Erikson, "'Identity Crisis' in Autobiographic Perspective," 27.
73. Friedman, *Identity's Architect,* 47.

other objects that came alive with vibrant energy resembled van Gogh's scenes:

> However, daring use of paint and color had been central to Van Gogh, and Erik bemoaned the fact that he "never learned to paint w[ith] color." He tried to move beyond "black and white drawings and woodcuts" and felt that if he wanted a significant career as an artist, he would have to do so, but he couldn't develop a facility for the use of color and paint; that "was where the inhibition was," he recalled.[74]

Significantly, Erikson ascribes to himself the same word—*inhibition*—that Freud uses in reference to Leonardo's difficulties as an artist. The word implies a mental or psychological process that restrains or suppresses an action, emotion, or thought. Thus, there is more going on here than merely a matter of technical skill. In fact, if Erikson's difficulties with color had been merely a matter of skill, he would have been helped by Leonardo's own recommendations to aspiring young artists on the use of color.[75]

In *Vital Involvement in Old Age* Erikson assigns a maladaptive and malignant tendency to each of the life cycle stages, the maladaptive being an excess of the positive dimension, and the malignant being an excess of the negative. Inhibition is the malignant tendency in the third stage (or play age) of the life cycle—*initiative vs. guilt*—while ruthlessness is the maladaptive tendency.[76] Thus, "in the third, the play age, an initiative not balanced by a sufficient empathic capacity for guilt may condone an all too guiltless *ruthlessness* (and eventually a militant self-extension), while an excessive tendency toward guilt and thus an impairment of purpose may result in a malignant *self-inhibition*."[77] In effect, excessive guilt is the critical factor in the child's inability to exercise initiative.

Freud traces Leonardo's inhibition to the *disappearance* of his mother between the ages of three and five (years that correspond to the play age in Erikson's life-cycle model). I suggest that Erikson's inhibition may also be traced back to the third stage of the life cycle, but that the inhibition had more to do with the *appearance* of his mother's husband, "that intruder, the bearded doctor, with his healing love and mysterious instruments."[78] Before young Erik knew this man as his stepfather, the boy had experienced him

74. Ibid., 47. These quotations are from various discussions with colleagues and personal letters.

75. Leonardo da Vinci, *Leonardo on Painting*, 70–84.

76. Erikson, et al., *Vital Involvement in Old Age*, 45.

77. Ibid., 43 (italics added).

78. Erikson, "'Identity Crisis' in Autobiographic Perspective," 27.

as his doctor, the man to whom his mother would take him for medical examinations and treatment. It was this very man who subsequently had "given me my last name (which I have retained as a middle name) and expected me to become a doctor like himself."[79] However, "like other youths with artistic or literary aspirations, I became intensely alienated from everything my bourgeois family stood for."[80]

Thus, it would appear that the inhibition from which Erikson suffered in the years when he believed himself to be an artist was prompted by guilt—guilt over what appeared to be a sense of ingratitude for the legitimacy his stepfather had bestowed upon him. His ingratitude was due in part to the fact that young Erik was falsely informed that his stepfather was his biological father. But a deeper reason was that his stepfather intruded on his singular relationship with his mother. Inhibited by guilt due to the fact that his pursuit of a career as an artist was in direct conflict with his stepfather's expectation that he would become a pediatrician, Erik eventually returned to his parents' home in Karlsruhe in utter despair, his aspirations as an artist in shambles.

In his concluding comments on Michelangelo in "Play and Actuality," Erikson acknowledges that the sketches of the Madonna "would seem to be only a subsidiary theme in Michelangelo's gigantic confrontations," for he "not only hammered away at his strangely tortured sculptures, sovereignly transcended by irate Moses, but also painted his own version of Adam and the Creator and of Christ at the Last Judgment in the Sistine Chapel."[81] Furthermore, "in a sonnet, he describes how, at the crippling expense of his whole physique, he gazed up at the ceiling, lifting arm and brush: 'my beard toward Heaven, I feel the back of my brain upon my neck.'"[82] What is going on here? Why this hammering? Why such intensity? Erikson comments:

> But whether or not a mighty compensatory force intensified Michelangelo's creative furor, we may well pause to wonder at the very fact of the singular fascination which these artistically created visual worlds painted on hallowed halls hold for us. *Could all this be ontologically related to the singular importance of that playfully structured visual field in the beginnings of childhood?*[83]

At great physical expense Michelangelo overcame whatever inhibition he may have felt toward the fathers who—whether through hate, love, or

79. Ibid.
80. Ibid., 28.
81. Erikson, *A Way of Looking at Things*, 317.
82. Ibid.
83. Ibid., 317–18 (italics added).

both—had the power to render their sons incapable of fulfilling their own dreams and aspirations. Michelangelo's contemporary, Leonardo, avoided this confrontation by painting women, children, and androgynous men (as in *Saint John the Baptist*).

FROM ASPIRING ARTIST TO CHILD ANALYST

If Michelangelo refused to be inhibited by the fathers, Erikson capitulated, but in his own way: Instead of becoming a pediatrician like his stepfather, he became a psychoanalyst who also focused on the healing of children. Though Erikson's introduction to Freud's group may seem to have been mere chance, it was providential that he was received into the psychoanalytic circle in Vienna. Here is the full text of what Erikson had to say in his autobiographical essay about his acceptance into the psychoanalytic community in Vienna:

> And if I ask myself in what spirit I accepted my truly astounding adoption by the Freudian circle, I can only surmise (not without embarrassment) that it was a kind of positive stepson identity that made me take for granted that I should be accepted where I did not quite belong. By the same token, however, I had to cultivate not-belonging and keep contact with the artist in me.[84]

Perhaps it helped—in both respects of belonging and not-belonging—that Erikson had become a member of a group whose founder confessed to having his own troubles with colors but at the same time had associated colors with children's play. In his chapter on color in psychology in *Color Codes*, Charles A. Riley II points out that Freud's references to color are few in comparison to those of Jung. He wonders why this was so:

> You may scour the works of Freud for any but the most offhand color references; even the monograph on Leonardo gives little notice of it. In *The Interpretation of Dreams* there is a brief paragraph on the importance of memory in the excitation of what he called the "psychical perceptual system of the visual organ" during dreams. He readily admits that his dreams are relatively impoverished in "sensory elements" like color. Could this explain why Freud pays scant attention to color?[85]

84. Erikson, "'Identity Crisis' in Autobiographic Perspective," 29.
85. Riley, *Color Codes*, 303.

In this paragraph from *The Interpretation of Dreams*, of which Riley speaks, Freud says that the best he can do as far as illustrating the role of color in dreams is concerned is to cite a dream of his own that *did* involve color. Riley notes that this was

> a dream in which he saw water of a deep blue, against which brown smoke rose from a ship's funnels by the red and dark brown buildings onshore. The colors were those of his children's toy blocks, shown to him the day before. The children's play buildings were linked with the recollection of a recent trip to Italy: "This was associated with color impressions from my last travels in Italy: the beautiful blue of the Isonzo and the lagoons and the brown of the Carso."[86]

Riley suggests that for Freud "the colors of the unconscious have a direct mimetic link to actual experience," and that "the conclusion drawn from the unusual experience with a colorful dream is an apt precis of his low-keyed views on the subject."[87] As Freud put it, "The beauty of the colors in the dream was only a repetition of something seen in my memory." For Riley, "this is a very literal-minded approach to color," and the message is that for Freud "colors are what they are, or were, and nothing more."[88]

However impoverished Freud's views of color may have been, one can well imagine that Erikson saw in this passage in *The Interpretation of Dreams* a vision of his own future: the colors that Freud saw in his dream were the very colors that Freud had recently seen on his children's toys and had previously seen in the natural world on his trip to Italy—colors that Erikson had so much wanted to be able to paint. It may appear to be a major diminishment of one's vocational aspirations to go from attempting to paint vibrant landscapes to observing children playing with their toys, but as Erikson writes in his autobiographical essay,

> To Freud, the *via regia* [royal road] to mental life had been the dream. For me, children's play became the first *via regia* to an understanding of growing man's conflicts and triumphs, his repetitive working through of the past, and his creative self-renewal in truly playful moments. I identified with Freud, then, not so much as the former laboratory worker who insisted on a terminology made for the observation of transformable quantities of drive enlivening inner structures, but as the discerner of verbal and visual configurations which revealed what

86. Ibid.
87. Ibid.
88. Ibid. Quotations are from Freud's *The Interpretation of Dreams*, 585–86.

consciousness wanted to enlarge upon, and what it attempted to disguise—and revealed.[89]

In effect, Erikson made a career of the insight that throughout our lives, we return to the conflicts and triumphs of the "play age." It is also important to note that, in embarking on this career, he identified with Sigmund Freud and, specifically, with the artistic side of Freud as "the discerner of verbal and visual configurations" that revealed what consciousness revealed in its very attempts at disguise and concealment. As Erikson goes on to confess,

> Freud's phenomenological and literary approach, which seemed to reflect the very creativity of the unconscious, held in itself a promise without which psychoanalytic theory would have meant little to me. . . . This may well have an admixture of a particular and maybe peculiar identification with Freud's freedom and enjoyment of inquiry.[90]

Erikson's identification with Freud brings us back around to the issue of inhibition and, specifically, to the excessive guilt that stands in the way of the child's—and young adult's—expression of initiative, that leaves him in the state of inactivity typical of the melancholic men Freud encountered in his psychoanalytic practice and writes about in "Mourning and Melancholia." Erikson's stepfather had expected—or strongly advised—his stepson to follow in his own footsteps. Perhaps Dr. Homburger envisioned that one day the two of them would work together, and that Erik would eventually take over his medical practice. However, this imposition of his plans for his stepson's future merely increased and fortified Erikson's determination to follow a different path altogether.

Freud did not do this. In fact, as Friedman notes, Sigmund and Anna Freud's offices were both on the second floor of the family apartment, and they were separated by a waiting room. As Erikson sat waiting for his appointment with Anna, he would look up as her father's door would open and he would invite his next patient into his office. Later, Erikson recalled feeling envious of Freud's own patients; sometimes Erikson "felt like a second-rate analysand who had been assigned to a 'female track' for his analytic training."[91]

To be so close yet so far from the man he had come to admire must have been difficult for him. Yet, as I will discuss in more detail in chapter 7, Erikson points out in *Toys and Reasons* that the infant's initial visual

89. Erikson, "'Identity Crisis' in Autobiographic Perspective," 39–40.

90. Ibid., 40.

91. Friedman, *Identity's Architect*, 78.

perception of the mother—whom he calls the "primary parent"—is later joined by the auditory perception of her presence, which "reinforces the hope that the voice heard will come 'around the corner' and be confirmed as the familiar face."[92] It is perhaps not unreasonable, then, to think that Erikson felt the voice of the father "around the corner" during his sessions with the daughter, and perhaps the very fact that they were not in the same visual field enabled Erikson to feel that the voice was not one of accusation and faultfinding but of encouragement and confidence in his ability to find his own way in life.

When Erik, Joan, and their two small sons left Vienna for Copenhagen in 1933, where he hoped he could set up a practice of his own, there was considerable tension between himself and Anna Freud, as she perceived that Joan, who was concerned that her husband would always be an "underling" in Vienna, was the primary instigator of the plan to leave.[93] It seems enormously significant therefore that Sigmund Freud was the only member of the psychoanalytic community to see Erikson and his family off. As they parted, Freud urged Erik "to have a kind and loving heart."[94] With this gesture, the younger man was the beneficiary of a paternal blessing, a blessing from the very person who exemplified for him the freedom and enjoyment of inquiry. It is noteworthy in this connection that Freud concluded his psychobiography of Leonardo da Vinci with the observation that in the way that Leonardo repressed his feelings toward his mother in childhood but later succeeded in sublimating these feelings into a craving for knowledge there is "a degree of freedom which cannot be resolved any further by psychoanalytic means."[95] And so with Erikson, there was a point where Freud was content to entrust the recipient of his paternal blessing to a future that neither man could clearly foresee.

92 Erikson, *Toys and Reasons,* 47.

93. Friedman, *Identity's Architect,* 96–97.

94. Ibid., 97.

95. Freud, *Leonardo da Vinci and a Memory of His Childhood,* 85–86.

3

The Resourceful Self

Erikson's *Insight and Responsibility* is a collection of six essays originally presented as lectures in the late 1950s and early 1960s in the United States, Germany, Vienna, and India. I will be focusing in this chapter on the essay titled "Human Strength and the Cycle of Generations."[1] This essay is an expansion of an address he gave for the Psychoanalytic Institute and Mount Zion Medical Center in San Francisco in 1960. In the lecture he presents what he calls "human strengths" or "virtues" that correspond to the eight stages of the life cycle. I want to make the case that the first four of these strengths or virtues, which correspond to the first four stages of the life cycle, play a critical role in the development of the *resourceful self*. I believe that they do so because *resourcefulness* relates not only to the capacity to avail oneself of external resources—resources provided by one's social and material environment—but also to the existence of inner resources, of strengths or abilities within oneself. In fact, an important inner resource is the capacity to avail oneself of external resources.

A SCHEDULE OF HUMAN STRENGTHS

Erikson's lecture on the human strengths is based on his well-known life-cycle model with its eight stages of development originally presented in his chapter titled "Eight Stages of Man" in *Childhood and Society*.[2] The chapter was expanded and titled "Eight Ages of Man" in the revised edition of *Child-*

1. Erikson, *Insight and Responsibility*, 109–58.
2. Erikson, *Childhood and Society*, orig. ed., 219–34.

48

hood and Society.[3] The life-cycle model was also presented in the chapter titled "Growth and Crises of the Healthy Personality" in *Identity and the Life Cycle.*[4]

The key feature of this model is that each stage is composed of a positive and negative pole, and ideally these interactive poles reflect a "balance of forces" with a "ratio" favoring the "positive" pole. Some of the terminology used to represent these poles was changed over the years, but the following chart lists the themes of the eight stages as presented in *The Life Cycle Completed.*[5] It also lists the human strengths.

Stage	Psychosocial Crises	Human Strengths
Infancy	Basic Trust vs. Mistrust	Hope
Early Childhood	Autonomy vs. Shame and Doubt	Will
Play Age	Initiative vs. Guilt	Purpose
School Age	Industry vs. Inferiority	Competence
Adolescence	Identity vs. Identity Confusion	Fidelity
Young Adulthood	Intimacy vs. Isolation	Love
Adulthood	Generativity vs. Stagnation	Care
Old Age	Integrity vs. Despair	Wisdom

Although the term "human strength" appears in the title, the essay begins with the heading "A Schedule of Virtues" and is followed by the acknowledgement that a psychoanalyst like himself "has good reason to show restraint in speaking about human virtue," for "in doing so lightly he could be suspected of ignoring the evidential burden of his daily observations which acquaints him with the 'much furrowed ground from which our virtues proudly spring.'" Moreover, one might "be accused of abandoning the direction of Freudian thought in which conscious values can find a responsible re-evaluation only when the appreciation of the unconscious and of the irrational forces in man is firmly established."[6]

However, Erikson defends his decision to focus on human virtues on the grounds that "the very development of psychoanalytic thought,"

3. Erikson, *Childhood and Society,* rev. ed., 247–74.

4. Erikson, *Identity and the Life Cycle,* orig. ed., 50–100; rev. ed., 51–107

5. Erikson, *The Life Cycle Completed,* 56–57.

6. Erikson, *Insight and Responsibility,* 111. This statement and several others that I will quote in this chapter do not use gender-inclusive language. The primary texts cited here were written and published before gender-inclusive language became an established norm. Later writings by Erikson are more reflective of this norm, but it is also worth noting that English was not his native language.

especially its current preoccupation with "ego strength," suggests that human strength be reconsidered, "not in the sense of nobility and rectitude
as cultivated by moralities, but in the sense of 'inherent strength.'" He adds
that psychoanalysts, having listened to life-histories for more than a half
century, have in fact "developed an 'unofficial' image of the strengths inherent in the individual life cycle and in the sequence of generations."[7] Erikson
thinks here "of those most enjoyable occasions when we can agree that a
patient has really improved—not, as the questionnaires try to make us say,
markedly improved, or partially improved—but essentially so."[8] On such
occasions, "the loss of symptoms is mentioned only in passing, while the
decisive criterion is an increase in the strength and staying power of the
patient's concentration on pursuits which are somehow right, whether it is
in love or in work, in home life, friendship, or citizenship."[9]

Why, then, do we shy away from any systematic discussion of these
human strengths? Why, instead of using words suggesting that the patient
has acquired or regained a sense of personal strength, do we merely say
that he or she is "relatively resistant to regression," or "somewhat freer from
repression," or "less given to ambivalence"? Why, in other words, do we talk
in terms of double negatives despite the fact that "we know that in a state of
health or of mental or affective clarity a process of order takes over which is
not and cannot be subsumed under the most complete list of negatives"?[10]

To be sure, Erikson acknowledges that psychoanalysts now use the
term "ego-synthesis" to express some of this process, but this term fails to
convey the fact that there are occasions when a person is endowed with "a
total quality which we might term 'animated' or 'spirited.'" Although this
quality is difficult to "classify," our failure to acknowledge the existence of
this quality makes us unable to "maintain any true perspective regarding the
best moments of man's balance, [or] the deepest of his tragedy."[11]

7. Ibid., 111.
8. Ibid., 111–12.
9. Ibid., 112.
10. Ibid.

11. Ibid. In his conversation with Richard I. Evans published in Evans, *Dialogue
with Erik Erikson,* Erikson notes that he decided, "somewhat challengingly," to call the
basic strengths "virtues" in order "to point to an evolutionary basis of man's lofty moral-
isms." For example, hope "is a very basic strength without which we couldn't stay alive,
and not something invented by theologians and philosophers." He acknowledges that
"many people are dubious of the attempt to tie anything which sounds like a virtue or
strength to an evolutionary process," and guesses that this is a reaction "against earlier
attempts to show that the highest form of evolution is Christianity or that values of
other systems are built into evolution." Nonetheless, he believes that humans are born
"with the capacity to learn to hope" and that "these virtues are as necessary in human

Thus, Erikson proposes in this essay to investigate "the developmental roots" and "the evolutionary rationale of certain basic human qualities" which he will call "virtues." Why "virtues"? One reason is that he finds the plural word "strengths" somewhat awkward. However, a more important reason is that "the word *virtue* serves to make a point."[12] Erikson rejects the Latin meaning of *virtue*—i.e. "virility"—because although it suggests "the combination of *strength, restraint* and *courage* to be conveyed here," it has the connotation of *manliness,* and it makes little sense "to consider manliness the official virtue of the universe, especially since it dawns on us that womanhood may be forced to bear the larger share in saving humanity from man's climactic and catastrophic aspirations."[13]

But "old English gave a special meaning to the word 'virtue' which does admirably," for it "meant *inherent strength* or *active quality,* and was used, for example, for the undiminished potency of well preserved medicines and liquors."[14] In effect, "*virtue* and *spirit* once had interchangeable meanings—and not only in the virtue that endowed liquid spirits." Therefore, the question with which he is concerned in this essay is "what 'virtue' goes out' of a human being when he loses the strength we have in mind, and 'by virtue of' what strength does man acquire that animated or spirited quality without which his moralities become mere moralism and his ethics feeble goodness?" To address this question, Erikson will focus on "certain human qualities of strength" and "relate them to that process by which ego strength may be developed from stage to stage and imparted from generation to generation."[15] To assist him in this task, he will avail himself of his recent efforts "to delineate the whole life-cycle as an integrated psychosocial phenomenon."[16]

As for the task of naming the basic virtues "with which human beings steer themselves and others through life," Erikson will resist the temptation to create neologisms out of Latin roots and instead use "the everyday words" that have been "ripened in the usage of generations."[17] Thus, he will "speak of *Hope, Will, Purpose,* and *Competence* as the rudiments of virtue

---

adaptation as instincts are among the animals." In fact, he "would go further and claim that we have almost an instinct for fidelity"—or any other of the human strengths (Evans, *Dialogue with Erik Erikson* 17, 30).

12. Erikson, *Insight and Responsibility,* 112.

13. Ibid., 113.

14. Ibid. (italics original)

15. Ibid.

16. Ibid., 114.

17. Ibid., 115.

developed in childhood; of *Fidelity* as the adolescent virtue; and of *Love, Care,* and *Wisdom* as the central virtues of adulthood."[18]

He notes that despite their seeming discontinuity, "these qualities depend on each other"; for example, the virtue of will "cannot be trained until hope is secure, nor can love become reciprocal until fidelity has proven reliable." Furthermore, "each virtue in its location in the schedule of all the virtues is vitally interrelated to other segments of human development." These segments include the *stages of psychosexuality,* the *psychosocial crises,* and the *steps of cognitive maturation.* But for the purposes of this essay Erikson will take these other "schedules" for granted and restrict himself to the "parallel timetable of the evolving virtues."[19]

DEFINING THE HUMAN STRENGTHS

In his discussion of the individual virtues or strengths, Erikson provides a brief definition (what he calls a "first formulation") of each one, then discusses its emergence at a particular stage in the life cycle. Although, as I indicated, he does not to consider their relationship to the other developmental segments in any systematic way, his earlier writings on these other developmental "schedules" are implicit in what he says about the various strengths. In the interests of space, I will simply provide here his definitions (or brief formulations) of the eight human strengths. While the subtleties of their meanings will perhaps be lost when they are presented in such truncated form, at least it will be evident from these definitions that each strength arises out of the individual's confrontation with the psychosocial crisis of the developmental stage to which this crisis relates.

(1) *Hope* is the enduring belief in the attainability of fervent wishes, in spite of the dark urges and rages which mark the beginning of existence.

(2) *Will* is the unbroken determination to exercise free choice as well as self-restraint, in spite of the unavoidable experience of shame and doubt in infancy.

(3) *Purpose* is the courage to envision and pursue valued goals uninhibited by the defeat of infantile fantasies, by guilt and by the foiling fear of punishment.

(4) *Competence* is the free exercise of dexterity and intelligence in the completion of tasks, unimpaired by infantile inferiority.

18. Ibid., 115.
19. Ibid.

(5) *Fidelity* is the ability to sustain loyalties freely pledged in spite of the inevitable contradictions of value systems.

(6) *Love* is mutuality of devotion forever subduing the antagonisms inherent in divided function.

(7) *Care* is the widening concern for what has been generated by love, necessity, or accident; it overcomes the ambivalence adhering to irreversible obligation.

(8) *Wisdom* is detached concern with life itself, in the face of death itself.

THE HUMAN STRENGTHS AS AN EPIGENETIC SYSTEM

Following his presentation of the schedule of the human strengths, Erikson expresses a concern that he had previously expressed about his psychosocial stages, namely, that some writers were turning the model into an achievement scale by focusing on the positive senses—trust, autonomy, initiative, and so forth—and blithely omitting the negative senses—mistrust, shame and doubt, guilt, and so on.[20] Erikson is similarly concerned that his list of human strengths or virtues "will be eagerly accepted by some as a potential inventory for tests of adjustment, or as a new production schedule in the manufacture of desirable children, citizens, and workers," and that others may "foresee the use of the schedule as a new set of ideals, to be held up with moral fervor."[21] He is convinced that neither of these will work, but this will not necessarily deter these persons from trying.

Then, however, he asks whether he should be even more concerned about the list itself, because to some persons the human strengths he has selected and their distribution throughout the cycle of life "may well appear rather arbitrary."[22] He can only hope that he has made clear that these emergent strengths "are not external ornaments easily added or omitted according to the fancies of esthetic or moral style"—that, in fact, this whole "body" of strengths is anchored in three different systems: *epigenesis* in individual development, the *sequence of generations*, and the *growth of the ego*.[23]

As the system of *epigenesis* has the most bearing on the emphasis of this chapter on the childhood origins of the *resourceful self*, I will confine the following discussion to this particular system. In doing so, I will make use of Erikson's earlier discussions of *epigenesis*, because his reflections on

20. Erikson, *Childhood and Society*, rev. ed., 273–74.
21. Erikson, *Insight and Responsibility*, 134.
22. Ibid.
23. Ibid., 135.

epigenesis in his essay on human strength and the cycle of generations refer to these earlier writings but do not present their points and conclusions as clearly, in part because he addresses Jean Piaget's view that the epigenetic process cannot be said to develop in identifiable stages.[24]

In his article "The Problems of Infancy and Early Childhood," originally published in 1940, Erikson describes *epigenetic development* as "the step by step growth of the fetal organs" and emphasizes that each organ has its time of origin, and that "this time factor is as important as the place of origin."[25] He cites the observation by Charles H. Stockard in *The Physical Basis of Personality* that if the eye, for example, does not arise at the appointed time, "it will never be able to express itself fully, since the moment for the rapid outgrowth of some other part will have arrived, and this will tend to dominate the less active region, and suppress the belated tendency for eye expression."[26] Furthermore, Stockard pointed out that the organ that "misses its time of ascendency not only is doomed as an individual but endangers at the same time the whole hierarchy of organs." Thus, "not only does the arrest of a rapidly budding part, therefore, tend to suppress its development temporarily, but the premature loss of supremacy to some other organ renders it impossible for the suppressed part to come again into dominance, so that it is permanently modified."[27] In short, epigenetic development has two essential features of *normal sequence* and *proper time*.

Erikson claims that the schedule of strengths he has presented in his essay on the human strengths and the cycle of generations is a reflection of this epigenetic ground plan. Under normal conditions, the strengths emerge in a predetermined sequence and each one has its appointed time of ascendance or dominance. If this sequence and/or proper time are disrupted for some reason or other, the whole system is weakened. The symptoms of this weakening are "disorder, dysfunction, disintegration, and anomie."[28] This is why Erikson uses the word "schedule" for the list of human strengths; for each of the strengths comes into its own "on schedule." This is also why he uses the phrase "process of order" to describe what is taking place when a patient has gained "a state of health or of mental and affective clarity."[29]

However, Erikson also wants to emphasize that the proper time of its ascendancy or dominance is also a time of crisis, for the human strengths or

---

24. Jean Piaget, in Osterrieth et al., *Le Problème des Studes en Psychologie de L'enfant*.

25. Erikson, *A Way of Looking at Things*, 549.

26. Ibid.

27. Ibid.

28. Erikson, *Insight and Responsibility*, 139.

29. Ibid., 112.

virtues are intimately related to the psychosocial crisis of the stage to which they have been assigned, and this means that their emergence is neither automatic nor without tension and possible conflict. Also, although each virtue has its proper time of ascendance and crisis, it does not then go into some sort of hiatus but continues to persist and undergo further developments. Erikson cites, for example, the strengths of hope and will:

> In an epigenetic development of the kind here envisaged, each item has its time of ascendance and crisis, yet each persists throughout life. Hope is the first and most basic and yet it is also the most lasting; it is the most stable and yet acquires new qualities, depending on the general stage reached. Thus, in adulthood, hope may have become invested in a formulated faith or endow an implicit one. Similarly, the rudiments of will become part of an adult's determination, both in the sense of his capacity to exert strong will over others and in his necessary self-control.[30]

Erikson claims that the strengths he has identified are integral to the *epigenetic* process of development. This is a rather bold claim. (His use of the word *virtues* makes it seem even bolder.) The claim is bold because the *epigenetic process* is fundamentally physical. That is, the epigenetic process concerns organic development or growth. In contrast, words like *hope, will, purpose,* and *competence* name "human qualities" whose connection to organic growth is certainly not obvious. But demonstrating the connection between organic growth and virtue development is the very task that he set for himself in his 1940 article on "Problems of Infancy and Early Childhood" and then went on to address in a more systematic way in his chapter "The Theory of Infantile Sexuality" in *Childhood and Society*.[31]

BODY ZONES, PHYSICAL MODES OF APPROACH, AND SOCIAL MODALITIES

In his chapter in *Childhood and Society* on the theory of infantile sexuality, Erikson endorses Freud's view that pregenital sexuality (i.e. from birth to puberty) has four "phases of development of the sexual organization."[32] The first phase is *oral* (i.e. involving sexual activity whose focus is the ingestion of food). The second phase is *sadistic-anal* (i.e., involving sexual aims asso-

---

30. Ibid., 140.
31. Erikson, *Childhood and Society,* rev. ed., 48–108.
32. Freud, *Three Essays on the Theory of Sexuality,* 63–66.

ciated with the erotogenic mucous membrane of the anus). The third phase is *genital* (i.e., involving sexual activity whose focus is the genital organs). Finally, the fourth is a *latency* period (i.e. a period when the external genitalia do not undergo further growth). These four "phases of development of the sexual organization" are the basis for the four childhood stages of Erikson's life-cycle model.

However, Erikson states that he wants to "build a bridge from clinical experience to observations on societies" (hence the title of his book, *Childhood and Society*), and this means that although it is vitally important to "speak of biologically given potentialities which develop with the child's organism" and to recognize that psychoanalysis cannot "remain a workable system of inquiry without its basic biological formulations," these formulations may also require "reconsideration."[33] The theoretical section of the chapter that seeks to formulate this reconsideration focuses on the *body zones*, the *physical modes of approach,* and the *social modalities.*

The *body zones* are the locus of the infant and child's interaction with the environment: these zones are the oral, the anal-urethral, and the genital regions of the body. (With the term *anal-urethral*, Erikson adds the function—*urethral*—of the bladder to Freud's anal phase.)

The *physical modes of approach* are the infant and child's forms of approach to the environment that occur within these body zones. These include *incorporation* (for the oral zone); *retention* and *elimination* (for the anal-urethral zone); and *intrusion* (for the genital zone). For Erikson, though, the *body zones* in each case are not as narrowly circumscribed as those identified in Freud's original formulations. Thus, not only the mouth (which is used for the ingestion of food) but also the whole skin surface and the sense organs (especially the eyes) are represented by the *incorporative mode* in its receptivity to outward stimulation. Similarly, the *retentive-eliminative mode* includes not only the anus and sphincter muscles but the whole muscular structure of the body; and the *intrusive mode* includes not only the genitalia but also the locomotor capacities of the growing child together with the capacity to intrude into other people's ears and minds by aggressive talking. In effect, these three *physical modes* of approach involve the whole body.[34]

33. Erikson, *Childhood and Society*, rev. ed., 70.

34. Ibid., 72–97. In his discussion of the genital phase of sexual development, Freud invites this expansion of the *body zones* to include the skin surface in general in the first stage, the muscular system in general in the second stage, and the locomotor capacities of the growing child in the third stage. In a section of this discussion subtitled "Muscular Activity," he writes: "We are all familiar with the fact that children feel a need for a large amount of active muscular exercise and derive extraordinary pleasure from

Finally, the *social modalities* are the expression of these *physical modes of approach* in ways that are personally and culturally significant. Thus, the *social modality* of the *incorporative mode* is *to get*, which essentially means "to receive and to accept what is given."[35] Erikson adds that 'in thus *getting what is given*, and in learning to *get somebody to do* what one wants to have done, the baby also develops the necessary ego groundwork to *get to be* the giver."[36] The *social modality* of the *retentive/eliminative mode* involves "the simple antithesis of *letting go* and *holding* on," and their "nature, ratio, and sequence" are "of decisive importance both for the development of the individual personality and for that of collective attitudes."[37] The *social modality* of the *intrusive mode* is *to make*, especially in the sense of *being on the make*, a phrase that suggests "head-on attack, enjoyment of competition, insistence on goal [and] pleasure of conquest."[38]

In setting forth these *zones, modes,* and *modalities,* Erikson emphasizes the critical role played by the first—or *incorporative*—stage. He discusses the fact that this stage is composed of two phases, the first involving a benign and relaxed interaction between the baby and mother (one of mutual regulation and reciprocity) and the second introducing a severe, traumatic change producing a lasting sense in the infant that something has gone terribly wrong. He emphasizes here the eruption of teeth, the infant's need to bite harder in order to alleviate the tension and pain caused by the teeth, and the proximity of this biting process to that of weaning and to the increasing separation from the mother or maternal person, who may go back to work, become pregnant again, or both. Unless the baby's faith in self and others "has already been shaken in the first stage by unduly provoked or prolonged paroxysms of rage and exhaustion," it is at this time "that 'good' and 'evil' enter the baby's world." Erikson adds:

> Our clinical work indicates that this point in the individual's
> early history is the origin of an evil dividedness, where anger
> at the gnawing teeth, and anger at the withdrawing mother, and

---

satisfying it. Whether this pleasure has any connection with sexuality, whether it itself comprises sexual satisfaction or whether it can become the occasion of sexual excitation—all of this is open to critical questioning. . . . It is, however, a fact that a number of people report that they experienced the first excitement in their genitals while they were romping or wrestling with playmates—a situation in which, apart from general muscular exertion, there is a large amount of conflict with the skin of the opponent" (Freud, *Three Essays on the Theory of Sexuality*, 68–69).

35. Erikson, *Childhood and Society*, rev. ed., 75.

36. Ibid.

37. Ibid., 82.

38. Ibid., 90.

anger with one's impotent anger all leads to a forceful experience of sadistic and masochistic confusion leaving the general
impression that once upon a time one destroyed one's unity with
a maternal matrix.[39]

In short, the oral stage—with its two phases—forms in the infant "the
springs of the *basic sense of trust* and the *basic sense of evil* which remain the
source of primal anxiety and of primal hope throughout life."[40] Note that
in addition to using similar wording both here and in the name he gives to
the first stage of psychosocial development (*basic trust vs. basic mistrust*),
Erikson also introduces the word—*hope*—that was to become the first human strength or virtue.

This sense of dividedness continues into the second stage. However, in
the second stage the existential sense of evil takes on a moral aspect relating
to good and bad behavior. Thus, in his discussion of the *social modality* of
the second stage, Erikson emphasizes that one develops a will of one's own,
and that it may be in the service of good, but that it may also produce bad
behavior.[41] Thus, Erikson anticipates his later identification of *will* as the
second human strength or virtue.

Erikson acknowledges that the culture of which the child's parents
or caretakers are the most immediate representatives plays a major role in
determining what makes a behavior good or bad, but he also notes that in
the specific case of the evacuation of the bowels and bladder, the child's own
physical comfort plays a significant—and pragmatic—role as well. Thus, the
sense of good and bad is not only derived from without but is also felt from
within. This, then, is a procedure that requires a cooperative attitude and
intention, and if accomplished successfully, produces a feeling of well-being
which says, "Well done."[42]

On the other hand, if one is so disposed, one can also produce a battle
of wills between oneself and the adult, despite the fact that the adult is acting

39. Ibid., 78–79. Erikson makes a connection between this "evil dividedness" and
the account in Genesis of Adam and Eve's act of disobedience (Gen 3:1–13): "This earliest catastrophe in the individual's relation to himself and to the world is probably the
ontogenetic contribution of the biblical saga of paradise, where the first people on earth
forfeited the right to pluck without effort what had been placed at their disposal; they
bit into the forbidden apple, and made God angry" (79). (*Ontogenetic* means the life
cycle of a single organism distinguished from the *phylogenetic*, i.e., the evolutionary
development of a species). We might add that the common belief that it was an apple
(whereas the biblical text simply says "fruit") suggests that their bite was forceful and
hard (which would be less likely if the fruit were a banana).

40. Ibid. 80.

41. Ibid, 81–82.

42. Ibid., 81.

in the child's own behalf. Much depends on how the adult handles this potentially volatile situation, for if the adult avoids rigid outer control and premature training, the child stands a much greater chance of developing "self-control" in terms of both letting go and holding on, and this is true not only in relation to the anal-urethral zone but also in relation to "the whole of the developing muscular system."[43]

Erikson concludes that the "enduring qualities" of the second developmental stage are a "sense of goodness" exemplifying autonomy and pride, and a "sense of badness" that takes the form of shame (the sense of having exposed oneself unnecessarily) and of doubt (the sense of looking back either literally or figuratively on what one has done).[44]

Finally, in his discussion of the *physical mode of approach* of *intrusiveness* in the third stage (which occurs near the end of the third year), Erikson notes that "walking is getting to be a thing of ease, of vigor."[45] To be sure, the child can walk much before this, but from the point of view of "ego progress" (i.e., of "a sense of coherence and security"), it is not really true than one can walk if one is only able to accomplish this feat more or less well, with more or fewer props, for short time spans. Thus, in the third stage the ego "has incorporated walking and running into the sphere of mastery where gravity is felt to be within," when one can forget the very fact that one is *doing* the walking and can instead find out what one can *do with* it. Only then do the legs become an unconscious part of oneself instead of being "an external ambulatory appendage."[46]

This ability "to move independently and vigorously" leads to the capacity to visualize new social roles.[47] In fact, Erikson suggests that this very ability enables the child at this stage to understand what roles are worth imitating, to associate with age mates, and (under the guidance of older children or adult guardians) to enter gradually into the politics of nursery school and neighborhood. The child's learning at this stage is inherently intrusive, leading to ever new facts and activities, and to an acute awareness of sexual differences, thus setting the stage for "infantile genitality." As for what "infantile genitality" means at this stage, it is at most "rudimentary, a mere promise of things to come." Moreover, if it is "not specifically provoked into precocious manifestation by special frustrations or special customs (such as organized sex play), it is apt to lead to no more than a series

43. Ibid., 81.
44. Ibid., 84–85.
45. Ibid., 85.
46. Ibid.
47. Ibid., 86.

of fascinating experiences which are frightening and pointless enough to be repressed during the stage which Freud called the 'latency' period—i.e., the long delay of physical sexual maturation."[48]

In his comments on the *social modality* of "making," Erikson notes that the child at this stage "develops the prerequisites for *initiative*, i.e., for the selection of goals and perseverance in approaching them." And although these goals may have a "sexual core" causing the child to develop "a deep sense of guilt" despite the fact that no overt "crime" has been committed (after all, it makes little sense to suggest that the child is capable of the crimes committed by King Oedipus), this secret guilt "helps to drive the whole weight of initiative toward desirable ideals and immediate practical goals."[49] Thus:

> At no other time than this is the individual more ready to learn quickly and avidly and to become big in the sense of sharing obligation and performance rather than power; in the sense of making things, not of 'making' people. At this stage the child learns to combine with other children for the purpose of constructing and planning instead of trying to boss and coerce them; and he is also able and willing to profit fully by the association with teachers and ideal prototypes.[50]

Thus, here again, Erikson not only introduces the terms he proposes for the psychosocial crisis of this stage (*initiative vs. guilt*), but he also uses the word—*purpose*—that was to become the third strength in his schedule of human strengths. The word *purpose* is especially significant, not only because this chapter in *Childhood and Society* on infantile sexuality was published a decade prior to his address on the human strengths, but also, and more importantly, because it shows the intimate connection between the human strengths and the epigenetic process of development. The human strengths of hope, will, and purpose are not merely—or even primarily—cultural values, but are qualities that originate in the way the body approaches and engages the world.[51]

Although Erikson does not discuss the fourth childhood stage in this chapter (other than to indicate that it is the *latency* period), he notes in his discussion of this stage in his later chapter, "Eight Stages of Man" (in the

---

48. Ibid., 86.

49. Ibid., 90.

50. Erikson, *Childhood and Society,* orig. ed., 86–87. These sentences have been eliminated from the revised edition.

51. One of Erikson's most compelling discussions of this intimate connection is the subsection of the "Play and Vision" section of *Toys and Reasons* titled "Seeing is Hoping," 41–51. I will focus on this discussion in chapter 7.

paragraphs on the psychosocial crisis of *industry vs. inferiority*) that with the oncoming latency period, the child "forgets, or rather sublimates, the necessity to 'make' people by direct attack" and "now learns to win recognition by producing things."[52] Having "mastered the ambulatory field and the organ modes" and having "experienced a sense of finality regarding the fact that there is no workable future within the womb of his family," he "becomes ready to apply himself to given skills and tasks, which go far beyond the mere playful expression of his organ modes or the pleasure in the function of his limbs," and "develops industry—i.e., he adjusts himself to the inorganic laws of the tool world." Thus, the child at this stage "can become an eager and absorbed unit of a productive situation," and bringing "a productive situation to completion is an aim which gradually supersedes the whims and wishes of his autonomous organism."[53] Erikson here cites Ives Hendrick's article on work and the pleasure principle, noting that "the work principle" teaches the child "the pleasure of work completion by steady attention and persevering diligence."[54]

The danger the child faces at this stage lies in "a sense of inadequacy and inferiority." He may despair "of his tools and skills or of his status among his tool partners," and his loss of hope in the tool world may reawaken "the more isolated, less tool-conscious familial rivalry" of the previous stage, causing him to think or believe that he is "doomed to mediocrity or inadequacy."[55] Extrapolating from Erikson's discussion of the *industry vs. inferiority* stage of psychosocial development, we may conclude—or at least suggest—that the *body zone* central in this stage includes the hands that hold or wield the tools, that the *mode of physical approach* is *steady attention* and *persevering diligence,* and that the *social modality* involves *cooperation* and *completion.*

BACK TO THE RESOURCEFUL SELF

This discussion of the epigenetic system brings us back to my suggestion that the human strengths that develop in childhood are the basis for the formation of *the resourceful self* (which will, of course, undergo further development in adolescence and adulthood). In order to show the relevance of this suggestion to Erikson's own work, I will briefly expand on my earlier

52. Erikson, *Childhood and Society,* rev. ed., 259.
53. Ibid.
54. Ibid., 259. See also Hendrick, "Work and the Pleasure Principle."
55. Erikson, *Childhood and Society,* rev. ed., 260.

comments about his view that the individual possesses a number of selves that make up his or her composite Self.

In chapter 5 of *Identity, Youth, and Crisis*, titled "Theoretical Interlude," Erikson discusses the fact that he has used the word *identity* in a variety of senses, but that one thing that can be said about *identity* is that identity formation has "a self-aspect and an ego-aspect."[56] *Ego-identity* has to do with "the ego's synthesizing power in the light of its central psychosocial function," and *self-identity* concerns "the individual's self- and role-images." If we understand the ego "as a central and partially unconscious organizing agency," this means that it must "at any given stage of life deal with a changing Self which demands to be synthesized with abandoned and anticipated selves." Thus, *identity confusion*—or, as he would prefer to say, *identity diffusion*—is a situation in which there is a "split of self-images," and therefore "a loss of center and a dispersion."[57] What the changing Self lacks is a coherent sense of *I*.[58]

Erikson goes on to suggest that "our composite Self" is made up of "various selves" and that there are "constant and often shock-like transitions between these selves." For example, there is the self who is "among friends" and the self who is "in the company of higher-ups or lower-downs," or "the body self in sexual excitement or in a rage; the competent self and the impotent one; the one on horseback, the one in the dentist's chair, and the one chained and tortured." He suggests that it takes "a healthy personality for the 'I' to be able to speak out of all of these conditions in such a way that it can testify to a reasonably coherent Self."[59]

While I would endorse Erikson's view of the Self as composed of "various selves" (selves that are not necessarily acting in concert with one another), I think his illustrations here of what we might call *occasional selves* fails to give adequate recognition to the fact that individuals have more *enduring selves* (i.e., selves that persist despite changing social conditions and circumstances). If this were not the case, it would be difficult to offer a reasonably accurate description of the personality of an individual, healthy or otherwise. And this brings us back to the *resourceful self.*

The dictionary defines *resource* as (1) something that lies ready for use or that can be drawn upon for aid or to take care of a need; (2) a means of accomplishing something; (3) a measure or action that can be resorted to, as in an emergency; (4) a source of strength or ability within oneself;

56. Erikson, *Identity, Youth, and Crisis*, 211.

57. Ibid.

58. Ibid., 217.

59. Ibid.

and (5) ability to deal promptly with problems, difficulties, etc. It defines *resourcefulness* as the ability to deal effectively and creatively with problems, difficulties, etc.[60]

In his 1940 article on the problems of infancy and early childhood, Erikson notes that humans are the "least prepared for rapid adaptation" among the animal species because they are "protected longer than any other being."[61] Yet, in his chapter in *Childhood and Society* on the theory of infantile sexuality, he does not present a picture of human infants or children as waiting passively for someone to come and provide them what they need by way of food and other necessities of life. On the contrary, Erikson portrays the infant as actively engaged in communicating his or her needs and expectation that these will be met. His very use of the phrase "mutual regulation" to characterize the relationship between the infant and the mother implies that the acquisition of resources is not a one-sided process.[62]

To be sure, if the mother does not appear, there is little that the infant can do but wait. However, this does not mean that the infant cannot signal—mostly by crying out—that he or she is hungry or otherwise uncomfortable or even in pain. Furthermore, the infant can use his or her mouth, not only as a means of crying out for nurturance or as a organ for ingestion when the nurturance arrives, but also as a positive means of attraction by means of a smile that few mothers can resist.

It is not surprising, then, that Erikson proposes that the *social modality* of the first stage of life is *to get,* and that even though he emphasizes the fact that *getting* is a *receptive* and *accepting* act, he also makes clear that this modality involves *getting somebody to do* what one wants to have done. Furthermore, the very fact that learning how to do this establishes the "necessary ego groundwork" for the capacity to *get to be* the giver at some later time implies the infant's recognition, perhaps on an unconscious level, that the other person *wants* to be the giver. Otherwise it would not occur to the infant and growing child that there are pleasures to be obtained by assuming the role of the one who gives.

Erikson notes that the mutual regulation formed in the first stage "faces its severest test" as the child enters the second stage and experiences the antithesis of *letting go* and *holding on.* But he also emphasizes the "self-preservative function" of this stage. Not only is there the "feeling of well-being"—and its accompanying sense of pleasure—that comes with successfully evacuating the bowels and bladder as completely as possible,

60. Agnes, *Webster's New World College Dictionary,* 1221.

61. Erikson, *A Way of Looking at Things,* 550.

62. Erikson, *Childhood and Society,* rev. ed., 73.

but there is also "the dimension of voluntary release" that accompanies "the arrival of better-formed stool and the general development of the muscle system," and thus the capacity not only to exercise self-will but also to exercise self-restraint or self-control. Throughout life, the capacity to exercise self-control is as likely to contribute to self-preservation as is the capacity to exercise self-will.[63]

The third stage introduces the social modality of *making* in the sense of *being on the make*. Although here again this capacity may create its own difficulties and problems for the growing child, it also has some clear and obvious benefits. Erikson's suggestion that this modality has the connotation of "head-on attack, enjoyment of competition, insistence on goal [and] pleasure of conquest," and his naming this stage "the play age," recall his earlier observation that the very fact that the childhood of humans is prolonged means that they engage in play more than do the species in which offspring enter adulthood more rapidly.[64] Also, with play there develops a tendency to experiment and speculate (hence, the emergence in this stage of an active imagination). Thus, although the word *intrusive*, which Erikson uses to describe the *physical mode of approach* in this stage, may have a negative connotation for those being intruded upon, this is not how the growing child experiences these behaviors and their accompanying thoughts and emotions. From the child's point of view, *intrusion* means active engagement, experimentation, curiosity; it also means testing boundaries (some of which may well be arbitrary or unnecessarily restrictive), and putting oneself to the test (i.e., discovering what one is capable of doing or accomplishing).

Finally, the *body zones, mode of physical approach,* and *social modality* of the fourth stage suggest that the child has or is developing the necessary dexterity to use tools effectively, to apply himself or herself to tasks and projects with steady attention and persevering diligence, and to cooperate with others on projects and to complete tasks and projects, whether these are the work of a group or of the individual child.

It has often been said that what distinguishes humans from other mammals is their capacity to use tools. Erikson would not disagree, though he might point out that tools, at least for children, were originally fabricated for the purposes of play. In any event, in his 1940 article on the problems of infancy and early childhood, he emphasizes the importance of play in the development of the infant and child, and the fact that play takes on new aspects and dimensions with growth and development. He writes:

63. Ibid., 81.
64. Erikson, *A Way of Looking at Things,* 550.

The changing aspects of his bodily growth and the constant increases in his ability to perceive, to touch, to grasp, to master, to make social contacts cause him to "invent" new forms of playful activity involving smaller systems (mouth, hands, speech organs, genitals, feces, etc.) or larger systems of his body (kicking, creeping, climbing, etc.), small or big objects (grasping, throwing, tearing, banging, smearing, filling, pushing, arranging, etc.), [and] imaginary or real persons (playing with nipples or face, smiling, holding, pulling, pushing, etc.). These activities are characterized by periods of exclusive fascination and endless repetition.[65]

Also, in his later discussion of the insecurities, anxieties, and fears experienced in early childhood, Erikson notes:

Except in play, the child rarely verbalizes his world. Only he who enters the child's world as a polite guest and studies play as a most serious occupation learns what a child thinks when he is not forced to adapt himself to the verbalized and classified world. It is the great function of fairy tales that they make play, in safety, of what is too big to be mastered in the child's own play.[66]

Thus, the child's engagement in play—whether with objects or through other forms of imaginative activity—is itself an expression of the child's resourcefulness. Erikson's emphasis on the resource of play will be expanded upon in chapter 5.

Human strengths or virtues of *hope, will, purpose,* and *competence* are integral to the epigenetic system as represented in the *body zones, physical modes of approach* and *social modalities* of the four developmental stages of childhood. They are also, in my view, central qualities of *the resourceful self.* Thus, *the resourceful self* has its basis in the enduring belief in the attainability of fervent wishes, in the unbroken determination to exercise free choice as well as self-restraint, in the courage to envision and pursue valued goals, and in the free exercise of dexterity and intelligence in the completion of tasks. That my proposal here is not intended to be a new version of a view of the human strengths as a "set of ideals, to be held up with moral fervor"[67] should be evident from the very fact that my proposal views the development of *the resourceful self* as occurring quite naturally and predictably as the child confronts and engages the challenges of the four stages of the life

65. Ibid.

66. Ibid., 556–57.

67. Erikson, *Insight and Responsibility,* 134.

cycle with their psychosocial crises of *basic trust vs. basic mistrust, autonomy vs. shame and doubt, initiative vs. guilt,* and *industry vs. inferiority.*

Also, given Erikson's suggestion that the strengths developed in child-hood and those that become central in adolescence and adulthood "depend on each other,"[68] we may assume that the *resourceful self* not only survives into adulthood but also undergoes further development as it interacts with the various other selves that make up the composite Self. I do not assume that adults are consciously aware of this self and of its significance in their lives. But neither do I assume that this is necessarily a problem, for this self can do its work even if adults are unaware of the fact that it is doing so.

Yet if adults cultivate greater awareness the *resourceful self* and of its role in their individual lives, such an awareness may assist adults in maxi-mizing the benefits of the self at work. Such a conscious awareness of this self may also help adults understand those times when things are not going as well as they would like. Furthermore, by becoming aware of the impor-tance of the *resourceful self*, adults may begin to give appropriate credit to the children they once were for what makes their lives more fulfilling—or potentially so—in adulthood. Appreciation of the importance of childhood for adulthood may, in turn, lead adults to treat today's children—whether their own or those of other parents—with greater understanding, respect, and appreciation.

PAIRING THE STRENGTHS

As we have seen, Erikson believes that the strengths or virtues that compose his schedule of strengths are intimately related. For example, he points out in "Human Strength and the Cycle of Generations" that the "will cannot be trained until hope is secure, nor can love become reciprocal until fidelity has proven reliable."[69] He also asserts in *The Life Cycle Completed* that "if developmental considerations lead us to speak of *hope, fidelity,* and *care* as the human strengths or ego qualities emerging from such strategic stages as infancy, adolescence, and adulthood, it should not surprise us (though it did when we became aware of it) that they correspond to such major creedal values as *hope, faith,* and *charity.*"[70] Referring to psychoanalysts like himself, Erikson admits that "skeptical Vienna-trained readers, of course, will be re-minded of the Austrian emperor who, when asked to inspect the model of a new flamboyant baroque memorial, declared with authority, 'You need a

68. Ibid., 115.

69. Ibid.

70. Erikson, *The Life Cycle Completed,* orig. ed., 58.

bit more faith, hope, and charity in the lower left corner!'" And yet, "such proven traditional values, while referring to the highest spiritual aspirations, must, in fact, have harbored from their dim beginnings some relation to the developmental rudiments of human strength."[71]

With these illustrations in mind, of how individual strengths may have special or particular relationships to one another, I would like to suggest in conclusion that contiguous strengths may especially "depend on each other."[72] So if one of these strengths has not developed for one reason or another, the contiguous strength is also jeopardized. Thus, I propose the following aphorisms for the human strengths of childhood: (1) *Hope* without *will* is *wishful,* and *will* without *hope* is *aimless*; and (2) *Purpose* without *competence* is *ineffectual,* and *competence* without *purpose* is *pointless*. If the *resourceful self* is to flourish, the four strengths must work together.

71. Ibid.

72. Erikson, *Insight and Responsibility,* 115.

II

The Primordial Resources

4

The Ease of Humor

ease:

(1) freedom from stiffness, formality, or awkwardness; natural;

(2) freedom from difficulty; facility, adroitness;

(3) freedom from pain, worry, or trouble; comfort.

W e turn, now, to the four primordial resources of humor, play, dreams, and hope. This chapter on humor and the following chapter on play will focus on resources that we often associate with children. Among psychoanalysts children's play has received far more attention than children's humor. Erikson too devoted more attention to children's play than to children's humor. But Freud himself wrote a book on jokes immediately after he wrote his book on dreams,[1] and years later he wrote an article on humor in which he made an interesting association between humor and children's play. He noted that the intention of humor is to convey the idea: "Look here! This is all this seemingly dangerous world amounts to. Child's play—the very thing to jest about."[2]

Martha Wolfenstein's *Children's Humor* picks up on Freud's view that humor challenges the idea that the world is dangerous and threatening. In

---

1. Freud, *The Interpretation of Dreams* was originally published in 1900; Freud, *Jokes and Their Relation to the Unconscious* was originally published in 1905.

2. Freud, "Humor," 268.

the introduction she points out that being a child is a predicament fraught with special difficulties:

> Children are little and they greatly long to have the bigness and powers of the adults and their marvelous-seeming prerogatives; they feel often oppressed by adult superiority and coerced by adult moral rules. Children undergo much frustration and disappointment; they experience many anxieties which are hard for them to master. From an early age children avail themselves of joking to alleviate their difficulties. They transform the painful into the enjoyable, turn impossible wishes and the envied bigness and powers of adults into something ridiculous, expose adult pretensions, make light of failures, and parody their own frustrated strivings.[3]

Wolfenstein adds that young children around the age of five employ joking to cope with their envy of adults and that school-age children turn their frustrated curiosity into a major theme of joking. And although the "particular exigencies which joking aims to alleviate vary with age, the basic motive of briefly triumphing over distress, of gaining a momentary release from frustration, persists."[4]

The frustration that especially interests us in this chapter is less the young child's envy of adult power and prerogatives and more the circumstances that give rise to the emergence of the melancholy self. Yet the exercise of adult powers and prerogatives and the imposition of adult moral codes on young children often contribute to and are manifestations of the emotional separation between mother and child, which, as we saw in chapter 1, is at the very heart of the development of the melancholy self. It is noteworthy, therefore, that Wolfenstein's opening chapter, on "Joking and Anxiety," begins with this illustration:

> At a quarter past three there was only one child left in the kindergarten classroom, the others having been called for by mothers or maids or older brothers and sisters. The teacher came over to where the little boy sat quietly waiting, and asked with some solicitude: "Who is calling for you today, Eugene? Your mother? Or Betty?" The boy smiled, "My mother is coming, and Betty is coming, and Kay is coming—the whole family is coming except me because I'm here already." He laughed.[5]

3. Wolfenstein, *Children's Humor*, 12.

4. Ibid., 12.

5. Ibid., 25.

Wolfenstein explains that in this joke "the little boy transformed an anxious feeling into one of amusement."[6] She adds,

> Under the strain of separation from the mother and sisters with whom he expected to be reunited at the moment . . . he is able to joke. He might instead have been overwhelmed with anxiety; he might have cried in the teacher's arms. Or he might have struggled to repress his painful feelings, to be apathetic. But he wants to continue to feel, and he insists on feeling something pleasant. He might then have forgotten his actual situation and become absorbed in play. He does not do this either; he remains aware of his situation of lonely waiting. While confronting this reality, he transforms his feeling about it from pain to enjoyment. This retaining of contact with a disappointing reality combined with the urgent demand to continue to feel, but to feel something pleasant, is decisive for joking.[7]

In light of Freud's observation in "Mourning and Melancholia" that one of the symptoms of melancholia is a profoundly painful dejection,[8] Wolfenstein's comment that Eugene wanted to continue to feel but wanted these feelings to be pleasant, not painful, is especially noteworthy. Also noteworthy is the suggestion that he might have taken refuge in playing, which is the subject of the next chapter.

This illustration of how humor becomes a resource for a child who anxiously awaits his mother's arrival brings us to the focus of this chapter on three articles by Erikson published in 1930–1931 in a psychoanalytic journal devoted to teaching. They were titled "Psychoanalysis and the Future of Education," "Children's Picture Books," and "The Fate of the Drives in School Compositions." The three articles have been republished in English translation (the third one in condensed form) in *A Way of Looking at Things*.[9] Only the third article is concerned with humor, but if we take seriously Martha Wolfenstein's contention that joking is a means for children to deal with the anxieties, exigencies, and frustrations of life as a child, then the first two articles set the stage for the article that deals with humor. Without the first two articles, we would probably overlook the fact that humor is a critically important resource in childhood.

The publication of these three articles in a psychoanalytic journal devoted to education reflects Erikson's niche in the psychoanalytic community

6. Ibid., 23.
7. Ibid., 24–25.
8. Freud, "Mourning and Melancholia," 165.
9. Erikson, *A Way of Looking at Things*, 14–69.

at the time. As I noted in chapter 1, Erikson's friend Peter Blos, director of the Hietzing School, in 1927 invited Erikson to teach there. During the five years it was in operation, the school averaged about sixteen children ranging from eight to fifteen years of age. Some were Americans whose parents had come to Vienna for analysis and perhaps training. A few were children of prominent European analysts. About 70 percent of the children were in analysis themselves, mostly with Anna Freud. For the most part, their parents had troubled marriages or were divorced.

Blos taught geography and the sciences while Erikson taught the humanities, especially art, history, and German literature. They employed John Dewey's educational methods borrowed from a progressive school in Winnetka, Illinois. This meant that the children were encouraged to follow their own interests and to become engaged in a project that unified diverse subjects.[10] Erikson also completed a teaching degree at the local Montessori during the time that he was an instructor at Hietzing School. As Lawrence Friedman notes, "He found Montessori training compatible with his earlier artistic experiences, for it focused on the objects that children made and arranged."[11] Erikson later recalled that "Montessori training induced him to 'pay attention to and to repeat with my own hands the simplest manipulation and the accompanying thought patterns which acquaint a child with the tangible world and permit him to reconstruct it in play.'"[12] Erikson also took courses at the University of Vienna, but his Montessori diploma, awarded in 1932, was the only formal degree he completed after receiving his diploma from the *gymnasium* in 1920.

Friedman indicates that Erikson's students "recalled that he was nervous, self-conscious, and even idiosyncratically funny," and that he "was tall, handsome, and well-groomed, attentive to his appearance, usually in suit and tie, and carried himself somewhat awkwardly."[13] Erikson also "seemed constantly to sip water, to hitch up his freshly pressed pants, and to blush 'ever so easily,'" and several students "found it amusing that he 'could not pass a mirror without looking at himself.'" Yet, "they all felt that he connected intuitively to their concerns."[14] The relevance of the last two observations—his narcissism and his intuitive connection with children—will

10. Friedman, *Identity's Architect,* 64–65.

11. Ibid., 67–68.

12. Ibid., 68.

13. Ibid., 65.

14. Ibid., 65.

become apparent in the following discussion of the first of the three articles, "The Fate of the Drives in School Compositions."[15]

NARCISSISM AND THE INTERFERING MOTHER

"The Fate of the Drives in School Compositions" centers on the essays that the adolescents in the Hietzing School wrote in response to the assigned question, "What would you do if you were suddenly alone in the world (you perhaps had no parents) and had to take care of yourself from then on?" This was one of the questions that Dorothy Burlingham, the school's founder, devised for student essays. Erikson explains in the article that the question "did not have to be answered too literally," for a story or fairy tale was also welcome. Thus encouraged, "the children let themselves go and followed their impulses and wishes beyond the confines of a usual school essay."[16] Erikson recalls that a number of the children allowed themselves a striking digression:

> They launched into such a detailed description of their fanta-
> sies of their parents' death and they lost sight of the point of
> the original question [which was how they would take care of
> themselves from now on]. Twelve children described the death
> of fifteen parents. Only six of these had died peaceful deaths,
> three had been murdered; four had died accidentally; two had
> ended in jail.[17]

Erikson guesses that "the children chose to write about what they wanted to be *free of* rather than what they wanted to be *free for*."[18]

The article focuses on four of the children: An eleven-year-old girl ("The Bright-Eyed One"), a fourteen-year-old boy ("The Adolescent"), a twelve-year-old girl ("The Gentle Girl"), and a ten-year-old boy ("The Inaccessible Boy"). I will limit my discussion to the eleven-year-old girl because her story and Erikson's interpretations of it particularly reflect his own struggle to come to terms with his early-childhood relationship with his mother, especially following her marriage to his stepfather, Dr. Theodor Homburger.

This young girl, whom Erikson calls "The Bright-Eyed One," wrote about the many things she would do if she were not subject to her mother's

15. Erikson, *A Way of Looking at Things,* 39–69.
16. Ibid., 39.
17. Ibid., 40.
18. Ibid.

prohibitions. For example, she would ride a wild horse and allow her hair to fly loose. For Erikson, the chance to let her hair fly loose was anything but trivial, for her mother had previously shortened her unusually beautiful hair, and this loss had made a profound impression on the young girl. For a long time it was the focus of all her resentment toward her mother.

Another thing that she thought she would do if she were not subject to her mother's prohibitions would be to become adept at carving wood. But then, having considered this desire, she quickly experienced a doubt: "'I hope my husband will approve, if not, then woe is me!'" Erikson observes, "She thinks someone will always fill the role of the no-sayer." However, he adds that her desire to carve wood was an aspect of her obvious talent in drawing and painting, and notes that her "productions are round and cheerful, like her handwriting and her sentences."[19] In a third fantasy, the girl returns to the theme of her hair, but this time she has sold her hair to a man who offered to buy it. He gave her "a very small sum, with which she ran to her mother, who was so happy and who found her daughter clever and kind."[20]

The thematic connection between the first and third fantasies is self-evident because both have to do with her hair. But how is the second one related? Erikson suggests that the "hair" and "artist" juxtaposition is significant. It makes "a somewhat vulgar association" because "many artists seem to value their hair and to set themselves apart from other people by their haircuts." He suggests that "we might call it a cult of the self, a kind of narcissism, which they reveal in this way."[21] Elaborating on this association, he notes that "it isn't necessarily the particular acts of personal vanity that document the narcissism of the artist; he has, after all, in his works a grander way of lifting the image of his being to the level of cultural refinement for all to share."[22] On the other hand, "We know from the lives of artists the setback, the kind of despair into which an artist is driven just when he has expressed his self-love most triumphantly, more triumphantly than his own culturally inhibited soul can bear, given its fear of its own hubris."[23]

These reflections on the artist's narcissism seem to go well beyond the artistic fantasies of a very young girl. But we need to consider that Erikson had been an aspiring artist through his midtwenties. Even after several years of association with the psychoanalytic community in Vienna, he declared

19. Ibid., 41–42.
20. Ibid., 40.
21. Ibid., 41–42.
22. Ibid., 42–43.
23. Ibid., 43.

more than once to Anna Freud "that I could not see a place for my artistic inclinations" in the "high intellectual endeavors" characteristic of this community.[24] Furthermore, the young girl had a particular desire to carve wood, and, as Robert Coles points out, Erikson in his early twenties executed "enormous woodcuts which demanded a good deal of physical energy as well as artistic imagination."[25] Erikson's personal identification with the young girl is also evident in the gender change—from the young girl to the male artist—precisely where he introduces the narcissism theme. Thus, his comments on the girl's struggle with narcissism, and on her mother's role in this struggle, are, to a significant degree, self-referential.

Erikson goes on to note that the young girl's fantasies evoke an *infantile* theme, that of "unlimited surrender to one's feelings and to nature as their soothing complement and then sudden fright." However,

> her fright springs not from the force of providence, nor is it a pang of conscience that warns from within; no, it is Mother who prevents her from acting on her sensual desires. That Mother cut her hair was the most active example of how she opposes all cravings; it struck at the girl's strongest wish: to find herself beautiful and to allow others to admire her.[26]

This conclusion prompts him to comment on the relationship between the child's personal beauty and subsequent desire to become an artist.

At this point he cites an article by I. Hermann, published the previous year in the same journal, who observes that physical beauty seems the necessary spark of a child's talent for drawing. One outstanding painter who was a patient of Hermann's was such a beautiful child that pregnant women "would come to feast their eyes on him."[27] Erikson wonders if hair played an important role in the childhood of Hermann's patients. Since Hermann does not address this possibility, he contributes a story of his own, one in which a

> little boy's fate seems somewhat analogous to the little girl's. Unusually beautiful as a child, the boy noticed in particular that people admired his full head of hair. When his mother had it all cut off, he thought he had lost all his charm, and in fact, he

---

24. Erikson, "'Identity Crisis' in Autobiographic Perspective," 30.

25. Coles, *Erik Erikson*, 11.

26. Erikson, *A Way of Looking at Things*, 43,

27. Ibid.

did eventually because of his grieving. Later he became gifted
in drawing.[28]

Since Erikson lived the first three years of his life near artists, returned
to visit them after he and his mother moved in with his stepfather, and
throughout his adolescent years and early twenties had every intention of
becoming an artist, it is possible that the little boy was Erikson himself. This
would account for his interest in the analogous fate of the little girl.

In any event, the story of the little boy's fate leads Erikson to comment
on another story: that of Absalom, "the narcissist of the Bible," who "would
not let go of his hair."[29] Erikson views this biblical story as a critique of narcissism, as intended by its author to portray how "self-love is punished." But,
for Erikson, the story of Absalom is more than a story about the punishment of self-love, and the very complexities of narcissism itself explain why
this is so. He notes that the story itself reveals

> how ineradicable is the power of those beings who manage to
> carry the certainty of their childish self-love throughout adult-
> hood. For people are constantly uncertain about whether they
> should be admiring or outraged (people admire what succeeds)
> when one among them reveals his impulsive drives for all to see,
> the very same impulses that had been buried within them early
> by taboos and feelings of guilt. The insurgent Absalom appar-
> ently had little sense of guilt. His upbringing had failed to fit him
> for a patriarchal society.[30]

Thus, Erikson's story of the little boy whose mother cut off his hair indicates
that it was her responsibility to "fit" him for a patriarchal society. However,
the biblical story says that Absalom cut off his own hair (2 Sam 14:26),
which suggests that *his* mother did not fulfill her responsibilities in this
regard, with the result that Absalom failed to learn the lesson in childhood
that "self-love is punished."

Erikson concludes that there are those who want to "elevate" the
narcissism they are unable to relinquish (as does Absalom), and there are
others who, artistically gifted, manage to raise their narcissism into the aesthetic sphere "where self-love clothed in beauty may silence the conscious
judgment of others." In either case, there is a real question whether this
"self-transcendence will entirely work for them or whether their efforts
will yet be weighed down by strains of vanity—and illness." This raises a

28. Ibid., 44.
29. Ibid.
30. Ibid.

"fundamental question," which, he says, he will not be able to discuss in detail, but it comes down to this:

> Both the little girl and the little boy who are gifted in drawing have been subjected to a mother's interference with their sense of beauty. Can this experience be viewed as a positive factor in the development of their talent? Is it a loss by which artistic effort will be spurred—in compensation?[31]

To address this question, however cursorily, Erikson cites a passage in Goethe's memoirs, cited also by Hermann, about the pain that young Goethe experienced as a result of his physical disfigurement by smallpox. An adoring aunt who had carried him around to show him off to others could scarcely see him in later years without exclaiming, "How ugly he has become!"[32] Erikson observes:

> One is tempted to see the mother behind the mocking, rejecting aunt in this example. As a matter of fact, Goethe, the great poet, was also a talented artist in drawing. Hermann speaks of his occasional "regression to artistic expression" when Goethe would turn to drawing at those times when a woman had disappointed him.[33]

If this is an example of the artistic talent spurred in a compensatory way when a child's mother has interfered with his sense of his own beauty, Erikson asks whether it could also be the case that "the experience of belittlement of their awareness of their own beauty does not contribute to the development of their talent but may yet limit it"?[34]

This possibility leads him into a brief discussion of guilt, the formation of conscience, and the transformation of rebellion into an act of sacrifice. In effect, this act of sacrifice is the little girl's third fantasy, in which she envisions herself sacrificing her hair, the very thing she loves the most about herself, and giving the proceeds to her mother as a kind of peace offering. But what is behind this self-sacrifice? On the one hand, the sacrifice may be viewed as one demanded by "a fear of one's own conscience," which means that it is not motivated solely, even primarily, by fear of the mother and her authority. Erikson asks, "Would the mother ever have demanded the sacrifice of the hair had she suspected what this meant to the child?"[35] Rather,

31. Ibid.
32. Ibid., 45.
33. Ibid.
34. Ibid.
35. Ibid., 46.

her conscience—"a part of her very self"—could demand what the mother had not demanded because *it* was capable of greater cruelty than the mother herself.

On the other hand, this cruel conscience came into being because of the child's fear of parental authority, "an authority that suddenly forbids tendencies which only a short while ago were displayed with the praise of the elders."[36] Thus, although fear of parental authority and fear of one's own conscience are distinguishable fears, they are related to one another, for the child's conscience begins to form when he or she is confronted by dramatically altered attitudes of the parent toward his or her narcissism, when the mother criticizes what she had earlier praised. The conscience is cruel because the child's initial narcissism has been replaced by a new narcissism—one of perfectionism designed to regain the parent's love and approval.

Thus, although the child's conscience is far more punitive than the mother's authority, this does not mean that the mother plays no role in the child's self-sacrifice. After all, her attitudes toward her child have changed. Features and qualities of the infant that previously evoked her admiring gaze are now treated negatively. While this change is not purely arbitrary, for it has much to do with fitting the child for a patriarchal society (one in which self-love is not ordinarily rewarded), the child finds it puzzling and does not know how to deal with it, especially because the child is not being disciplined for misbehavior, but is being confronted by "an authority that suddenly forbids tendencies which only a short while ago were displayed with the praise of elders."[37]

Thus, although "fear of parental authority" and "fear of one's own conscience" are distinguishable fears, they are related, for the child's conscience began to form when he or she was confronted by dramatically altered parental attitudes toward his or her narcissism: when mother criticized what she had earlier praised. The conscience is cruel because the initial narcissism of the child has been replaced by the narcissism of self-sacrifice, a sacrifice designed to regain the parent's love and approval.

Another theme in Erikson's response to the question of the mother's interference with the child's narcissism is that of "hidden gratification." In the concluding paragraph of his discussion of the child's self-sacrifice, he notes:

> The puzzle of the sacrifice would still not be solved if we did not also discover the gratification hidden within it. Just as we could say about the artist that he *withdraws behind his art even while*

36. Ibid., 45.
37. Ibid.

offering an image of himself in his work, so does the little girl
present herself to the eyes of the public through her hair, as if to
say, "See, this is how beautiful I am." And an audience imagined
by her will accept what the real people around her will no longer
grant.[38]

The "hidden gratification" is that the narcissism is not entirely relinquished,
but takes a different form—one that has its own satisfactions. In the artist's case, he "withdraws behind his art," thus allowing his art to express his
"sense of beauty." At the same time, he "offers an image of himself in his
work," thus incorporating himself in his art in both direct (most directly
through self-portraiture) and indirect ways (for example, in the uniqueness
of his artistic style).

If Erikson's story of the little boy whose mother cut off his hair is autobiographical, this very story illustrates how the process of "withdrawing
behind his art even while offering an image of himself in his work" may
occur and, for Erikson personally, have hidden gratification. This anecdote,
in fact, may be a clue to the subtle process of self-representation Erikson
has employed throughout his discussion of the artist, for discerning readers
cannot fail to see that he is writing self-referentially. Thus, like the little girl,
Erikson presents himself to an imagined audience of readers who, he hopes,
will accept a degree or form of narcissism that the real people around him
(beginning with his mother in childhood) would no longer grant.

In developing a capacity for drawing, the boy sacrifices his narcissism
in its original terms but finds an alternative medium through which he
preserves his narcissism in a form that the adult world will accept and approve. In this way, he arranges his own reward for sacrificing the happiness
and security of face-to-face recognition, a sacrifice that was, in any event,
inevitable. Unlike the charismatic leader, who "elevates" his narcissism by
appealing to an admiring public, the artist clothes his self-love in the beauty
of what he fashions.

This "hidden gratification," however, is extremely fragile, and is always
subject to a melancholy reversal. Following the sentence about the little girl's
imagining an audience that will accept what the real people around her will
no longer grant, Erikson adds: "The very words which have barely awakened
feelings of triumph immediately dim it by devaluing the desires of the child,
saying 'How beautiful is your hair! But it is dirty.'"[39] This "devaluing" of the
child's desires refers to an episode in her story in which her offer to sell her

38. Ibid., 46 (italics added).
39. Ibid.

hair to a hairdresser elicited the response that it was dirty and needed to be washed. Even after it was washed, its sale netted a very small sum.

So, in a sense, the cruel conscience takes the radiance out of the moment of triumph by pointing to the flaw in the artist's work. The melancholy conclusion is, if only one could have continued to be the object of the mother's unconditional approval and admiration, one would not now be subject to the vicissitudes inherent in the interplay between one's imagined triumph before an admiring audience and a punitive conscience that points out that one's work is flawed.

THE DREAD OF THE DESTRUCTIVE MOTHER

The second of Erikson's articles, "Psychoanalysis and the Future of Education," was originally presented before the Vienna Psychoanalytic Society in 1930.[40] It focuses on one child, Richard, a seven-year-old pupil at Hietzing School. Richard's mother had asked Erikson to talk with him, explaining that Richard demonstrated such a drive to ask questions about everything that she felt unable to satisfy his curiosity. Also, she wanted a man to answer his questions about sexual matters. Erikson agreed, and throughout the ensuing months, he answered Richard's questions, scrupulously avoiding any temptation to give any more information than Richard asked for so that he would not inhibit Richard from asking the next question that was already forming in his mind. It became clear that Richard's questions involving sexuality were posed in a much more anxious tone of voice than those relating to any other subject; questions about blood and hair were especially anxiety producing.

Erikson concludes from "this very limited insight into one child's mind which Richard's questions have provided" that "the formation of anxieties, fantasies, and unconscious and conscious theories continues regardless of sexual enlightenment."[41] Why is this so? Why doesn't sexual enlightenment *reduce* the child's anxieties and fantasies about sexual matters? Erikson in-

---

40. Ibid., 14–30.

41. Ibid., 21 (italics added). Erikson's use of the phrase "sexual enlightenment" is noteworthy because "The Sexual Enlightenment of Children" is the title of an open letter that Freud wrote to the editor of *Sociale Medizein und Hygiene* in 1907. In it Freud emphasized the importance of providing children sexual enlightenment but suggested that if parents offer such explanations "in mysterious and solemn language," this is worse than not providing explanations at all. He also suggested that explanations about the specific circumstances of human sexuality and of its social significance should be provided before the child is eleven years old (Freud, *The Sexual Enlightenment of Children*, 23–24).

vokes the psychoanalytic oedipal theory to explain this continued anxiety and fantasy formation, noting that the child's sexual curiosity preceded the development of the Oedipus complex, which brought about a repression of the now dangerous sexual questions. Questions previously asked openly and freely "are now set carefully, half dreamily and disinterestedly, and behind the words which would endeavor to hide the sexual content lurks a general permeation of sexual anxiety, born of the conviction that a catastrophe must take place."[42]

Erikson points out that this foreboding sense of catastrophe remains a fixture of the adult psyche, and sexual enlightenment as such has little if any effect on this foreboding. He also observes that although psychoanalysis "has recommended sexual enlightenment as of very real assistance," what this enlightenment actually offers "remains a fairy tale for the affects of the child, just as the story of the stork remains a fairy tale for his intellect."[43] Thus, "modern teachers forsake the symbol-filled darkness of ancient tales which combined so attractively the uncanny and the familiar, but in doing so they have no reason to be optimistic."[44] Why?

> Because in replacing these ancient tales with more logical interpretations expressing some facts more directly and clearly, they neglect to include even vaguely much that is more fundamentally important. Neither fairy tale nor sexual enlightenment saves the child from the necessity of a distrustful and derisive attitude toward adults, since in both cases he is left alone with his conflict.[45]

Erikson contends, in fact, that the fairy tale has a certain advantage over sexual enlightenment because it addresses the feelings of dread and impending catastrophe that sexuality evokes in children. He cites a recent article by Hans Zulliger, a Swiss analyst, who argues that the

> complete stork tale, as a more exact psychoanalytic examination is capable of showing, contains anal and genital birth theories

42. Erikson, *A Way of Looking at Things,* 22.

43. Ibid., 23–24.

44. Ibid., 24. Erikson's reference to ancient tales that combine "the uncanny and the familiar" is a direct allusion to Freud's essay "The Uncanny." In the essay Freud argues that the reason something appears "uncanny" or strange is that it was originally experienced as "familiar." He notes in this regard the tendency of some male patients to feel that there is something uncanny about the female genital organs, and suggests that they are uncanny because they are reminiscent of one's original home in one's mother's body, from which one is now estranged.

45. Erikson, *A Way of Looking at Things,* 24.

(the chimney, the stove and the pond), the idea of the forceful and sadistic in connection with the acts of begetting and bearing (biting in the leg), castration idea (leg biting), and genital begetting idea (stork-bird as masculine symbol), etc.[46]

Hence, the fairy tale articulates the sense of dread with which children associate sexuality. In contrast, in enlightened responses to children's questions,

> the sexual act as represented to the child is rationalized and made more or less gentle and noble according to the personal attitude of the adult. In any case, sleeping restfully together is sure to be emphasized by the adult as the only pleasure involved, but it is just this feeling of protected rest from which the child is drawing away into the tumultuous fight for existence. Only yesterday he forsook his mother's arms and his possessive share of her body. Today he has a respite in which to accustom himself to his loss, but tomorrow, so he feels, something quite new and different and dangerous will present itself.[47]

Therefore, the child "accepts sexual enlightenment exactly as he accepts general enlightenment in other fields—passing it off with an almost patronizing gesture."[48]

But why does the child have this sense of impending catastrophe, of something quite new and different and dangerous? Why this sense of foreboding? The answer to this question appears when the child's questions about sexual matters "reach a complicated and dangerous point," as they did in Richard's case:

> Softly the child [Richard] speaks of the purple snail and fire engines, the food tube of the hen and the goiter that some women have. And still more softly come the inmost questions of the child which only barely make themselves heard to his interpreter: 'What about the desire and the fear of destroying, and the fear and desire of being destroyed?' With his most earnest questions, then, the child still remains alone.[49]

In the concluding pages of the essay, Erikson focuses on the issue of "inwardly directed aggression" and the need of the child to deal with "the dangers within himself." He notes that the effort to provide sexual enlightenment (as Richard's mother had requested of Erikson) leads to the discovery

46. Ibid.
47. Ibid., 22–23.
48. Ibid., 23.
49. Ibid., 25.

of a self-punitive aggression within the child. The child feels alone because he experiences himself as "wicked in an apparently noble and purposeful world," and this sense of wickedness sets him on a "vicious circle of guilt and expiation."[50]

Erikson notes in this regard that the children in their own progressive little school had admitted "that their desire for punishment was not satisfied by us [the teachers]."[51] So Erikson decided to have a talk with some of the older children (twelve- and thirteen-year-olds) about the fact that much of the unsocial behavior among them lay in outbursts of rage (rage that was often unreasonable), and that this rage was actually "inwardly directed" and had the effect of excluding them from participation in the activities of the group. Erikson alluded to what the children had been studying in their history classes, specifically to the Eskimos who have a "singing contest" instead of a law-court procedure, in which the two opponents are forced to make fun of one another until the laughing observers declare one party or another "knocked out."

One of the girls, he notes, immediately had "the correct idea": "They can do that," she declared, "because they haven't any nasty names. We would say 'pig' or 'idiot' right away and then everyone would be mad again." With this acceptance of rage as a general fact, and not as something that is merely the fault of the individual who carries it within him, "a variety of thoughts began to stir in the children's minds," and they spoke "of aggression that is displayed and of aggression that is felt, of guilt and the desire for punishment, with an inner comprehension of which adults are hardly capable."[52]

On the other hand, this discussion with the older children did not directly answer the question that Richard posed to Erikson, "What about the desire and the fear of destroying, and the fear and desire of being destroyed?" Specifically, it did not identify the person or persons whom Richard imagines himself destroying and/or being destroyed by. The traditional psychoanalytic answer to Richard's question would be that, with Richard having left his mother's protective arms and his possessive share of her body, his unconscious mind is preparing for the inevitable battle with his father. Erikson, in fact, employs this interpretation in his comments on Richard's difficult family situation, noting that Richard's mother, who seemed to be unhappy, had married in England but shortly after the war had been compelled by various circumstances to leave his father and settle in Vienna. Richard explained this change by making a connection between the war,

50. Ibid., 26–27.
51. Ibid., 27.
52. Ibid.

the fights he overheard in his parents' bedroom, and his mother's flight to Vienna to escape from his father's aggression. Thus, the unconscious identification in Richard's questions "of the country in which one lives with the threatened or suffering mother, and the enemy with the brutal father against whom the boy, the young hero, has to defend her may be pointed out as a common one," and "it is important to see where Richard's fantasies are based on his special Oedipus situation. 'The sun and the moon,' he once remarked, 'can never be in the sky at the same time. They would eat each other up.'"[53]

If, however, Richard understands this allusion to the sun and moon as his way of explaining why his parents cannot live together, this also suggests that he fears not only his father (who, after all, is no longer present) but also his mother, who is no less capable of "eating up" the other. It is also noteworthy that Erikson was drafted by Richard's mother to answer her son's questions because she "felt unable to satisfy his curiosity" and "preferred to have a man answer his questions concerning sexual matters."[54] Had her husband been around, he, no doubt, would have been drafted instead.

But why did Richard have "such a drive to ask questions" in the first place? In my view, the aggression that Erikson ascribes to children at the end of the article is already evident at the beginning of the article. Richard's almost manic need to ask questions betrays a verbal aggressiveness toward his mother, and this may be his way of defending himself against what he experiences—consciously or unconsciously—as her capacity to destroy him. By this questioning mania, he forces her into a defensive position, prompting her to turn to Erikson, a man, for help. Is this what we would expect from a son who is his mother's defender against a brutal father? Or is it instead the case that what we see here is a boy who has a very powerful need to overwhelm his mother with a barrage of questions that she is "unable to satisfy"? Because Richard's "fantasy" of the sun and moon eating each other up and his aggressive behavior are orally oriented, it is not far-fetched to suggest that Richard is using his verbal facility to defend himself against being "eaten up" by his mother. As long as he continues to ask questions which put her on the defensive, he is able to fend off her powers to destroy him. The feared catastrophe is not that his *father* may brutalize him, but that his *mother*, the giver of life, may become the agent of death.[55]

53. Ibid., 19.

54. Ibid., 15.

55. As Freud points out in the concluding paragraph of his essay "The Theme of the Three Caskets," a psychoanalytic interpretation of Shakespeare's *The Merchant of Venice* and *King Lear*: "One might say that the three inevitable relations man has with woman are here represented: that with the mother who bears him, with the companion of his bed and board, and with the destroyer. Or is it the three forms taken by the figure

Thus, the aggression so apparent in Richard's incessant questioning may well be a defense against the impending catastrophe that he perceives his mother may visit upon him. In a sense, the catastrophe cannot occur as long as he continues to distract her with questions. Fantasies of destruction at her hands also underlie his self-directed aggression, as he hopes thereby to forestall the dreaded event by attempting to fashion himself into the child that she can at least tolerate, thereby saving himself from her own destructive rage. Or perhaps he believes that his own self-punishment will inhibit her from inflicting further punishment of her own. This is the "logic," as it were, of the punitive conscience.

THE SELF-DIRECTED SADISM OF THE SOUL

Erikson's third essay, "Children's Picture Books," originally presented at the House of Children in Vienna, reflects the fact that he was concerned at the time to find connections between his psychoanalytic work and his training as a teacher in Montessori methods.[56] He begins the essay by noting that in the Montessori seminar in which he had participated, a number of highly diverse children's picture books were reviewed. This review led to the impression that on the whole, the books "constitute a small, circumscribed world that reflects the big real world—with specific distortions."[57]

First, Erikson takes up the books about a character named Struwelpeter who, he notes, some readers consider sadistic. But he points out that sadism lends itself to two different interpretations. On the one hand, it may apply to picture books that seek "to deplore animal torture by showing a tortured creature on every page," thus unwittingly stirring up "cruel impulses rather than revulsion."[58] On the other hand, the Struwelpeter books "not only present scenes in which a creature (a creature identifiable with the child reader) is tormented but also some in which a child is punished." Thus, "we expect that any reader will identify with the hero," and that the children reading this book "feel punished when Struwelpeter is punished,

---

of the mother as life proceeds: the mother herself, the beloved who is chosen after her pattern, and finally the Mother Earth who receives him again? But it is in vain that the old man yearns after the love of woman as once he had it from his mother; the third of the Fates alone, the silent goddess of Death, will take him into her arms" (Freud, "The Three Caskets," 75).

56. Erikson, *A Way of Looking at Things*, 31–38.

57. Ibid., 31.

58. Ibid., 31–32.

and we know how lasting such an impact can be, and how unforgettable the perverse enjoyment" for "even terrified children return to this book."[59]

Erikson suggests that the second form of sadism is far more danger-ous, "for cruelty to others is checked by the strength of these other creatures, who defend themselves." But what resources are available to curb "the para-doxical tendency to be cruel to oneself?" He indicates that he will return to this issue of self-directed sadism later in the essay, "for it seems to me that if we condemn certain effects, we should try to recognize their root causes. Otherwise, they will return along unforeseen paths."[60]

First, though, he takes up the question of why adults draw cruel pic-tures for children's books in the first place. If teachers and parents object to such depictions, the artist, in self-defense, "will merely cite the appeal of his drawings and suggest that artists probably know more about children than we do." Acknowledging that "this seems true in some way," Erikson nonetheless suggests that "we have to try to find the common ground that draws them together, artist and child."[61] In search of this common ground, Erikson draws attention to certain medieval paintings of the Mother of God or the Holy Family in which the faces of the little Savior or of other children are strangely distorted: "ill; somewhat embryo like; somewhat senile." Our initial impression is that the Christ Child was meant to be depicted "as an 'old infant,' mature at birth and childlike in death," and yet "we cannot help feeling that here the adult artist, ascetically and mystically earnest about the true nature of childhood, has unconsciously shrunk back, refusing to recognize a child as he really is."[62]

A similar distortion, a tendency to deny childhood, is evident in picture books. Why this distortion of the child image? Why this refusal to recognize a child as he or she really is? Erikson suggests that the artists are, perhaps unwittingly, revealing a truth about the child's own self-perception, which itself is reflective of a deep split within the child's own psyche:

> In reality, the very young infant certainly evinces nothing of this. He delights in himself and in the growing radius of his move-ments and impulses. His psyche seems to say "This is good" to everything that he produces with his body and perceives with his senses. And he is accustomed to having the big people (the

59. Ibid., 32.
60. Ibid.
61. Ibid.
62. Ibid.

powerful adults on whose love he depends) applaud his behavior—until he reaches an age at which he can be educated.[63]

Now the situation changes: When he expresses his most genuine and favorite behavior, adults more and more often say, "You mustn't do that. We won't love you when you're like that." Thus, he learns that certain actions are no longer lovable and must find some way "of maintaining his old self-love (which is necessary for survival) while also keeping the love of adults which he needs just as badly."[64]

Erikson interprets the child's new situation in terms of the psychoanalytic concept of the superego, noting,

> The child condemns some of his impulses on his own; by some enigmatic mechanism, he internally develops an authority that appropriates and represents the prohibitions of adults. One part of his ego is transformed—psychoanalytic theory calls it the superego—and repudiates the part that remains as it was originally. The positive aspect of this development is that the prohibiting part, too, belongs to the child's mind, representing the prohibition as his own desire, with which his self-love can side. But such disparate self-love survives at the price of one's inner unity.[65]

This is the same dynamic Erikson discussed in his article on children's essays. But here he relates it to children's enjoyment of picture books, books in which "good children are rewarded and bad ones punished." Because some of the child's "bad behavior" was directed toward much younger children viewed as rivals for their mother's love and affection, the older child's "inner authority" now views the younger children as "sweet" and "cute." Thus, the older children enjoy those picture books that "delicately render a pale, sweet, mimosa-like world."[66] No doubt, this warm response to these pictures of younger children reflects the older children's nostalgia for that period in their lives when they, too, were considered "sweet" and "cute," so that their reaching out to the children in these pictures is an attempt to repair the damage of their loss of inner unity.

However, Erikson's main concern is with the common ground that draws together the adult artist and the child old enough to appreciate the

63. Ibid., 33.

64. Ibid.

65. Ibid.

66. Ibid. Mimosa is "any of a large genus of trees, shrubs, and herbs that grow in warm regions and usually have heads or spikes of small white, yellow, or pink flowers" (Agnes, *New World College Dictionary*, 916).

picture books. He points out that the adult who drew these pictures "went through the same transformation" and then "forgot what had happened."[67] Thus,

> repressed childhood wishes are replaced by paradisiacal surrogate images or moralistic prejudices, as though one had been born a well-behaved creature. The adult (impelled by some urgent memory) feels the desire to draw a picture book for a child. He either establishes good and evil in his book or makes up a world of such doll-like infantility that it is without punishment only because it has no drives.[68]

Therefore, picture books where children are punished and those that use "a delicate or schematic depiction to strip the world of flesh and blood" are not all that different from one another: "The former books show the world as threatening and advise caution; the latter advise capitulating immediately to the threat by behaving like a doll or a delicate mimosa, the kind of child so many adults like to see." Both, of course, reflect the formation of conscience, and the distinct advantage of this mechanism is that the child "catches up in a short time with thousands of years of upbringing," an advantage so self-evident that adults minimize its disadvantages to the child, claiming, "A normal child doesn't suffer all that much from this process."[69]

But Erikson dissents from this sanguine view, noting that the "disadvantages are great as they pile up with the growth of civilization." He adds, "They threaten to turn into the mountain with which modern education, after a bold approach, finds itself unable to cope." These disadvantages all result from the fact that a child can be educated only because of a split in his or her mental makeup. Under the pressure of either remaining what he is or becoming like the adult to please him, the child undergoes a transformation in the psyche. An inner voice arises, taking over the prohibitions of the adult milieu and making sure that the child's instinctual energy is tamed, and, whenever necessary, punished for unruliness.[70]

This inner voice "censors all memories of the original and now-condemned world of the senses" and the "page of the psyche is blank again—not because nothing was written on it but because the censor has meticulously pasted over the primeval writing."[71] Thus, in order to become "civilized," capable of being educated, the child has become alienated from nature, and

67. Erikson, *A Way of Looking at Things*, 33.
68. Ibid., 34.
69. Ibid., 34.
70. Ibid.
71. Ibid.

suffers from the "dangerous self-directed sadism of the soul."[72] The "cruel and deadly hatred that the small infant once aimed at the overpowerful adults" is "internalized in the course of capitulation, and since the child must despair of any resistance, his hatred is turned against his own flagging inner world."[73]

Erikson concludes that while children's picture books depicting cruelty toward others are certainly to be disparaged, they are not as problematic as those that promote "self-directed sadism." The reason for this is that adults are far more likely to praise the second type of children's books for their moral content. In fact, "what is expressed as moralistic cruelty against others is merely a reflection of the effects of that internal sadistic impulse," and as far as the person who "moralizes" against others is concerned, "we may assume that he presumably keeps his own instinctual impulses calm only by means of heavy fetters."[74]

HUMOR AND THE GENIAL SIDE OF THE SUPEREGO

In a sense, Erikson's analysis of children's picture books simply underscores what he has already noted in the two other essays: that the punitive conscience emerging from the loss of the child's primitive narcissism internalizes the child's rage against parental (and other adult) authority and redirects it against the self. But, in a footnote, he observes that he has necessarily omitted from his consideration certain psychologically significant features of children's picture books—such as their fantasy elements—and in the concluding paragraphs of the essay he shifts to another type of picture book that was also reviewed in the Montessori seminar: books that are intentionally humorous.

Although these humorous books, *Max and Moritz* and *Adamson,*[75] were not written for children, their appeal to children was well-known. On one page of *Adamson,* the hero wants to smoke his cigar, but his "better self," which stands behind him (and is identifiable by its angel wings) takes the cigar from his mouth and tosses it out the window. For a moment the

72. Ibid., 35.

73. Ibid.

74. Ibid.

75. Sebastian Smee mentions that the painter Lucian Freud and his grandfather, Sigmund Freud, "liked *Max and Moritz*, the antic prank-filled comic strip by Wilhelm Busch that dated back to Sigmund's childhood." In later years, Lucian "always claimed not to have read much of his grandfather's work, and yet he speaks of him with fondness and a certain protectiveness. 'You know how laughter often seals your memory of someone?' he said. 'He made me laugh a lot'" (Smee, *Lucian Freud,* 9).

Adamson self is stunned, but then it races downstairs and catches the cigar before it reaches the ground. Erikson comments: "Rebellion has acted faster than conscience and the force of gravity. Immoral? Yet the most conscientious person laughs."[76]

Observing that what has happened here is that the ego has defended itself, Erikson alludes to Freud's only recently published (1928) essay on humor and quotes the following statement:

> The wonderful thing [about humor] is obviously the victoriously defended invulnerability of the ego. The ego refuses to be offended and forced to suffer any provocation in reality. It insists on not letting the traumas of the outer world get too close for comfort; indeed, it shows that they are merely an occasion for pleasure.[77]

Erikson adds that several external features of the Adamson figure show the great extent to which it depicts the child—the infantile ego—in a human being who struggles with hindrances, prohibitions, and accidents:

> In the ratio of his head size to his torso Adamson is a childlike figure; he has a big hat, like a child acting grownup; he is always alone; he has no manly adventures. And his adversaries, human beings ("the big man"), are all taller than he to the same degree that an adult is taller than a child.[78]

How, then, does humor speak through the depiction of "this sly, struggling ego"? Erikson suggests that it "confronts the nasty superego with a kindly laugh," and then Erikson quotes the comment from Freud's essay on humor previously cited: "Look here! This is all that this seemingly dangerous world amounts to. Child's play—the very thing to jest about." He concludes that we can see, therefore, what is so liberating about these books:

> For an instant they relieve the ego of the pressure of the superego. Max and Moritz and Adamson are stupidly sly and cruel, as all of us feel we are at some point. But humor smiles at this, and we smile, too. We like ourselves a bit more and perform some tiny detail better than we would have managed without that bright moment.[79]

76. Erikson, *A Way of Looking at Things*, 36.
77. Ibid.
78. Ibid.
79. Ibid.

Here, Erikson makes the case for humor as enabling the ego to liberate itself, if only for a fleeting "bright moment," from the pressures of the sadistic conscience that demands so much and promises so little. But, interestingly enough, he seems to misread Freud on this point. What Freud actually says in reference to the "Child's play, the very thing to joke about" remark is that "it is really the superego which, in humor, speaks such kindly words of comfort to the intimidated ego," and this, Freud suggests, "teaches us that we have still very much to learn about the nature of that energy."[80]

In Freud's view, when we use humor, we adopt "the attitude of an adult towards a child, recognizing and smiling at the triviality of the interests and sufferings which seem to the child so big," and this means that "if the superego does try to comfort the ego by humor and to protect it from suffering, this does not conflict with its derivation from the parental function."[81]

Yes, the superego often expresses itself in the form of a punitive conscience, but it also has a more genial side, for, in humor, it speaks kindly words of comfort to the intimidated ego. The "bright moments" afforded by the capacity for humor testify that the child's superego is able to relax its moral grip from time to time and allow some breathing space, and even, occasionally, the freedom to run down the stairs and catch the cigar before it hits the pavement. As Erikson has shown that hair may be more than hair, so the Adamson character shows that sometimes a cigar is much more than a cigar: in fact, it may be the very symbol of the restoration—if only a fleeting bright moment—of the child's inner unity.

CONCLUSION

What is remarkable about these three articles of Erikson's is how comfortable he has become with psychoanalytic ideas in a relatively short period of time. After all, just three years prior to his writing of these articles he was an unemployed artist living at home in Karlsruhe, Germany, and apparently

---

80. Freud, "Humor," 268. Quite possibly, this was not a misreading of Freud but the expression of a different viewpoint; that is, that it is not the superego (or internalized parental function) that comforts the ego, but the ego that stands up to the superego and, in a sense, comforts it. In a footnote, Erikson suggests that fairy tales "appeal, with their reconciling strength, to all human beings, not just children, and they possess the magically solid form that has always been the brighter condition for a comforting touch on the stern superego" (Erikson, *A Way of Looking at Things*, 37). Erikson may be suggesting that humor has a similar effect on the stern superego. In any event, Freud's idea that the superego has a genial side and that humor is perhaps the best illustration of this fact, is quite revolutionary and has yet to be fully recognized as such by his successors.

81. Freud, "Humor," 269.

had little if any knowledge, much less interest, in Freud or psychoanalysis. When one reads these articles, one cannot avoid thinking of his account of how Martin Luther, who had come to a dead end, began to come alive again when he began, quite reluctantly at first, to teach at the new university in Wittenberg at the insistence of Dr. Johann von Staupitz, the vicar-general of the province "and the man who was the fatherly sponsor of Martin's late twenties."[82] Erikson notes that Luther took on the lectures "not with pious eagerness, but with a sense of tragic conflict; but as he prepared and delivered them, he became affectively and intellectually alive."[83] Furthermore, Staupitz had employed humor to overcome Martin's resistance to taking on the lectures. When Martin complained that Staupitz was "killing him" with his demand that he prepare himself for the professorship, Staupitz casually responded, "That's all right, God needs men like you in heaven, too."[84]

Erikson's early articles, especially the first of the three—"Psychoanalysis and the Future of Education"—give the distinct impression that he had found his vocation in life, which was to be a teacher, an educator. In fact, this essay begins by noting that of all those who through their analytic training hope to make some fundamental contribution to therapeutic or educational work, "the teacher is the least able to foresee what he may achieve through analytical insight, which he gains from his own clinical analysis," the reason for this being that the analyst "is obliged for the most part to remain a silent observer while the teacher's work involves continuous talking."[85] Furthermore, the teacher not only has to deal with affects in his children, the ultimate forms of which are not yet fully determined, "but he also cannot avoid registering his own affective response."[86] Moreover, although he knows that he, like the analyst, is the object of transference, "he cannot eliminate his own personality, but must play a very personal part in the child's life."[87]

Noting that the teacher, unlike the child guidance workers, accomplishes "his educational purposes chiefly through the imponderables of his attitude in the pursuit of his work as teacher," and that "his duty is to train, to present, to explain, and to enlighten," Erikson suggests that enlightenment is the point where "teaching and psychoanalysis can be seen to come to a fundamental convergence."[88] He concludes the article with the observation

82. Erikson, *Young Man Luther*, 165.

83. Ibid., 220.

84. Ibid., 166.

85. Erikson, *A Way of Looking at Things*, 14.

86. Ibid., 15.

87. Ibid.

88. Ibid.

that modern enlightenment can best be achieved through psychoanalysis because psychoanalysis has demonstrated "the truth of the healing power of self-knowledge."[89]

If Erikson could write years later of the fact that his adoption by the Freudian circle was "truly astounding," we might say the same of his adoption of it. There can be little doubt that a major reason why he adopted Freud's teaching was that it was so deeply committed to the truth of the healing power of self-knowledge. Of course, Erikson experienced this truth in his analytic sessions with Anna Freud, but the articles that we have considered here suggest that he experienced this truth even more profoundly in his interactions with the children at the Hietzing School. If so, an important aspect of these interactions was the humor that was an integral part of them (and may well have been at the core of Anna Freud's view that Erikson's teaching style was too permissive). In any case, as noted earlier, the children later recalled that Erikson was nervous, self conscious and idiosyncratically funny, and that he carried himself somewhat awkwardly, and they also remembered their own amusement that he could not pass a mirror without looking at himself. This was a man with whom they could identify. His very awkwardness made them laugh, and this, in turn, made them feel better, less anxious, about themselves, their problems, and their own lowly status in the world.

89. Ibid., 29.

5

The Power of Play

power:

(1) the ability to do, act, or produce;

(2) the capacity to affect, control, or enforce.

Erikson's first book, *Childhood and Society,* was originally published in 1950. Two decades later, Robert Coles wrote that he doubted "that any other book by a student of Freud is as well known over the world." He added that it has been translated into eleven languages, that it sold steadily for thirteen years and was then reissued in a second, revised edition in 1963, and that in a recent study of the reading lists given to young residents of 140 psychiatric training centers, it was one of only eighteen of 2800 recommended books that appeared in all of the reading lists.[1]

Chapter 7 of *Childhood and Society*, "Eight Stages of Man," retitled "The Eight Ages of Man" in the revised edition, presents Erikson's conception of the human life cycle. This chapter is unquestionably the best-known chapter in the book.[2] Given its singular importance, the fact that it is the third of three chapters in part 3 "The Growth of the Ego" is easy to overlook. Chapter 5, "Early Ego Failure: Jean," focuses on Erikson's case of a five-year-old schizophrenic girl,[3] and chapter 6, "Toys and Reasons,"

---

1. Coles, *Erik Erikson,* 118.

2. Erikson, *Childhood and Society,* rev. ed., 247–74.

3. Ibid., 195–208.

focuses on several "cases": Ben Rogers in Mark Twain's *Tom Sawyer*; Freud's account in *Beyond the Pleasure Principle* of the "gone-there" game played by his five-year-old grandson;[4] and Erikson's own cases of a three-year-old girl who was having nightmares, a five-year-old boy with an urge to set fires, and an African American boy who listened every night to the radio program, *The Red Rider*—a cowboy devoted to righting wrongs and challenging the bad guys—and imagines himself to be the Red Rider.[5]

I will discuss here the cases of the five-year-old schizophrenic girl and of Freud's grandson (which I alluded to in chapter 2). Both cases focus on the child's relationship with the mother and on Erikson's proposal that, through play, children find ways to master their sense of emotional separation from their mothers, the experience that, as I have been suggesting, is primarily responsible for the development of a melancholy self among the various selves that comprise one's "composite Self."[6] The first case centers on the issue of maternal rejection, while the second concerns the issue of maternal absence due to circumstances beyond the mother's control. Following these discussions, I will focus on another case of Erikson's in *Childhood and Society*: that of a young boy named Sam, which Erikson presents in the first chapter, titled "Relevance and Relativity in the Case History."

THE THEME OF THE REJECTING MOTHER

Erikson begins his chapter on Jean, the five-year-old schizophrenic girl, with this observation:

> To come face to face with a "schizophrenic" child is one of the most awe-inspiring experiences a psychotherapist can have. It is not the bizarreness of the child's behavior which makes the encounter so immediately challenging, but rather the very contrast of that behavior with the appeal of some of these children. Their facial features are often regular and pleasing, their eyes are

4. Freud, *Beyond the Pleasure Principle*, 31–38.

5. Erikson, *Childhood and Society*, rev. ed., 209–246.

6. Erikson, *Identity, Youth, and Crisis*, 217. In chapter 1 I focused on the formation of the melancholy self in young boys, but I hope to show by means of Erikson's case of the five-year-old preschizophrenic girl that young girls are no less prone to develop a melancholy self. The French psychoanalyst Julia Kristeva makes this very point in *Black Sun: Depression and Melancholia*, 41–42. She suggests that the young girl's melancholia is traceable to the two-to-three-year-old girl's need to begin adopting the dominant ("symbolic") language of her culture, which is male-oriented, and thus to leave the security of her mother's language world (which is "semiotic").

"soulful" and seem to express deep and desperate experience, paired with a resignation which children should not have.[7]

This impression of the child, he adds, can be seductive, for it "immediately convinces the observer, often against the better knowledge of previous experience that the right person and the right therapeutic regime could bring the child back on the road to coherent progress."[8] Furthermore, "this conviction has the more or less explicit corollary that the child has been in the wrong hands and, in fact, that he has every reason to mistrust his neglectful and rejecting parents." Erikson alludes to a previous chapter in which he demonstrated how far adult members of various cultures "would go in accusing one another of doing deliberate harm to their children: *our occupational prejudice is 'the rejecting mother.'*"[9] He returns to this issue of the "rejecting mother" in the final paragraph of the chapter.

Initially, however, he focuses on Jean herself, noting that he first saw her when she was almost six years old:

> I did not see her at her best. She had just made a train trip, and my house was strange to her. What glimpses I could catch of her (for she was frantically on the move through garden and house) showed her to be of graceful build, but tense and abrupt in her movements. She had beautiful dark eyes which seemed like peaceful islands within the anxious grimace of her face.[10]

Erikson noticed that she ran through all the rooms of the house, uncovering all the beds she could find, as if she were looking for something: "The objects of this search proved to be pillows, which she hugged and talked to in a hoarse whisper and with a hollow laugh."[11] She *was*, most certainly, "schizophrenic." This was apparent in the fact that her "human relationships were centrifugal, away from people."[12]

He had observed "this strange phenomenon of a 'centrifugal approach,' often interpreted as mere lack of contact, years before in the behavior of another little girl who was said to 'notice nobody.'"[13] When this other little girl had come down the flight of stairs toward Erikson, "her glance drifted in an absent way over a series of objects, describing concentric circles around

---

7. Erikson, *Childhood and Society,* rev. ed., 195.

8. Ibid.

9. Ibid. (italics added)

10. Ibid., 195–96.

11. Ibid., 196.

12. Ibid.

13. Ibid.

my face. She focused on me negatively, as it were."[14] He suggests that this "flight" is the common denominator

> for a variety of other symptoms, such as the preoccupation with things far away and imagined; the inability to concentrate on any task at hand; violent objection to all close contact with others unless they fit into some imaginary scheme; and immediate diffused flight from verbal communication, when it happens to become more or less established. Meaning is quickly replaced by parrot-like repetition of stereotyped phrases, accompanied by guttural sounds of despair.[15]

Jean's "mad rush" through the house, pausing long enough to concentrate her attention and to lavish her affection on bed pillows, "seemed important" to Erikson for the following reason:

> Her mother had told me that Jean's extreme disorientation had begun after the mother had become bedridden with tuberculosis. She was permitted to stay at home in her own room, but the child could speak to her only through the doorway of her bedroom, from the arms of a good-natured but "tough" nurse.[16]

During this period Jean's mother had the impression that there were things that her daughter urgently wanted to tell her. She had regretted at the time that, shortly before her illness, she had let Jean's original nurse, a gentle Mexican girl, leave them. As she watched from her bed, she noticed that the tough nurse, Hedwig, was always in a hurry, moved the baby with great energy, and was very emphatic in her disapprovals and warnings. Her favorite remark was, "Ah, baby, you stink!" and her holy war was her effort to keep the creeping infant off the floor so that she would not be contaminated by dirt. If the child were slightly soiled, she scrubbed her "as if she were scrubbing a deck."[17]

When, after four months of separation, Jean, now thirteen months old, was permitted to reenter her mother's room, she spoke only in a whisper. Her mother noted that she shrank back from the chintz pattern on the armchair and cried. She tried to crawl off the flowered rug and cried all the time, looking very fearful. She was terrified by a large, soft ball rolling on the floor and of paper crackling. These fears spread. First, she did not dare to touch ashtrays and other dirty objects, then she avoided touching

14. Ibid.
15. Ibid.
16. Ibid.
17. Ibid., 197.

or being touched by her elder brother and gradually by most people around her. Although she learned to feed herself and to walk at the normal time, she gradually became sad and silent.

Erikson surmises that her frantic affection for pillows had to do with that period when she was prevented from approaching her mother's bed: "Maybe, for some reason, she had not been able to take the separation, had 'adjusted' to it by a permanent pattern of fleeing from all human contact, and was now expressing her affection for the bedridden mother in her love for pillows."[18]

Jean's mother confirmed that Jean had a fetish, a small pillow or sheet which she would press over her face when going to sleep. Erikson adds:

> For her part, the mother seemed desirous of making restitution to the child for what she felt she had denied her, not only during those months of illness, but by what now seemed liked a general kind of neglect by default. This mother by no means lacked affection for the child, but she felt that she had not given Jean the relaxed affection she needed most *when* she needed it most.[19]

Erikson notes that "some such maternal estrangement may be found in every history of infantile schizophrenia," but what

> remains debatable is whether the maternal behavior could possibly be a "cause" for such a radical disturbance in a child's functioning; or whether such children, for some intrinsic and perhaps constitutional reasons, have needs or need stimulations which no mother would understand without professional help—and professional people, until very recently, were utterly unable to spot these children when they were young enough to perhaps be saved with special dosages of well-planned mother love.[20]

He indicates that he will take up this issue again later in the chapter.

Jean's mother supplied further information about Jean's feeding history, which indicated that she had tried to nurse her for a week but gave up due to a breast infection. Also, when she was ten days old Jean began to suffer from thrush (a disease, especially common in infancy, caused by a fungus and characterized by the formation of milky-white lesions on the mouth, lips, and throat) which remained an acute condition for three weeks and a low-grade chronic infection for the remainder of her first year.

18. Ibid.
19. Ibid.
20. Ibid., 197–98.

Erikson comments, "No doubt the oral trauma had been severe," and that it had direct bearing on the fact that her fetish consisted of a sheet "which she made into a ball and pressed against her mouth with one piece between her teeth."[21]

Erikson also observes that besides pillows and sheets, Jean loved instruments and machines. She smiled at egg-beaters, vacuum cleaners, and radiators: "She smiled at them, whispered to them, and hugged them, and was impelled by their very presence to a kind of excited dancing—all this, while she remained completely uninterested in people unless they invaded her preoccupations, or unless she wished to invade theirs."[22]

Jean's mother shared with Erikson the observation of a psychologist who tested Jean when she was four years old: that she seemed to have "turned against speech."[23] Erikson found this statement highly relevant because it suggested that children with a schizophrenic tendency in early childhood repudiate their own organs and functions as though they are hostile and external to them. Thus, "they have a defective screening system; their sensory contacts fail to master the overpowering impressions as well as the disturbing impulses which intrude themselves upon consciousness," and they therefore "experience their own organs of contact and communication as enemies, as potential intruders into a body ego which has withdrawn 'under the skin.'"[24] This is why these children close their eyes and hold their hands over their ears, or hide their heads under a blanket.

Erikson asks whether there any way in which a favorable view of one's own organs of contact and communication might be restored? He suggests that "only a carefully dosed and extraordinarily consistent application of maternal encouragement could enable the child's ego to reconquer, as it were, its own organs, and with them to perceive the social environment and to make contact with it more trustingly."[25] This conviction led him to propose the following preliminary treatment plan: Noting that Jean had not been living with her parents for many months (she had been living in a foster home), he proposed that Jean should be restored to her family home "and that, for some extended time, the mother should take over Jean's care under my guidance to be given on regular trips to their home in a college

21. Ibid., 198.
22. Ibid., 172.
23. Ibid., 198.
24. Ibid., 198–99.
25. Ibid., 199.

town."[26] This family-treatment plan, he felt, should precede any direct therapy with Jean.

Back within the family, and with her mother in constant attendance, Jean expressed her appreciation by "a determined and goal-directed attempt to restore contact."[27] These attempts, though, were often too determined and too specific, as they involved grabbing her brothers' penises, invading her father's shower so that she could grab at his genitals, concentrating on the bump on her father's head, and tearing his cigarettes from his lips and throwing them out the window. In other words, "she knew where people are vulnerable; these children, so vulnerable themselves, are masters at such diagnosis."[28]

In addition to grabbing, she "used her fingers for poking people and came so near to hurting a visitor's eyes [Erikson's?]" that "she had to be energetically stopped."[29] Erikson adds that Jean "especially liked to poke her father, obviously as a sequence to her penis- and cigarette-grabbing activities." When, at this point, her father had to go on a trip, "she regressed to whining, resumed her sheet fetish (saying 'blanket is mended'), spoke only in a soft voice, and ate little, even refusing ice cream." Apparently, she believed that she had again made somebody go away by touching him, and she "seemed particularly desperate because she had, in fact, begun to respond to her father's devoted efforts to help her." On the other hand, her mother gave her "appropriate explanations concerning her father's 'disappearance,'" and this seemed to help.[30]

Jean's interest in her mother focused on her breasts, and as she took sly pokes at them, she would say "not touch a bandage—throw away a chest—hurt a chest," which led both mother and Erikson to "surmise that she communicated an impression according to which she had hurt the mother when she developed 'chest trouble' and that she had been banished from her mother's room for this reason."[31] This assumption that she was reliving the time, five years earlier, when her mother was ill, was also supported by the fact that she "became outspokenly self-punitive and asked to be 'thrown away,'" and in solitary games "would go back to her old fears of dirt, and

26. Ibid.
27. Ibid.
28. Ibid., 200.
29. Ibid., 205.
30. Ibid.
31. Ibid., 200.

would act as if she were brushing away a cobweb or throwing away something disgusting."[32]

Her mother continued to explain patiently to Jean that her illness was not her fault, and Jean seemed to begin to believe her: "After several months, she showed marked improvement," becoming "more graceful in her movements; her vocabulary increased, or, as one should say in such cases, became apparent, for it is usually there before its presence is suspected."[33] Erikson adds, "And she began to play!"[34] She especially liked to play "nurse and baby" with her little toy dog, saying, "Go to sleep, dog, stay under covers; shut your eyes, have to spank you, dog." She also began to build long block trains which were "going east." During one of these games she looked her mother in the eyes "with one of her rare, completely contact-seeking glances and said, 'Not go on long ride on the train sometime,'" to which her mother replied, "No, we are going to stay together."[35]

Although her ability to play indicated marked improvement, these improvements were also interrupted by crises that led to emergency calls. Erikson would then visit the family and talk with everyone until he had ascertained what was going on in all of their lives. He notes:

> A whole series of difficulties arose in this one-patient sanitarium. One can live with schizophrenic thought only if one can make a profession out of understanding it. The mother had accepted this task, which demands a particular gift of empathy and at the same time the ability to keep oneself intact. Otherwise one must refute such thinking in order to be protected against it. Each member of the household, then, in being forced to take a glance into Jean's life, characterized as it was by the alternation of naked impulsiveness and desperate self-negation, was endangered in his own equilibrium and self-esteem. This had to be pointed out repeatedly, because Jean would constantly change the direction of her provocation. And she would withdraw repeatedly for no apparent reason.[36]

Erikson describes in some detail one such crisis that followed upon her mother's attempt to make Jean sleep by herself. This resulted in the development of a fetishistic attachment to the small spoon-like shade attached to

---

32. Ibid., 200–201.
33. Ibid., 202.
34. Ibid. This sentence was added in the revised edition.
35. Ibid.
36. Ibid.

the dim lightbulb in her room, and her subsequent touching of a plug in the living room that caused an electrical short circuit in the house.

Erikson also notes that Jean's improvements underscored the fact that she was simply unable to integrate her experiences. For example, she became adept at playing the xylophone, and her parents found a piano teacher for her who based her methods on Jean's auditory gifts and ingenuity in imitating. On his next visit, Erikson heard someone practicing some phrases of Beethoven's first piano sonata, and thought that a gifted adult was playing: "To find Jean at the piano was one of the surprises which are so gripping in work with these cases—and which often prove so misleading, because again and again they make one believe in the child's total progress where one is justified in believing only in isolated and too rapid advances of special faculties." Erikson adds that he says this "with feeling and conviction, for Jean's piano playing, whether it was Beethoven, Haydn, or boogie-woogie, was truly astounding—until she turned against this gift, just as she had 'turned against speech,' in the words of the first psychologist who had seen her."[37]

Erikson concludes that this case illustrates "the essential ego weakness which causes these children to be swayed at one time by a 'drivenness' focused on a part of another person; and at another by cruel self-punitiveness and paralyzing perfectionism."[38] It is not, in his view, "that they fail to be able to learn, to remember, and to excel—usually in some artistic endeavor which reflects the sensory counterpart of their essentially oral fixation," but that "they cannot integrate it all: their ego is impotent."[39]

What eventually happened to Jean? As she grew older, the discrepancy between her chronological age and her behavior became so marked that associations with children anywhere near her own age were impossible. Then, other difficulties which Erikson does not specify arose, and these required an interval in a special school, and "she quickly lost what she had gained in the years of her mother's heroic effort." At the time of writing, her treatment has resumed "under the best residential circumstances and under the guidance of one of the most devoted and imaginative child psychiatrists in this particular field."[40]

Erikson concludes the chapter with a paragraph on the issue of "maternal rejection." He notes that the role played by "maternal rejection" or "special circumstances of abandonment" in these cases is still debatable, but he thinks that one should consider that "these children may very early and

37. Ibid., 206.
38. Ibid.
39. Ibid., 206–207.
40. Ibid., 207.

subtly fail to return the mother's glance, smile, and touch; an initial reserve which makes the mother, in turn, unwittingly withdraw."[41] Thus, the "truism" that the original problem is to be found in the mother-child relationship holds only in so far as one considers "this relationship an emotional pooling which may multiply well-being in both but which will endanger both partners when the communication becomes jammed or weakened."[42]

As far as the cases of infantile schizophrenia which he had seen are concerned, "there was a clear deficiency in 'sending power' in the child."[43] In a footnote Erikson recalls that in the first edition of *Childhood and Society* he had said that "the primary deficiency in 'sending power" was in the child," and adds that this statement "referred only to those few cases that I had seen; and such cases were rare then in psychoanalytic practice." This statement was intended to counter "certain facile interpretations then in vogue which claimed that rejecting mothers could cause such malignancy in their offspring." Unfortunately, the statement "has been quoted out of context in support of a strictly constitutional etiology of infantile psychosis." But this was not his intention. On the contrary, the careful reader of this and other chapters will see that "I am not trying to isolate first causes and therapeutic effects, but to delineate a new conceptual area encompassing both the struggles of the ego and of social organization." He acknowledges that this new conceptual approach may bypass "details in parent-child interaction in which constitutional and environmental defects aggravate each other malignantly," but "first causes can be isolated (or ruled out) only where rigorous diagnostic criteria exist and where anamneses in quantity permit comparison."[44] Such work, he suggests, is being undertaken in the growing literature of psychoanalytic child psychiatry, but this, he implies, cannot and should not be imposed retrospectively on the case he has reported in this chapter.

Also, in the first edition of *Childhood and Society* Erikson had mentioned that the child may share with the parent "some frailty of contact and communication which may appear in malignant form in the younger mind and organism, while in the adult it may have found a compensatory expression in superior intellectual or artistic equipment."[45] In the revised edition he changed this to read: "Because of the very early failure in communication, however, the child may only betray in more malignant form a

41. Ibid.
42. Ibid.
43. Ibid.
44. Ibid.
45 Erikson, *Childhood and Society*, orig. ed., 181.

frailty of affective contact which already exists in the parent(s), although in them it may be compensated for—at least in other relationships—by a special character make-up or by superior intellectual endowment."[46] Thus, he now wants to suggest that the frailty of affective contact may exist in both parents—not only the mother—but that the compensations that one or both of the parents experience may have little to do with the parent-child relationship itself.

Finally, in the original version Erikson suggested that this superior intellectual or artistic equipment" can be used "to develop in mother and nurses that surplus of curative and creative effort of which Jean's mother was capable, and which alone may be expected to make up for a deficiency of such magnitude." He had also cautioned that "only a therapist with faith as well as experience in the matter, and only a sturdy and enlightened mother, should undertake to pioneer on this frontier of human trust."[47] In the revised edition, he merely says that regarding "the procedure described in this chapter, it should be clear that Jean's mother was capable of that exceptional curative effort which is a prerequisite for all experimentation on this frontier of human trust."[48] This change emphasizes that Jean's mother was, in fact, capable of making the effort (albeit unsuccessful) to help her daughter get well, and it eliminates the reference to the therapist, perhaps because the very fact that his curative efforts were ineffective may raise questions as to whether even a therapist "with faith as well as experience in the matter" *should* attempt what he had attempted.

THE 'SENDING POWER' OF PLAY

One of the most interesting aspects of this case concerns the occasions when Jean abandoned her preoccupation with fetish objects and progressed to genuine child's play. In her "nurse and baby" play with her toy dog (itself reminiscent of the days when she was under nurse Hedwig's charge), she assumed the role of the adult in putting the child to bed, instructing him to go to sleep, remain under the covers, and shut his eyes. If he did not comply, she would have to spank him. Given "the immense self-punitive tendency in these driven children" and their tendency to "take the dictum, 'if thine eye offend thee, pluck it out,' literally and quite seriously," the fact that the punitive focus shifted from herself to her dog is especially noteworthy.[49]

46. Erikson. *Childhood and Society*, rev. ed., 207–8.

47. Erikson, *Childhood and Society*, orig. ed., 181.

48 Erikson, *Childhood and Society*, rev. ed., 208.

49. Ibid., 201.

Also, the play involving the train recapitulated experiences when Jean had been separated from her family, and elicited her mother's promise that there would be no more train rides, for "we are going to stay together."[50] The first instance of child's play, then, enabled Jean to project her self-punitive impulses onto another object, while the second allowed her to express her deep anxieties about being separated from her family, especially her mother.

What about her grabbing and poking behavior? This play, aggressive enough to hurt the other, reflected an opposite impulse to her play with the long train. By grabbing and poking, she fantasizes that she can make the *other person* go away, and is therefore no longer the passive victim of their actions and intentions toward her. Although Erikson notes that her mother gave her "appropriate explanations concerning her father's 'disappearance,'" Jean must have gained secret satisfaction from being able to "make somebody go away by touching him."[51] This particular "ability" gives an ironic twist to Erikson's suggestion that "a clear deficiency in 'sending power' was in the child." From her own point of view, Jean had the power to send others away, and thus to avenge the times when they had sent *her* away. On the other hand, Erikson's discussion of the case indicates that, time and again, Jean's ability to play—games or the piano—was eventually arrested or disrupted, and she regressed to fetishistic behaviors instead. Her play did not have lasting curative effects. In the chapter in *Childhood and Society* that follows this one, Erikson discusses the case of Ernest, the grandson of Sigmund Freud, and the effects of play in his case are very different.

THE THEME OF THE ABSENT MOTHER

Erikson begins chapter 6—"Toys and Reasons"—with the observation that even as Freud noted that the "interpretation of dreams is the royal road to a knowledge of the unconscious activities of the mind,"[52] so "play [is] the royal road to the understanding of the infantile ego's efforts at synthesis."[53] Having presented an example of the failure of such synthesis in the case of Jean, Erikson will now shift to "childhood situations which illustrate the capacity of the ego to find recreation and self-cure in the activity of play;

50. Ibid., 202.

51. Ibid., 205.

52. Freud, *The Interpretation of Dreams*, 647.

53. Erikson, *Childhood and Society*, rev. ed., 209. The chapter title "Toys and Reasons" was derived from these lines in a poem by William Blake: "The Child's Toys and the Old Man's Reasons / Are the Fruits of the Two Seasons." It may have special relevance to the case that I will be discussing here: the case of Sigmund Freud's reflections on a game invented by his grandson.

and to therapeutic situations in which we were fortunate enough to be able to help a child's ego to help itself."[54]

As I indicated earlier, this chapter consists of several cases. Three of these cases were Erikson's own, the most fully developed of which was that of Mary, a three-year-old girl who was having nightmares, and with whom Erikson engaged in "play therapy." Unlike the case of Jean, this case concluded on a positive note, largely because the play therapy enabled Mary to transfer onto Erikson (the man with the toys) "a conflict which had disturbed her usually playful relationship with her father."[55] Summarizing the effects of the play therapy, Erikson says that Mary "reassured herself, reaffirmed her femininity—and told the big man off," and adds, "Such play peace gained must, however, be sustained by new insight on the part of the parents."[56]

The case that I propose to consider here, however, is that of Ernest Freud's grandson, which, as indicated in chapter 2, focuses on a game that Ernest invented.[57] Ernest was his daughter Sophie's first child, and eighteen months old at the time that Freud observed his play behavior. Erikson provides an extensive quotation from Freud's text and then offers his own understanding of what Freud saw in the game that his grandson played.

Freud's own discussion of his grandson's improvised game follows his observation that the "study of dreams may be considered the most trustworthy method of investigating deep mental processes," and that "dreams occurring in traumatic neuroses have the characteristic of repeatedly bringing the patient back into the situation of his accident, a situation from which he wakes up in another fright."[58] Then, however, he indicates that he wants "to leave the dark and dismal subject of the traumatic neurosis and pass on to examine the method of working employed by the mental apparatus in one of its earliest *normal* activities—I mean in children's play."[59]

Freud notes that the various theories of children's play have only recently been summarized and discussed from the psychoanalytic point of view by S. Pfeiffer. Although he recommends the article, he notes that none of the theories presented emphasize the "economic motive" in play. That is, they fail to consider "the yield of pleasure involved." He feels that by focusing on the economic motive in play, he can "throw some light on the

54. Ibid.
55. Ibid., 232.
56. Ibid., 232–33.
57. Freud, *Beyond the Pleasure Principle*, 32–38.
58. Ibid., 30.
59. Ibid., 31–32.

first game played by a little boy of one and a half and invented by himself." His observation of the boy's game was more than fleeting because he "lived under the same roof as the child and his parents for some weeks, and it was sometime before I discovered the meaning of the puzzling activity which he constantly repeated."[60]

Describing the boy himself, Freud says that he was not at all precocious in his intellectual development. He could say only a few comprehensible words. But he was on good terms with his parents and their servant-girl, and tributes were paid to his being a "good boy." He did not disturb his parents at night, he conscientiously obeyed orders not to touch certain things or go into certain rooms, and "above all he never cried when his mother left him for a few hours."[61] At the same time, "he was greatly attached to his mother, who had not only fed him herself but had also looked after him without any outside help."[62] He *did,* however, have an occasional disturbing habit of taking any small objects he could get hold of and throwing them away from him into a corner, under the bed, and so on, so that hunting for his toys and picking them up was something of a hassle for others. As he did this, he gave vent to a loud, long-drawn-out "*o,*" accompanied by an expression of interest and satisfaction. Freud notes that his mother and Freud himself agreed "that this was not a mere interjection but represented the German word '*fort*' ['gone']."[63]

Freud eventually realized "that it was a game and that the only use he made of any of his toys was to play 'gone' with them." One day Freud made an observation which confirmed his view:

> The child had a wooden reel with a piece of string tied round it. It never occurred to him to pull it along the floor behind him, for instance, and play at its being a carriage. What he did was to hold the reel by the string and very skillfully throw it over the edge of his curtained cot, so that it disappeared into it, at the same time uttering his expressive "o-o-o-o." He then pulled the reel out of the cot again by the string and hailed its reappearance with a joyful "*da*" ["there"]. This, then, was the complete game—disappearance and return.[64]

Ordinarily, one witnessed only its first act, "which was repeated untiringly as a game in itself, though there is no doubt that the greater pleasure was

60. Ibid., 32.
61. Ibid., 32–33.
62. Ibid., 33.
63. Ibid.
64. Ibid.

attached to the second act."[65] In a footnote, Freud indicates that a further observation confirmed this interpretation: One day the child's mother had been away for several hours and on her return was met with the words "Baby o-o-o-o." At first, this seemed incomprehensible. But it soon turned out that during this long period of solitude the child had found a method of making *himself* disappear: "He had discovered his reflection in a full-length mirror which did not quite reach to the ground, so that by crouching down he could make his mirror-image 'gone.'"[66]

The footnote also refers the reader to another footnote added to Freud's *The Interpretation of Dreams* in the 1919 edition, the same year that he was writing *Beyond the Pleasure Principle*. In this footnote, Freud refers to "the first dream that I was able to pick up from my grandson, at the age of one year and eight months."[67] On the night before the day on which his father was due to leave for active military duty, Ernest cried out, sobbing violently, "Daddy! Daddy!—baby!" Freud suggests that the only meaning this could have is that "Daddy and baby were remaining together." He observes that at this time Ernest "was already quite well able to express the concept of separation," and mentions the game of "gone" that he had played with his toys, a game that "went back to a successful piece of self-discipline which he had achieved at an early age in allowing his mother to leave him and be 'gone.'"[68]

Reflecting on his observation that "the greater pleasure was attached to the second act" of the game, Freud suggests that the interpretation of the game becomes quite obvious:

> It was related to the child's great cultural achievement—the instinctual renunciation (that is, the renunciation of instinctual satisfaction) which he had made in allowing his mother to go away without protesting. He compensated himself for this, as it were, by himself staging the disappearance and return of the objects within his reach.[69]

Obviously, the child could not "possibly have felt his mother's departure as something agreeable or even indifferent," and this being the case, Freud asks: "How then does his repetition of this distressing experience as a game fit with the pleasure principle?" He thinks the answer lies in the fact that "her departure had to be enacted as a necessary preliminary to her joyful

65. Ibid., 33–34.
66. Ibid., 34.
67. Freud, *The Interpretation of Dreams*, 498.
68. Ibid.
69. Freud, *Beyond the Pleasure Principle*, 34.

return," and that the "true purpose of the game" was therefore expressed in the second act ("there").[70] Thus, the game is an example of the pleasure principle at work.

On the other hand, there is the fact that "the first act, that of departure, was staged as a game in itself and far more frequently than the episode in its entirety, with its pleasurable ending."[71] Freud believes, therefore, that something more than the pleasure principle is operating here, and that the game had another motivation besides that of giving the child pleasure: "At the outset he was in a *passive* situation—he was overpowered by the experience; but, by repeating it, unpleasurable though it was, as a game he took on an *active* part." In effect, these efforts indicate "an instinct for mastery that was acting independently of whether the memory was in itself pleasurable or not."[72]

Although this instinct for mastery interpretation seems entirely plausible, Freud suggests another explanation that seems no less plausible, namely, that the motivation behind the game was that of revenge: "Throwing away the object so that it was 'gone' might satisfy an impulse of the child's, which was suppressed in his actual life, to revenge himself on his mother for going away from him. In that case it would have a defiant meaning: 'All right, then, go away! I don't need you. I'm sending you away myself.'"[73] In support of this interpretation, Freud notes that a year later Earnest would take a toy, and if he was angry at it, he would throw it on the floor, exclaiming, "Go to the fwont!" He had heard at that time that his absent father was "at the front," and "was far from regretting his absence; on the contrary he made it quite clear that he had no desire to be disturbed in his sole possession of his mother."[74]

To provide further support for this interpretation, Freud refers the reader to his brief essay on Goethe's recollection of merrily throwing all of his miniature dishes and saucepans out of the window.[75] As Freud notes in the essay, the objects thrown out the window were a substitute for a younger brother who stood in the way of his sole possession of his mother. In a footnote in *Beyond the Pleasure Principle*, Freud points out that Ernest's mother—Freud's daughter Sophie—died when he was almost six years old. Freud adds that now that she was really gone, he "showed no signs of grief,"

70. Ibid.
71. Ibid., 35.
72. Ibid.
73. Ibid.
74. Ibid., 35–36.
75. Freud, "A Childhood Recollection from Goethe's *Dichtung und Wahrheit*." 112.

noting that in the interval "a second child had been born and had roused him to violent jealousy."[76]

In the end, Freud suggests that we need not choose between the interpretations that he has put forward, for any or all of them may be appropriate to a particular game that a child invents. He concludes that children, in their play, "repeat everything that has made a great impression in real life" and, in doing so, they relive the impression and "make themselves master of the situation." He also notes that all of their play "is influenced by a wish that dominates them the whole time—the wish to be grown-up and to be able to do what grown-up people do."[77] And, finally, he observes that the fact that an experience was not pleasurable does not necessarily make it unsuitable for play:

> If the doctor looks down a child's throat or carries out some small operation on him, we may be quite sure that these frightening experiences will be the subject of the next game; but we must not in that connection overlook the fact that there is a yield of pleasure from another source. As the child passes over from the passivity of the experience to the activity of the game, he hands on the disagreeable experience to one of his playmates and in this way revenges himself on a substitute.[78]

In the example cited, he plays "doctor" on a playmate, preferably a younger sibling with whom he is in competition for possession of the mother.[79]

In his own commentary on Freud's discussion of the game that Earnest played, Erikson suggests that in order to understand what Freud saw in this game we need to consider the fact that he was interested in the strange phenomenon of the "repetition compulsion," that is, "the need to re-enact painful experiences in words or acts." Erikson points out,

> We have all experienced the occasional need of talking incessantly about a painful event (an insult, a quarrel, or an operation) which one might be expected to want to forget. We know

---

76. Freud, *Beyond the Pleasure Principle*, 36. Sophie was expecting her third child when she died of influenza. Freud was completing *Beyond the Pleasure Principle* at the time. See Gay, *Freud: A Life for Our Times*, 391.

77. Ibid.

78. Ibid., 37.

79. In the concluding paragraph of his discussion of children's play Freud reminds his readers that dramatic plays created by adults present the audience with the most painful experiences, but in such a way that they are felt to be enjoyable. This is "convincing proof that, even under the dominance of the pleasure principle, there are ways and means enough to making what is in itself unpleasurable into a subject to be recollected and worked over in the mind" (ibid., 37).

of traumatized individuals who, instead of finding recovery in sleep, are repeatedly awakened by dreams in which they re-experience the original trauma. We also suspect that it is not so innocently accidental that some people make the same mistakes over and over again; that they "coincidentally" and in utter blindness marry the same kind of impossible partner from whom they have just been divorced, or that a series of analogous accidents and mishaps always must happen just to *them*.[80]

Erikson adds that in all of these cases, Freud concluded that "the individual unconsciously arranges for variations of an original theme which he has not learned either to overcome or to live with: he tries to master a situation which in its original form had been too much for him by meeting it repeatedly and of his own accord."[81]

Continuing his commentary on Freud's discussion of the game his grandson played, Erikson notes that as Freud was writing about the "repetition compulsion," he became aware of the solitary game invented by his grandson and of the fact that "the frequency of the main theme (something or somebody disappears and comes back) corresponded to the intensity of the life experience reflected—namely, the mother's leaving in the morning and her return at night."[82] This dramatization "takes place in the play sphere" where, utilizing his mastery over objects,

the child can arrange them in such a way that they permit him to imagine that he is master of his life predicament as well. For when the mother had left him, she had removed herself from the sphere of his cries and demands; and she had come back only when it happened to suit her. In his game, however, the little boy has the mother by a string. He makes her go away, even throws her away, and then makes her come back at his pleasure. He has, as Freud puts it, *turned passivity into activity*; he plays at doing something that was in reality done to him.[83]

Then, having noted this transformation of the experience from one of passive endurance to active mastery, Freud mentions three items that may guide us in a further social evaluation of this game:

First, the child threw the object away. Freud sees in this a possible expression of revenge—"If you don't want to stay with me,

80. Erikson, *Childhood and Society*, rev. ed., 216.
81. Ibid., 216–17.
82. Ibid., 217.
83. Ibid. (italics original)

I don't want you"—and thus an additional gain in active mastery by an apparent growth of emotional autonomy. In his second play act, however, the child goes further. He abandons the object altogether and, with the use of a full-length mirror, plays "going away" from himself and returning to himself. He is now both the person who is being left and the person who leaves. He has become master by incorporating not only the person who, in life, is beyond his control, but the whole situation, with *both* its partners.[84]

He seems to say, "If you can go and return at will, so can I." In so doing, he internalizes the other, and, in effect, plays *her* role.

Erikson notes that this is "as far as Freud goes with his interpretation," and that a further point may also be made, one concerning the fact that "the child greets the returning mother with the information that he has learned to 'go away' from himself."[85] This, to Erikson, is very important, for the game alone "could be the beginning of an increasing tendency on the child's part to take life experiences into a solitary corner and to rectify them in fantasy, and only in fantasy." What if the child were to have shown complete indifference when the mother returns, thus "extending his revenge to the life situation and indicating that he, indeed, can now take care of himself, that he does not need her"?[86] In fact,

> This often happens after a mother's first excursions: she rushes back, eager to embrace her child, only to be met by a bland face. She may then feel rejected and turn against or away from the unloving child, who is thus easily made to feel that the vengeance in the game of throwing away and his subsequent boast has hit its mark too well, that he has indeed made the mother go away, whereas he has only tried to recover from being abandoned by her. Thus the basic problem of being left and leaving would not be improved by its solution in solitary play.[87]

This, however, did not happen in the case that Freud presents: Instead, the little boy "told his mother of his play, and we may assume that she, far from being offended, demonstrated interest and maybe even pride in his ingenuity." This would mean that "he was then better off all around" because "he had adjusted to a difficult situation, he had learned to manipulate new

84. Ibid. (italics original)

85. Ibid., 217.

86. Ibid., 217–18.

87. Ibid., 218.

objects, and he had received social recognition for his method."[88] In effect, Ernest's mastery of a difficult situation was even better than his grandfather realized, for although mastery by incorporating the other into oneself is a noteworthy achievement, even better is the mastery of taking the other into one's confidence, at least with regard to the game he plays upon himself. What Ernest has taken out of play is the possibility that his mother may feel rejected and withdraw from him.

THE RETRIEVAL POWER OF PLAY

The contrast between Ernest's and Jean's invented games is unmistakable, for, unlike Jean's games, Ernest's games evidenced a mastery of a difficult life situation. An episode that Erikson reports in his case of Jean captures the contrast in a dramatic way. Noting that Jean had not lived with her parents for many months prior to the time he was asked to accept her for treatment, Erikson comments:

> Most of the time she appeared not to care. Yet, on the previous Christmas, after attending a party at her parents' house, the child had thrown all the presents which she had received from her parents on the street outside her foster home, stamped on them, and cried wildly. *Maybe she did care.*[89]

Similarly, Ernest had thrown his toys away, but this was only the "first act" in what became a two-act play, the second act being the return of the toys that he had sent away. Thus, the critical difference between his play and Jean's was that his consisted of two acts: the act of disappearance but also the act of recovery. Her play involved the first act of making others go away, but there was no corresponding second act of making them return. She had "sending power" but lacked retrieval power. Her play reflected the "repetition compulsion" of which Freud writes (the need to reenact painful experiences in words or acts), but unlike Ernest's games, which reflect various forms of mastery of the situation (and not merely revenge), her play illustrates what Erikson, in his "Toys and Reasons" chapter, calls "play disruption," i.e., the situation in which a child becomes "trapped by his overpowering emotions in the middle of the game," and the ego, "flooded by fear," is unable to continue.[90]

88. Ibid., 218.
89. Ibid., 199 (italics added).
90. Ibid., 224.

MOURNING, MELANCHOLIA AND PLAY

A common feature of these two cases of children's play is the issue of the mother's absence. The absence of the father also arises in both cases, but his absence seems rather easy to account for, and, in any case, does not seem to trouble the child nearly as much as the mother's absence. In the case of Jean, there were times when the mother was physically absent or inaccessible (when she was ill with tuberculosis and when Jean was living in a foster home), but the much deeper issue that Erikson raises is the question of her emotional absence. In the case of Ernest, the mother is physically absent, but neither Freud nor Erikson raises any questions concerning her emotional availability when she *was* at home. On the other hand, Freud mentions the fact that several years after Ernest devised his "gone-there" game, his mother died, resulting, of course, in her permanent physical absence. He adds that the boy did not grieve, attributing this, at least in part, to the fact that Sophie had given birth to her second child, toward whom Ernest felt a "violent jealousy."

Both cases, then, leave their readers with some unanswered questions, questions that arise because the authors of the cases raise these questions themselves. In the case of Jean, Erikson raises the question of "the rejecting mother," and although he is concerned to dissociate himself from the then popular view that the mother is primarily to blame for a schizophrenic child, he presents circumstantial evidence that would appear to suggest that there was an element of "maternal estrangement" from almost the very beginning of Jean's life. In the case of Ernest, Freud's observation that Ernest did not grieve is more absolute than is typical of Freud, and even he does not appear to believe that his explanation for this claim is entirely satisfactory. I suggest, therefore, that we return to Freud's essay "Mourning and Melancholia" to shed some light on these unanswered questions, and, in doing so, to enable us to gain further insight into the restorative role of children's play.[91]

As we saw in our discussion of this essay in chapter 1, Freud believes that a major reason why mourning and melancholia have such different effects on the individual who has suffered the loss of the loved object is that, in the case of mourning, the loved object is permanently, irrevocably gone, whereas in the case of melancholia, the loved object is "usually to be found in [the person's] near neighborhood," and is therefore physically present but emotionally withdrawn or absent.[92] This leads the person who is bereft of the loved object to internalize the other and to direct one's feelings of

91. Freud, "Mourning and Melancholia."
92. Ibid., 173.

having been abandoned and mistreated toward this internalized object. In Freud's view, this internalization of the other accounts for the fact that the melancholic person engages in so much self-reproach, for the real object of the reproach is the person from whom one has become estranged. Thus, the self-punitive tendencies of the melancholic person are, in a sense, a disguised form of rage against the "lost object."

I suggest that the case of Jean reflects the melancholic condition, or, put another way, that her melancholy self looms very large among the various selves that comprise her "composite Self."[93] By endorsing this suggestion, we can agree with Erikson's resistance to the tendency of some to blame "the rejecting mother" for the fate of children like Jean. At the same time, we can recognize that *Jean herself* blames her mother for her own sense of abandonment, with such blaming disguised, at least in part, behind her own self-punitive behaviors. If Jean's melancholy self is especially dominant, her one-act games simply reinforce its dominance, and, as Erikson points out, leave her with an ego that is weak and impotent. Moreover, her mother's "exceptional curative efforts" are ineffective, in part at least, because her daughter blames the very one who is trying to help her for the condition in which she finds herself.

In contrast, the case of Ernest illustrates the mourning condition. He, too, feels bereft of his mother when she is away, but, much in the same way that grieving persons overcome their "grave departures from the normal attitude to life," he overcomes his painful self-dejection through the mastery that he realizes through his two-act games, and through his capacity to tell his mother, when she returns, about the game in which he makes himself appear and disappear. In effect, the two-act game takes a potentially melancholia-producing situation and turns it into a situation of ego-mastery.

The view that Ernest's games enabled him to engage in the mourning process during his mother's physical absences also sheds light on his grandfather's observation that he seemed not to grieve over the death of his mother. Although his violent jealousy of his younger sibling may have been a factor in this failure to grieve, I think that a more fundamental explanation is that he had already developed the capacity to grieve through his invented games, and that the memory of these earlier occasions of grieving sustained him when his mother died. If we "re-enact painful experiences in words or acts" under the aegis of the "repetition compulsion,"[94] a similar re-enactment of earlier experiences in which we achieved mastery over such

93. Erikson, *Identity, Youth, and Crisis*, 217.
94. Erikson, *Childhood and Society*, rev. ed., 216.

painful experiences, turning passivity into activity, might also occur. In this case, play—whether child's or adult's—is an act of self-restoration.

WORDS OF REASSURANCE

The following case, presented in the first chapter of *Childhood and Society*, provides an illustration of how Erikson worked with troubled children through play. It also illustrates how one boy struggled with the issue of alienation and estrangement from his mother, and how Erikson, in the role of surrogate father, helped to relieve the boy of guilt and thereby enabled him to look toward the future with refound hope. He titles this case "A Neurological Crisis in a Small Boy."[95]

Erikson was a faculty member of the Department of Psychiatry at the University of California in Berkeley when he encountered Sam. He became Sam's therapist when the boy was five years old. Sam's difficulties had begun two years earlier, and he had had two therapists prior to Erikson. At the time, Erikson was using a great deal of play therapy in his work with children.

When he was three years old, Sam began to suffer convulsions shortly after the death of his grandmother. His first attack occurred five days after her death, the second happened a month later when he found a dead mole in the backyard of his home, and a third took place two months after that, following his accidental crushing of a butterfly in his hand. After the second attack, the hospital staff diagnosed the affliction as idiopathic epilepsy ("idiopathic" meaning that the cause was unknown or uncertain), possibly due to a brain lesion in the left hemisphere. However, EEG tests following the third attack were inconclusive. They indicated only that "epilepsy could not be excluded."[96]

As he became acquainted with the case, Erikson learned that Sam's mother had been extremely nervous about her husband's mother's visit shortly after they had settled into their new home in a new town: "The visit had the connotation of an examination to her: had she done well by her husband and by her child?"[97] Aware that Sam enjoyed teasing people, she warned him that his grandmother's heart was not very strong. He promised not to tease the older woman, and at first everything went well. Still, his mother seldom left the two of them alone together, especially because the enforced restraint seemed to be hard on the vigorous little boy, causing him

95. Ibid., 25–38.
96. Ibid., 26.
97. Ibid., 26.

to appear pale and tense. Then, one day, she slipped away for a while, leaving him in his grandmother's care, and returned to find the older woman lying on the floor. She had suffered a heart attack. Sam's mother was later informed by her mother-in-law that he had climbed up on a chair and had fallen. Erikson notes, "There was every reason to suspect that he had teased her and had deliberately done something which she had warned against."[98] Sam's grandmother was ill for several months, during which she remained at her son's and daughter-in-law's home. But she failed to recover, and eventually died. Five days later, Sam suffered his first attack.

Sam's parents did not disclose to him that his grandmother had died. Instead, the following morning, his mother told him that his grandmother had gone on a long trip north to Seattle. He cried and asked, "Why didn't she say goodbye to me?" Then, when her body was removed from the house in a casket, his mother compounded the deception by telling him that his grandmother's books were in the big box. But Sam had not seen his grandmother bring so many books with her, and could not understand why the relatives who had gathered in their home would have shed so many tears over a box full of books. Sam's mother told Erikson this story, but when he heard it from her, he "doubted that the boy really believed the story."[99] His doubts were confirmed by other remarks by "the little teaser." Once when his mother had wanted him to find something that he did not want to look for, he had said, mockingly, "It has gone on a lo-oong trip, all the way to Se-attle." Also, in the play-therapy group that he later joined as part of the treatment plan, he would build innumerable variations of oblong boxes, the openings of which he would carefully barricade: "His questions at the time justified the suspicion that he was experimenting with the idea of how it was to be locked up in an oblong box."[100]

Belatedly, his mother decided to tell him the truth, informing him that his grandmother had, in fact, died. But he now refused to accept it. Instead, he responded to her, "You're lying. She's in Seattle," and "I'm going to see her again."[101] Thus, if he questioned his mother's earlier story, he also refused to believe her retraction of the earlier story and substitution of the true story. It was as if Sam wanted his mother to know that he had no idea what he could believe anymore.

Erikson also learned through conversations with Sam's mother that he had lost his good-natured mischievousness and sense of humor at about

98. Ibid., 26.
99. Ibid., 27.
100. Ibid.
101. Ibid.

the time of his grandmother's arrival, and had become uncharacteristically aggressive. He had hit another child, hard enough to cause bleeding, and his punishment was that he would have to remain at home with his grandmother and not go outside and play. He had also thrown a doll at his mother and the impact loosened one of her teeth. In reaction, she had struck him back, displaying "a rage which neither she nor he had known was in her."[102]

One day, "in order to test his threshold," Erikson arranged for Sam to lose consistently to him at a game of dominoes. As his losses mounted, his face grew very pale. Suddenly, he stood up, grabbed a rubber doll, and hit Erikson in the face with it. At that very moment, his eyes took on an aimless state, he gagged as if about to vomit, and he swooned slightly, thus suffering "one of his minor spells." After regaining consciousness, he rearranged the dominoes into an oblong, rectangular configuration, a miniature version of his grandmother's casket. Erikson said to him, "This must mean that you are afraid you may have to die because you hit me." Sam replied, breathlessly, "Must I?" and Erikson reassured him: "Of course not." Then he added: "But you must have thought that you did make your grandmother die and therefore had to die yourself. That's why you built those big boxes in your school, just as you built this little one today. In fact, you must have thought you were going to die every time you had one of those attacks." He simply replied, "Yes."[103]

Erikson presented this case in the first chapter of *Childhood and Society* to illustrate the relationships that he would be exploring throughout the book between the *somatic process* (reflected in Sam's seizures and convulsions), *the ego process* (reflected in Sam's effort to protect his individuality by adopting the role of the little teaser), and the larger *social process* (reflected in the fact that Sam's parents had chosen to live in a town in which they were the only Jewish family).[104]

It is reasonable to assume that Erikson also gave this case history such prominence in this, his first book, because it had significant similarities to his own early childhood, especially as reflected in his own change of residence at the age of three, and his own mother's deception about the identity of his biological father. The fact that Erikson says he "played in" with this deception[105] suggests that he was no more deceived by it than was Sam when his mother told him that his grandmother had taken a long trip to Seattle. Erikson may also have noticed the similarities in the fact that both mothers, aware that their sons did not believe the initial story, tried to amend their stories. But whereas Erikson's mother did not tell him the real truth—that he was neither the son of his stepfather nor the son of her estranged husband—Sam's mother tried to convince her son that the original story was false, that his grandmother had in fact died.

Why, then, did Sam reject the true story, especially when it was supported by his own perceptions and judgments, such as the size of the box that was allegedly filled with books that he knew his grandmother did not own? Was it because he wanted to serve his mother notice that once she had lied to him, he could never trust what she said to him? Or was he so conscience-stricken over the role he had played in precipitating his grandmother's heart attack that he wanted to believe that her original story was true? Or was it both? And why did she lie to him in the first place? Had she wanted to spare her son the guilt he felt for having been responsible, at least in part, for his grandmother's heart attack? Or was she struggling with her own guilt for having slipped out that day, leaving her son in the older woman's care? Or was it both?

One thing seems reasonably clear: Sam's mother's deception would have made it very difficult for Sam to work through his feelings of guilt through direct conversation with her. He would have to deal with them on his own, in his own way. So we should not be surprised that Sam's sense of guilt took a physiological form, and that he would suffer attacks similar to that of his grandmother (which he had personally witnessed). The similarity of these attacks was congruent with his mother's later recollection that on the evening before his first attack, he had piled up his pillows the way his grandmother had done to avoid congestion and had gone to sleep in nearly the same sitting position that his grandmother had adopted following her heart attack.[106] Also, because his grandmother lived a few months following her initial attack, he may have viewed his own survival of several attacks as merely a temporary reprieve. As Erikson learned through their play together, it was apparent that Sam believed he would eventually have to die for having brought on or at least contributed to her heart attack.

Then, however, Erikson, the third of three therapists called in to help the family, uncovered the psychodynamic roots of Sam's physical seizures, making the critical connection between the boy's symptoms and the death of his grandmother. But Erikson did much more than diagnose the problem. His therapeutic interventions, especially on the day that he caused Sam to lose at dominoes, were decisive for Sam's recovery. By reassuring him that he would not need to pay with his life—one death begetting another—for

106. Erikson, *Childhood and Society*, rev. ed., 27.

what he had done, Erikson became the one person in the whole scenario surrounding his grandmother's death to whom the young boy could confide and acknowledge his deep sense of guilt and expectation of ultimate punishment.

In *Young Man Luther*, Erikson suggests that when we "look through a glass darkly" (an allusion to 1 Cor 13:12) we find ourselves "in an inner cosmos in which the outlines of three objects awaken dim nostalgias": the "affirmative face" of the mother, graciously inclined; the "paternal voice of guiding conscience"; and the pure self itself, the unborn core of creation. The third dim nostalgia envisions the self as "no longer sick with a conflict between right and wrong."[107] I suggest that Erikson represented the paternal voice of guiding conscience, which, as Erikson notes, provides "sanction for energetic action,"[108] action based on the boy's recovery of a sense of hope. As Erikson says of hope in his essay "Human Strength and the Cycle of Generations":

> The gradual widening of the infant's horizon of active experience provides, at each step, verifications so rewarding that they inspire new hopefulness. At the same time, the infant develops a greater capacity for renunciation, together with the ability to transfer disappointed hopes to better prospects; and he learns to dream what is imaginable and to train his expectations on what promises to be possible.[109]

Sam was no longer an infant. He was five years old. Nonetheless, new and different seeds of hope were sown that day when a small boy was unable to control his dark urges and rages and the man he hit on the face with a rubber doll communicated to him that he fully understood. We sense that in that moment of reassurance the boy was enabled to transfer disappointed hopes to better prospects.

In his *Introductory Lectures on Psychoanalysis* Freud addressed the skepticism with which he was so frequently confronted by the relatives of his patients. They doubted that "anything can be done about the illness by mere talking." But Freud drew attention to the power of words: "Words were originally magic and to this day words have retained much of their ancient magical power. By words one person can make another blissfully happy or drive him to despair."[110] Given his focus on children, Erikson could not take the royal dream road to the unconscious. Instead, he followed Freud's ex-

---

107. Erikson, *Young Man Luther*, 263–64.

108. Ibid., 264.

109. Erikson, *Insight and Responsibility*, 117.

110. Freud, *Introductory Lectures on Psychoanalysis*, 20.

ample in *Beyond the Pleasure Principle* when he analyzed his grandson's play behavior and took the royal play road to the unconscious. Both, however, shared the conviction that the voice is an organ of happiness and of despair, and Erikson's fatherly voice in this case evoked in the small boy a deep sense of happiness based on the sanction he had received for energetic action instead of seizures, swoons, and aggressive attacks on undeserving others.

CONCLUSION

Erikson continued to write about play in the course of his career, and one of the topics he addressed was the issue of the relationship between play and work. In his essay "Human Strength and the Cycle of Generations" he noted that "play is to the child what thinking, planning and blueprinting are to the adult, a trial universe in which conditions are simplified and methods exploratory, so that past failures can be thought through, expectations tested."[111] Thus, if play to the child is far from being frivolous and random activity and is, instead, purposeful, then purpose is also the human strength that he assigns to the third stage of the life cycle, which is also the "play age."

By the same token, Erikson suggested in his 1972 essay "Play and Actuality" that "creative" people know that the there is no real division between play and work.[112] In support, he cites Robert Frost's poem "Two Tramps in Mud-Time," in which Frost tells about two strangers who noticed that he was splitting wood in his yard, and one of them made it apparent to Frost that he wanted to take over the task for pay. Erikson quotes the lines in which Frost says that "My object in living is to unite / My avocation and my vocation / As my two eyes make one in sight."[113] Erikson observes:

> We may for the moment ignore the fact that the men thus addressed were looking for work; we know that one man's play and work may be another's unemployment. But taking Frost's creativity as a measure, we may add to his formulation the postulate that the adult, in combining vocation and avocation, creates leeway for himself while creating leeway for those within his scope of mutuality.[114]

111. Erikson, *Insight and Responsibility,* 120.
112. Erikson, *A Way of Looking at Things,* 311–45.
113. Frost, *The Poetry of Robert Frost,* 275–77.
114. Erikson, *A Way of Looking at Things,* 332–33.

Erikson invokes the idea of "leeway" again in his book *Toys and Reasons* when he notes that of all the formulations of play, the briefest and best is to be found in Plato's *Laws*. Plato, he notes,

> sees the model of true playfulness in the need of all young crea-
> tures, animal and human, to leap. To truly leap, you must learn
> how to use the ground as a springboard, and how to land resil-
> iently and safely. It means to test the leeway allowed by given
> limits; to outdo and yet not escape gravity. Thus, wherever play-
> fulness prevails, there is always a surprising element, surpassing
> mere repetition or habituation, and at its best suggesting some
> virgin chance conquered, some divine leeway shared.[115]

He goes on to say that Plato's association of playfulness with "young" creatures is perpetuated in adult views of play as neither serious nor useful,
in the division of play and work, and in avoidance of "the often awesome
suggestion that playfulness—and, thus, indeterminate chance—may occur
in the vital center of adult concerns, as it does in the center of those of
children."[116]

The cases we have considered in this chapter are those of young children, and they reflect, therefore, the fact that Erikson himself was considered a child analyst. But one of the things that impressed him about Jesus
was that Jesus used stories about children—for example, the story of the
children sitting in the marketplace who called to their playmates and said,
"We piped to you, and you did not dance; we wailed, and you did not mourn"
(Matt 11:16–19)—to help adults gain insights into their own attitudes and
behaviors.[117] The same point applies to the cases we have considered here.

115. Erikson, *Toys and Reasons*, 17.
116. Ibid., 18.
117. Erikson, "The Galilean Sayings and the Sense of 'I,'" 350.

6

The Beneficence of Dreams

beneficence:
(1) the fact or quality of being kind or doing good;
(2) a charitable act or generous gift.

In his autobiographical essay Erikson asks how it was that an artist like himself was able to find a place in a clinical and scientific movement that is so intensely verbal. The answer, he suggests, is that his "first acquaintance with the psychoanalytic view of childhood coincided with a period of daily contact with children, and my first study of dreams with the observation of children's play."[1] He also notes that he soon detected in Freud's writings "vivid manifestations of an indomitable visual curiosity," which was reflected in his description of his patients' memories and dreams, as they "reveal that he deeply empathized with their imagery before he entered what he had heard and seen into the context of verbal nomenclature."[2]

Thus, even as children's play involves the creation of observable configurations, so dreams are visual configurations. The persons (or animals) in dreams may speak, but the dreams themselves are visual. Thus a person with artistic capacities and training may, in fact, be an ideal psychoanalytic candidate. As noted in chapter 2, when he mentioned to Anna Freud that he could not see a place for his artistic inclinations in such high, intellectual

1. Erikson, "'Identity Crisis' in Autobiographic Perspective," 29.
2. Ibid., 30.

endeavors as those reflected in psychoanalysis, she quietly replied, "You might help to make them see."[3] Thus, to move from our consideration of the resource of play to that of dreams is not the large leap that it may appear to be.

As I previously noted, Erikson's *Insight and Responsibility* is a collection of six lectures, presented on three separate continents. In the preface he indicates that they "all converged on a common theme," which was "the light thrown by clinical insight on the responsibilities which each generation has for all succeeding ones."[4] The second lecture, "The Nature of Clinical Evidence," which Erikson presented at an interdisciplinary symposium on evidence and inference at the Massachusetts Institute of Technology in 1957, and the fifth lecture, "Psychological Reality and Historical Actuality," which was originally presented in a more condensed form to the American Psychoanalytic Association in New York in 1961, have in common a focus on dreams. The third lecture concerns the dream of one of Erikson's patients, a young man in his early twenties. The fifth lecture treats two of Sigmund Freud's own dreams. I will focus on these two lectures in this chapter.

THE DREAM OF THE EMPTY FACE

The letter that invited Erikson to participate in the symposium on evidence and inference asked him to address the question, "How does a good clinician really work?" He chose to focus on a single case, that of a young man who was "on the borderline of psychosis," and, more specifically, on a dream that the patient reported in a session that took place several months into therapy. At the time, Erikson was on the staff of the Austen Riggs Center in Stockbridge, Massachusetts. According to Erikson, this young man was "one among a small group of our patients who came from theological seminaries"; he added that "he had developed his symptoms when attending a Protestant seminary in the Middle West where he was training for missionary work in Asia."[5]

Erikson quotes the following from the original test report on the patient and notes that the course of treatment confirmed these test results:

> The tests indicate border-line psychotic features in an inhibited,
> obsessive-compulsive character. However, the patient seems
> to be able to take spontaneously adequate distance from these

3. Ibid. For a different account, also noted in chapter 2, see Friedman, *Identity's Architect*, 69–70.

4. Erikson, *Insight and Responsibility*, 9.

5. Ibid., 65.

border-line tendencies. He seems, at present, to be struggling to strengthen a rather precarious control over aggressive impulses, and probably feels a good deal of anxiety.[6]

Erikson's account of the session in which the young man reported the dream begins in this way: "A young man in his early twenties comes to his therapeutic hour about midway during his first year of treatment in a psychiatric hospital and reports that he has had the most disturbing dream of his life."[7] The patient noted that the dream vividly recalled "his state of panic at the time of the 'mental breakdown' which had caused him to interrupt his studies for missionary work abroad and enter treatment." Given the fact that the dream seemed painfully real on awakening, and that even now the dream-state seems vivid enough to threaten his sense of reality, he expressed the fear that this was "the end of his sanity."[8]

The dream image itself was quite brief. According to the patient, "there was a big face sitting in a buggy of the horse-and-buggy days. The face was completely empty, and there was horrible, slimy, snaky hair all around it. I am not sure it wasn't my mother." The dream was followed by "a variety of seemingly incidental reports of the events of the previous day" and these eventually gave way "to a rather coherent account of the patient's relationship with his deceased grandfather, a country parson," in which "he sees himself as a small boy with his grandfather crossing a bridge over a brook, his tiny hand in the old man's reassuring fist."[9] At this point, the patient's mood changed "to a deeply moved and moving admission of desperate nostalgia for the rural setting in which the values of his Nordic immigrant forebears were clear and strong."[10]

Erikson notes his own need to make an initial prediction as to whether the dream was a sign of an impending collapse or a potentially beneficial clinical crisis: "The first would mean that the patient is slipping away from me and that I must think, as it were, of the emergency net; the second, that he is reaching out for me with an important message which I must try to understand and answer."[11] He decided on the latter alternative, for although the patient acted as if he were close to a breakdown, Erikson "had the suspicion that, in fact, there was a challenge in all this, and a rather angry one." This impression was based to some extent on a comparison between the

6. Ibid., 60–61.
7. Ibid., 57.
8. Ibid.
9. Ibid.
10. Ibid., 57–58.
11. Ibid., 61.

present therapeutic hour and the previous one, in which the patient had seemed markedly improved: "Could it be that his unconscious had not been able to tolerate this very improvement?" Also, "does the dream-report communicate, protesting somewhat too loudly, that the patient is still sick? Is his dream sicker than the patient is?"[12]

With this preliminary prediction in mind, Erikson focuses on the dream image itself, noting that there are no spoken words, no motion, and no people. Clearly, then, there are omissions. This being the case, the dream interpreter should be especially wary of the urge to look for the most plausible explanation of the dream image, and instead allow his free-floating clinical attention and judgment "to lead him to all the *possible* faces which may be addressed in this one dream face and then decide what *possible meaning* may explain their combined presence."[13] He suggests that these possible faces include his own, God's, the patient's mother and grandfather, and Medusa's, of whom Freud had written an essay in 1922 in which he argued that the decapitated head of Medusa suggests the terror of castration as punishment for seeing something that one ought not to have seen.[14]

Erikson's Face

Erikson considers his own face first, noting that the empty face had something to do with a certain tenuousness in their the therapist-patient relationship due, in large part, to the fact that in the third month of therapy Erikson had "abandoned" his patient to have an emergency operation for which the patient believed himself to be responsible due to his "evil eye."[15] So one message of the empty face is that the patient is asking how he can have or gain what he needs most—a coherent personality, an identity, a face of his own—if his therapist is thinking more of his own discomfort following surgery than that of his patient's, or if the therapist may again absent himself when his patient needs him?

The Face of God

Erikson turns next to God's countenance, and notes that the young theological student had not found the expected transformation of his symptoms

12. Ibid., 61–62.
13. Ibid., 62–63.
14. Freud, "Medusa's Head."
15. Erikson, *Insight and Responsibility*, 63.

through prayer, a practice "which both for reasons of honesty and of inner need, he had taken more seriously than many successful believers."[16] Noting that "the wish to gaze through the glass darkly and to come 'face to face' was a desperate need not easily satisfied in some modern seminaries," he says that he needn't remind his listeners and readers "of the many references in the Bible to God's 'making his face to shine upon' man, or God's face being turned away or being distant."[17] He concludes that the patient's report of an anxiety dream in which a face was horribly unrecognizable seemed to echo his "religious scruples at the time of the appearance of psychiatric symptoms—the common denominator being *a wish to break through to a provider of identity.*"[18]

The Grandfather's Face

Erikson's observation that the patient wanted desperately to "break through to a provider of identity" leads him from the immediate clinical situation "to the developmental crisis typical for the patient's age (and the possible meaning of facelessness as 'identity-confusion'), to the vocational and spiritual crisis immediately preceding the patient's breakdown (and the need for a divine face, an existential recognition)." Thinking of this developmental crisis prompts him to focus on the "buggy" in the dream, which leads a further step back to "an earlier identity crisis—and yet another significant face."[19] A historical symbol of cultural change, *horse-and-buggy* may be "a derisive term connoting hopelessly old-fashioned ways or it is a symbol of nostalgia for the good old days." For this patient, it meant the latter. The young man's family had come from Minnesota, where his mother's father had been a rural clergyman of character, strength, and communal esteem. When his parents moved the family to Pittsburgh, his mother had especially found it impossible to overcome an intense nostalgia for the rural ways of her youth. In fact, she had imbued her son with this nostalgia for a rural existence and had demonstrated marked disappointment when, "at the beginning of his identity crisis (maybe in order to cut through the family's cultural conflict)," he "had temporarily threatened to become somewhat delinquent."[20] The

16. Ibid., 65.
17. Ibid.
18. Ibid., 65–66 (italics original).
19. Ibid., 66.
20. Ibid.

horse and buggy might therefore signify "something like being stuck in the middle of a world of competitive change and motion."[21]

In any event, even as Erikson had begun to infer in his own mind that the face sitting in the buggy must also represent the patient's deceased grandfather, the patient spontaneously embarked on "a series of memories concerning the past when his grandfather had taken him by the hand to acquaint him with the technology of an old farm in Minnesota. Here the patient's vocabulary had become poetic and his description vivid, and he had seemed to be breaking through to a genuinely positive emotional experience."[22] On the other hand, as a reckless youngster, he had defied his grandfather shortly before his grandfather's death, and, knowing this, Erikson "sympathized with his tearfulness which, nevertheless, remained strangely perverse, and sounded strangled by anger, as though he might be saying: 'One must not promise a child such certainty, and then leave him.'" Thus, the immediate clinical situation, the history of the patient's break-down, and a certain period in the patient's adolescence when he defied his grandfather all have "as their common denominator the idea that the patient wishes to *base his future sanity on a countenance of wisdom and firm identity* while, in all instances, he seems to fear that his anger may have destroyed, or may yet destroy, such resources." So the patient's "desperate insistence on finding security in prayer and, in fact, in missionary work, and yet his failure to find peace in these endeavors belongs in this context."[23]

The Mother's Face

Finally, Erikson suggests that the rural symbol of the horse-and-buggy created a possible connection between the nostalgic mother and her dead father, and this connection leads Erikson to the fact that the patient, half denying what he was half suggesting, said that he wasn't sure the face was *not* that of his mother. Erikson notes that this comment has direct bearing on "the most repetitious complaint of the whole course of therapy."[24] He explains: "While the grandfather's had been, all in all, the most consistently reassuring countenance in the patient's life, the mother's pretty, soft, and loving face had since earliest childhood been marred in the patient's mem-

21. Ibid., 67.

22. Ibid.

23. Ibid. (italics original). Note Erikson's observation that "a countenance of wisdom and firm identity" were *resources*—resources that his grandfather had represented to him and, in a sense, had bequeathed to him.

24. Ibid., 68.

ory and imagination by moments when she seemed absorbed and distorted by strong and painful emotions."[25]

The Thematic Apperception Test given to the patient before any history taking occurred suggested that the mother figure was one who sought to control her son by her protectiveness of him and by her own self-pity and demonstrations of her frailty at any aggressive act on his part. The test also noted that there appeared to be a great deal of aggression on the patient's part toward the mother figure. This picture of the mother figure was supported by the patient's tendency to describe with anger and horror "the mother of his memory as utterly exasperated, and this at those times when he was too rough, too careless, too stubborn, or too persistent."[26]

Erikson hastens to note that the actual mother is not being accused of having behaved this way, for "we can only be sure that she appeared this way in certain retrospective moods of the patient," and that such memories "are typical for a certain class of patients," which raises the question "whether this is so because they have in common a certain type of mother or share a typical reaction to their mothers, or both."[27] Whatever the case may be, "many of these patients are deeply, if often unconsciously, convinced that they have caused a basic disturbance in their mothers," and that in cases where corporal punishment and severe scolding have become less fashionable and parents resort "to the seemingly less cruel means of presenting themselves as deeply hurt by the child's willfulness," the "violated" mother "tends to appear more prominently in images of guilt."[28]

In some cases, this guilt over having been the cause of a basic disturbance in the mother becomes an obstacle in the resolution of adolescence, and those young persons who in late adolescence face a breakdown on the borderline of psychosis "all prove to be partially regressed to the earliest task in life," which is the acquisition of a sense of basic trust strong enough to balance the sense of basic mistrust to which the newborn is subject in infancy. Also, while others relive earlier stages of their existence in dreams, artistic experience, and religious devotion, and emerge stronger than before, these patients "experience such partial regression in a lonely, sudden, and intense fashion, and most of all with a sense of irreversible doom," and this sense of doom is also reflected in the dream.[29]

25. Ibid.
26. Ibid.
27. Ibid., 68–69.
28. Ibid., 69.
29. Ibid., 69.

Medusa's Face

Next, Erikson notes that the face also calls to mind the Medusa: "the angry face with snake-hair and an open mouth."[30] In support of Freud's view that the Medusa is a symbol of the feminine void and an expression of the masculine horror of femininity, Erikson cites instances when the patient's memories and dream associations could easily be traced to infantile observations and ruminations concerning "female trouble," pregnancy, and postpartum upsets. These could certainly support the idea that the facelessness of the dream image can mean a sense of inner void and, from the male point of view, of castration anxiety.

Erikson believes, however, that the facelessness may also mean the absence or lack of identity, and that the two interpretations are not mutually exclusive. The issue, then, is which interpretation reflects the present context most adequately. In Erikson's view, the most pressing issues related to "acute interpersonal needs," and he adds that the sexual symbolism of the dream was taken up later, when it reappeared in another context, "namely that of manhood and sexuality," and "revealed the bisexual confusion inherent in all identity conflict."[31] In other words, at this point in the therapy, the empty face especially reflected the patient's need for "a provider of identity."

The Father's Face

Having discussed "all the *possible* faces which may be condensed in this one dream face," Erikson notes that the one face that seems to have been completely omitted is that of the patient's father. He notes, however, that the patient's father images "became dominant in a later period of the treatment and proved most important for the patient's eventual solution of his spiritual and vocational problems," and from this "we can dimly surmise that in the present hour the grandfather 'stands for' the father."[32] Erikson does not explain exactly how the patient's images of his father aided the eventual solution of his spiritual and vocational problems. If, however, the grandfather "stands for" the father in this dream, we can guess that the patient perceived his father as the provider of identity for which he had been searching all along.

30. Ibid., 70.
31. Ibid.
32. Ibid., 69.

The Four Stages of the Patient's Longing for a Trustworthy Other

Erikson concludes that the tracing of a main theme of the dream of the empty face retrospectively has revealed this theme's presence in four periods of the patient's life, each of which "left him with anger and fear over what he was to abandon rather than with the anticipation of greater freedom and more genuine identity."[33] There was the present treatment "and the patient's fear that by some act of horrible anger (on his part or on mine or both) he might lose me and thus his chance to regain his identity through trust in me."[34] Then there was the immediately preceding religious education and the patient's "abortive attempt at finding through prayer that 'presence' which would cure his inner void." Preceding that was his earlier youth and his "hope to gain strength, peace, and identity by identifying himself with his grandfather." And, finally, much earlier, there was his early childhood and his "desperate wish to keep alive in himself the charitable face of his mother in order to overcome fear, guilt, and anger over her emotions."[35]

The earliest of these four periods established the theme, which then continued to manifest itself throughout his life and relationships. The theme is, "Whenever I begin to have faith in somebody's strength and love, some angry and sickly emotions pervade the relationship, and I end up mistrusting, empty, and a victim of anger and despair."[36] What was needed, therapeutically speaking, was a fundamental variation of the theme in which the angry and sickly emotions are not allowed to sabotage his faith in somebody's strength and love.[37]

What Did Erikson Say to His Patient?

Viewing this anxiety dream as a symptom of a derailed wish fulfillment, and perceiving that the young man was "still smarting in his twenties under what he considered his mother's strange emotions in his infancy," Erikson felt that he needed to review with the patient some of what he had presented in the lecture, and then to help his patient "learn to delineate social reality

33. Ibid., 70.

34. Ibid., 71.

35. Ibid.

36. Ibid.

37. In *Pastoral Care: A Thematic Approach* I noted Erikson's association with Henry Murray at Harvard University, and the fact that Murray was the originator of the Thematic Apperception Test. I suggested that Erikson's life stages may be viewed as themes, and that positive growth occurs when an individual who is struggling with a particular theme discovers a variation on this theme.

and to tolerate emotional tension" by communicating to the patient how he (Erikson) responded emotionally to the patient's dream. Thus, Erikson told his patient that his own response to the dream had included a feeling of being attacked, and went on to explain that the patient "had worried me, had made me feel pity, had touched me with his memories, and had challenged me to prove, all at once, the goodness of mothers, the immortality of grandfathers, my own perfection, and God's grace."[38] In other words, he implied that the patient was asking an awful lot from him and that there was no way that he—or anyone else—could meet this challenge.

How did the patient respond to this? Erikson says that he "was amused, delighted, and encouraged when I told him of my thoughts and my feelings over his unnecessary attempts to burden me with a future which he could well learn to manage—a statement which was not meant to be a therapeutic 'suggestion' or a clinical slap on the back, but was based on what I knew of his inner resources as well as of the use he made of the opportunities offered in our clinical community."[39] Erikson adds, "The patient left the hour—to which he had come with a sense of dire disaster—with a broad smile and obvious encouragement."[40]

Erikson goes on to explain that he did not belittle the dream as representing sham despair, but instead acknowledged that the patient "had taken a real chance with himself and with me," and because he had done so, "a sense of mutuality and reality was thus restored."[41] This very restoration was reinforced by the fact that, although Erikson accepted the implied dream faces as meaningful, he had refused to become drawn into them: "I had played neither mother, grandfather, nor God (this is the hardest), but had offered him my help as defined by my professional status in attempting to understand what was behind his helplessness." Also, "by relating the fact that his underlying anger aroused mine, and that I could say so without endangering either myself or him, I could show him that in his dream he had also confronted anger in the image of a Medusa—a Gorgon which, neither of us being a hero, we could yet slay together."[42] This concluding comment implies an association between the faceless dream image and the patient's mother, and that the patient had begun to challenge his mother's emotional power and control over him.

38. Erikson, *Insight and Responsibility,* 72,

39. Ibid., 74.

40. Ibid.

41. Ibid., 75.

42. Ibid.

What Became of the Patient?

Except for his observation that the patient's images of his father eventually enabled him to resolve his spiritual and emotional problems, Erikson does not say what became of the patient. However, Lawrence Friedman mentions that the "seminarian was successfully discharged in 1957 after four years of intermittent treatment," and that he "eventually abandoned his religious training" and entered the medical profession.[43]

Friedman also notes that "the case left a deep and lasting impression on Erikson," and that it "would serve as a springboard for [his] new book, which would focus on the identity crisis of Martin Luther, another young seminarian." He adds that Erikson came to call this the case of the "Medusa dream" and that it "deepened Erikson's interest in the psychology of religious experience and silenced his residual doubts that by treating religion seriously, he was being disloyal to Freud." After all, "the seminarian had revealed his personal quest for identity through prayer and missionary work; Erikson understood that religious expression was hardly antithetical to psychoanalytic insight."[44]

Friedman notes, further, that Erikson had begun his work with the seminarian with some trepidation because of his limited experience with psychotic or even borderline patients, and his uncertainty about what course to follow if the seminarian became fully psychotic. But as the case proceeded, he became more confident in his clinical skills, and felt that his own personal experiences "had helped him to understand the seminarian."[45] Friedman mentions in this connection his insight that when the seminarian played a jazz saxophone melody, he was "essentially representing his mother's loving voice combined with his own noisy infantile voice." Friedman concludes, "The young man, who had never established a bond of trust or mutuality with his mother, had established one between himself and his elegant if enigmatic therapist."[46]

The New Person

In summing up the case in relation to the question he had been asked to address—"How does a good clinician really work?"—Erikson commented: "I would also acknowledge the power of *transference*, i.e., the patient's transfer

43. Friedman, *Identity's Architect*, 267–68.
44. Ibid., 267.
45. Ibid., 268.
46. Ibid.

to me of significant problems in his past dealings with the central people in his life; but I would know that only by playing my role *as a new person in his present stage of life* can I clarify the inappropriateness of his transferences from the past."[47] Thus, the therapeutic process was one in which the patient journeyed back into his past, but being accompanied by a *new person* made a world of difference, enabling him to see *himself* as a new person in the stage of life that was even then unfolding.

What is especially significant about this case for the present study is what Erikson describes as the patient's half denial of his own half suggestion that the face in the dream may have been that of his mother. The very face-lessness of the face stands in marked contrast with the charitable face of his mother that the patient wants to keep alive in himself in order to overcome fear, guilt, and anger over *her* emotions. By refusing to play the mother, Erikson communicated to the patient that he need not be devastated or overwhelmed by the emotions of the other, that he can in fact survive the experience of the loss of his mother's charitable countenance.

This is not, of course, to say that the patient will not continue to long for what Erikson had earlier described in *Young Man Luther* as "the affirmative face of charity, graciously inclined, reassuring the faithful of the unconditional acceptance of those who will return to the bosom."[48] What this therapeutic hour represented, however, was a step forward, and, as Erikson's observation regarding the "complete omission" of the patient's father in the dream and associated themes suggests, the very facelessness of the others paved the way for the appearance of the father images that "became dominant in a later period of the treatment and proved most important for

47. Erikson, *Insight and Responsibility*, 78 (italics added). Freud emphasized in his writings on transference that the therapist's knowledge of the role that transference plays in the therapeutic process is critically important, for without this knowledge comes the danger that the feelings that the transference expresses will be treated in an exploitative or unethical manner; see Freud, "Further Recommendations"; and Freud, "The Dynamics of the Transference." In his discussion of Freud's case of Dora in his lecture on psychological reality and historical actuality in *Insight and Responsibility*, Erikson notes that at the time Dora was his patient, Freud was "becoming aware of the singular power of transference and he pursued this in his evidence." Erikson observes, however, that today we would go beyond the issue of transference and recognize that the transference is "always complemented by the patient's relation to the analyst as a 'new person,'" and that young patients in particular "appoint and invest the therapist with the role of mentor." Erikson adds that the patient's demands do not obligate the analyst to "play a part," as Freud "so firmly refused to do." On the other hand, "true mentorship," which is "far from being a showy form of emotional sympathy," is always part of "a discipline of outlook and method," and no "good therapist or teacher need protest 'human' respect, personal friendship, or parental love" (Erikson, *Insight and Responsibility*, 173–74).

48. Erikson, *Young Man Luther*, 264.

the patient's eventual solution of his spiritual and vocational problems."[49] A critical factor in this paving of the way for the appearance of the father images was, however, that the patient was able to relate his dream to a *new person* in his life. The therapeutic process was one in which the seminarian journeyed back into his past, but being accompanied by a *new person* made a world of difference, as it enabled him to see *himself* as a new person in the stage of life that was unfolding.[50]

FREUD'S DREAM OF THE THREE FATES

In his "Psychological Reality and Historical Actuality" lecture Erikson discusses two of Freud's dreams—"The Dream of the Three Fates" and "Count Thun"—which were among the nearly fifty of Freud's own dreams presented in *The Interpretation of Dreams*.[51] I will focus here on the dream of the three Fates because it is more relevant to the theme of this book, i.e., the emergence of the melancholy self and its corollary resourceful self.

Before he begins his reflections on the dream itself, Erikson notes that Freud's dreams offer an invaluable "testing ground" for his own life-cycle theory, and confesses that "it is easier for me to recognize the criteria of the life stages in some of Freud's dreams than in those of my patients or my students."[52] Why? Because he is no exception to the rule that every "trained psychoanalyst has studied Freud's dreams during the formative years of his training and has usually, more or less consciously, seen in them something more than, or different from, what his instructors saw."[53] Often, what he

---

49. Erikson, *Insight and Responsibility*, 69.

50. This case suggests that Erikson was especially drawn to dreams that were enigmatic. This may well have been the consequence of the fact that he had initially aspired to be an artist and, as an artist, he would have been intrigued by a dream in which a person sitting in a buggy was faceless. In his chapter titled "The Dream Screen" in *Toys and Reasons* he focuses on his case of a young woman who had a dream that consisted only of the word S[E]INE lit up against a dark background. His analysis of this dream, which "eventually proved strategic in helping to clarify the patient's early neurosis and personality development," focused on the fact that the Seine river flows through Paris and that it was when the patient was leaving the Louvre that she had her first symptoms of agoraphobia, the reason she had come to therapy. But the bracketed E, Erikson's own initial, suggested that the dream involved a transference, i.e., "a transfer on the psychoanalyst of highly conflicted feelings originally attached to a significant figure in childhood," namely, her pediatrician father (Erikson, *Toys and Reasons*, 127–37).

51. Freud, *The Interpretation of Dreams*.

52. Erikson, *Insight and Responsibility*, 177.

53. Ibid.

himself saw contained a theoretical change he was to formulate much later, for

> Freud's dream productions are suggestive far beyond the points Freud himself made explicit in first reporting them. For the same reason, one sometimes thinks that one has learned from Freud what he has not really made explicit—while also, of course, continually rediscovering points mentioned by Freud only in passing. Beyond this, Freud's dreams suggest themselves for further analysis for the same reason for which he chose to publish them.[54]

Thus, although matters pertaining to the stages of life are "latent trends" in Freud's dreams, "much of this is to be found in the manifest dream, or rather, in a continuum reaching from the formal surface to the unconscious content." For this reason,

> it will not be necessary for me to indulge in the sport of newly interpreting what might be presumed to have been unconscious to Freud himself. Quite on the contrary, my evidence rests rather on the fact that Freud, while focusing on matters of his concern, and admittedly leaving out much that he considered irrelevant enough to be kept from the gossipy public, yet sketched into the general outline of his material what is relevant for our contemporary trend of investigation.[55]

Having established how he will use—and not use—Freud's dreams, Erikson moves into his discussion of the dream.

Freud's Dream Account

In his presentation of the dream, Freud indicates that it occurred when he was on a trip. Tired and hungry after a day's journey, he went to bed, and "the major vital needs began to announce their presence in my sleep."[56] During the night, he had the following dream:

> I went into a kitchen in search of some pudding. Three women were standing in it; one of them was the hostess of the inn and was twisting something about in her hands, as though she was making dumplings. She answered that I must wait until she was

54. Ibid., 177–78.
55. Ibid., 178.
56. Freud, *The Interpretation of Dreams*, 237.

ready. I felt impatient and went off with a sense of injury. I put on an overcoat. But the first I tried on was too long for me. I took it off, rather surprised to find it was trimmed with fur. A second one that I put on had a long strip with a Turkish design. A stranger with a long face and a short pointed beard came up and tried to prevent my putting it on, saying it was his. I showed him then that it was embroidered all over with a Turkish pattern. He asked, "What have the Turkish designs to do with you?" But we then became quite friendly with each other.[57]

When he first began analyzing this dream, Freud says that he unexpectedly thought of the first novel he ever read when he was about thirteen years old. He could not recall the title or author, but he had a vivid memory of its ending: "The hero went mad and kept calling out the names of the three women who had brought the greatest happiness and sorrow into his life."[58] He wasn't at all sure what this recollection would lead to in the dream analysis. In connection with the three women, however, he "thought of the three Fates who spin the destiny of man, and I knew that one of the three women—the inn-hostess in the dream—was the mother who gives life, and furthermore (as in my own case) gives the living creature its first nourishment." Thus, love and hunger, he thought, "meet at a woman's breast."[59] He mentions at this point the quip by a young man who was a great admirer of feminine beauty; the young man was describing his good-looking wet nurse: "I'm sorry that I didn't make a better use of my opportunity." Freud adds that he had often quoted this anecdote to explain the factor of "deferred action" in the mechanism of psychoneuroses.[60]

Continuing the dream analysis, he observes that one of the three Fates was rubbing the palms of her hands together as though she were making dumplings: a strange occupation for a Fate "that cried out for explanation."[61] The explanation was provided by another and earlier memory from his childhood. When he was six years old and was receiving his "first lessons" in life from his mother, he was informed that we are all made of earth and must return to earth. This "doctrine" did not appeal to him, and he expressed doubts as to its validity. His mother responded by rubbing the palms of her hands together and showing him the blackish scales of skin produced by the

57. Ibid.
58. Ibid., 238.
59. Ibid.
60. Ibid.
61. Ibid.

friction as proof that we are made of earth.[62] This demonstration astonished him to such a degree that he "acquiesced in the belief" which he was later to hear expressed in the words: "Thou owest nature a death."[63] Freud concludes that "they really were Fates that I found in the kitchen when I went into it—as I had so often done in my childhood when I was hungry, while my mother, standing by the fire, had admonished me that I must wait until dinner was ready."[64]

Freud's analysis focuses next on the suggestion that the woman appeared to be making dumplings (*Knödl* in German). He was reminded that one of his University professors had taken legal action against a man named Knödl for plagiarizing his writings. This idea of plagiarizing—of appropriating whatever one can, even though it belongs to someone else—led to the second part of the dream, in which Freud "was treated as though I were the thief who had for some time carried on his business of stealing overcoats."[65]

A whole chain of associations followed, linking "several elements of the dream's manifest content," and involving the "childish naughtiness" of playing with other persons' names (Pélagie, Knödl, Brücke, Fleischl), a naughtiness that Freud excuses on the grounds that his own name had been "the victim of feeble witticisms like these on countless occasions," due to the fact that *Freud* is the German word for "joy" (and, as Erikson notes in his commentary on the dream, the "joy" implied in this instance is the joy of illicit sexual behavior). Freud also found himself thinking of cocaine, "a drug which removes *hunger*."[66] An especially significant feature of this train of thoughts was that one of the name associations (Brücke) reminded him of the Vienna Institute of Physiology where he spent the happiest years of his student life, "free from all other desires."[67] This prompted him, in turn, to recall the words from Goethe's *Faust*: "Thus, at the breasts of Wisdom

---

62. It is possible that his mother's action was intended to counteract the influence of Freud's nanny, a Catholic woman who took him with her to church. In a letter to his friend Wilhelm Fliess Freud writes: "I asked my mother whether she still remembered the nurse. 'Of course,' she said, 'an elderly person, very clever, she was always carrying you off to some church; when you returned home you preached and told us all about God Almighty'" (Freud, *The Complete Letters of Sigmund Freud to Wilhelm Fliess 1887–1904*, 271).

63. In footnote 2 on page 238 of Freud's *An Interpretation of Dreams*, James Strachey, the editor, suggests that this was a recollection of Prince Hal's remark to Falstaff in Shakespeare's *Henry IV*: "Thou owest God a death."

64. Freud, *The Interpretation of Dreams*, 238–39.

65. Ibid., 239.

66. Ibid., 240 (italics original)

67. Ibid., 239.

clinging / you will find each day a greater rapture bringing."[68] He adds that the desire for Wisdom was "in complete contrast to the desires which were now *plaguing* me in my dreams."[69]

Admitting that this train of thoughts was rather confusing, Freud returns to the stranger who tried to prevent him from putting on the overcoat, and notes that this stranger "bore the features of a shop-keeper at Spalato [a town on the Dalmatian coast] from whom my wife had bought a quantity of *Turkish* stuffs."[70] Her purchase reminded him of another potential purchase at Cattaro, also on the Dalmatian coast, which he had been too cautious over, "so that I lost an opportunity of making some nice acquisitions."[71] This seemed to be related to the earlier allusion to the neglected opportunity with the wet-nurse, and led to the following thoughts relating to his hunger: "One should never neglect an opportunity, but always take what one can even when it involves doing a small wrong"; and "One should never neglect an opportunity, since life is short and death inevitable."[72] Freud suggests that this lesson of seizing an opportunity when it presents itself "had among other meanings a sexual one, and because the desire it expressed did not stop short of doing wrong, it had reason to dread the censorship and was obliged to conceal itself behind a dream. All kinds of thoughts having a *contrary* sense then found voice: memories of a time when the dreamer was content with *spiritual* food, restraining thoughts of every kind and even threats of the most revolting sexual punishments."[73]

Erikson's Review of Freud's Dream

Erikson begins his discussion of Freud's dream with the observation that the dream occurred after a day of traveling and after an evening when Freud had to "'seek his bed' without an evening meal—tired and hungry."[74] His "review" of the dream will therefore focus on this question: "If in the analysis of a dream we come to the conclusion that it reaches back into problems of the *oral stage*, do we find evidence for the assumption that the dream, besides references to *food*, to *mouth* and *skin*, also concerns itself with the

68. Ibid.
69. Ibid.
70. Ibid., 240.
71. Ibid., 241.
72. Ibid.
73. Ibid. (italics original)
74. Erikson, *Insight and Responsibility*, 178.

first vital virtue of *hope*, and with the *cosmic order*?"[75] He is referring here to his proposal in his preceding lecture in *Insight and Responsibility* on "Human Strength and the Cycle of Generations" (which I discussed in chapter 3) that the human strengths that correspond to the first four stages of the life cycle, are *hope, will, purpose,* and *competence*. In noting that the dream concerns itself with the cosmic order, he is also referring here to his schema of the elements of the social order corresponding to the eight life stages in *Identity and the Life Cycle*.[76]

Erikson indicates that the first part of the dream—Freud's encounter with the three women in the kitchen—will be his main illustration, for the second part is "less clear both in its manifest form and in the extent of Freud's associations."[77] He adds that this is not the dream of a person who is "pathologically regressed," one for whom "all frustrations of the day turn into insults on the oral level." On the contrary, this is the dream of a person who had "faced an acute oral problem just before going to sleep," and "was apt, therefore, to meet this problem in his dream with the resources of a well functioning ego." This very fact "permits us to ask whether in the total context of the dream report—i.e., the dream itself and the dreamer's 'associated' afterthoughts—our criteria for the first stages of all the developmental schedules are discernible."[78]

Erikson begins with the manifest form of the dream, noting that it suggests much of the imagery and peculiar tension of an *oral crisis*: "The locality is that part of a house in which food is prepared; the mode of approach is demanding reciprocity—for contrary to the [English] translation, which pictures the dreamer as being 'in search of food,' the German original says that he goes there in order to let somebody give him food."[79] The "dream population consists of women exclusively" and one of them is the "hostess of the inn" who, as "every connoisseur of German song will recognize," is "the prototype of the food-and-drink-dispensing, all-maternal and yet on occasion romantic woman, who invites the lonely wanderer to her table, at least."[80] Her dual role accounts, in effect, for the fact that Freud recognized that the latent content of the dream was sexual, and sheds light on Freud's

75. Ibid., 178–79.

76. Erikson, *Identity and the Life Cycle,* orig. ed., 64–65.

77. Erikson, *Insight and Responsibility,* 179.

78. Ibid. Note Erikson's observation that Freud's ability to address the problem of his hunger through the dream itself indicated that he possessed the *resources* of a well-functioning ego.

79. Ibid., 179–80.

80. Ibid., 180.

use of the plural form when he says that after going to bed, "the major vital *needs* began to announce their presence in my sleep."[81]

But Erikson's analysis continues with the image of the woman twisting something about in her hands "as though she were making dumplings," and centers on the fact that she tells the dreamer that he must wait until she is ready: "Here, of course, we have the all important *delay* which must be faced in the oral stage, and which exposes the child to tests of faith as to whether it can trust or learn to trust that the 'hostess' will finally come and bring him his food on time, or whether she will leave him to the gnawing pain of his empty stomach."[82] He adds that "in a manner obviously childish, the dreamer feels impatient and goes off with a sense of injury, that is with that pessimistic *sulkiness* which can be characteristic of a certain oral type in broad daylight."[83]

Does this scene in the kitchen support Erikson's own formulation of the first stage of the life cycle, with its psychosocial crisis of *basic trust vs. basic mistrust*, its ego strength of *hope,* and its association with the *cosmic order*? In Erikson's judgment, it does. He notes that the dream reenacts the *bipolar relationship* with the mother who, at this stage, is the very totality of the "comprehensible world, and therefore becomes, and in many ways remains, the model for the [cosmic] powers which, because they can give, can also withhold everything."[84] As for the psychosocial crisis of *basic trust vs. basic mistrust,* the dreamer "prefers deliberate *mistrust* to unsure trust" as he "refuses to wait and leaves the scene—to turn elsewhere and, in fact, to men, as will be seen in the dream's second part."[85] This does not mean that he abandons *hope,* "for he obviously directs his hopefulness elsewhere and away from the sources of edible nutriment."[86]

At this point, Erikson adds another element that supports the relationship of the dream to his formulation of the first life-cycle stage. This is the dream's *psychopathology,* or what occurs when there is "a malignant failure of the oral stage."[87] The psychopathology of the oral stage may take the form of *delusion,* or turning to a fictitious reality; of *addiction,* which seeks supplies of intense but short-lived hope in toxic substances; and of paralyzing

---

81. Freud, *The Interpretation of Dreams,* 237.

82. Erikson, *Insight and Responsibility,* 180 (italics original).

83. Ibid. (italics original)

84. Ibid.

85. Ibid. (italics original)

86. Ibid., 181.

87. Ibid.

depression, in which hope is abandoned altogether. He suggests that all of these are found in Freud's associations to the dream.

Erikson alludes to three of Freud's associations to the first part of the dream before moving on to the second part of the dream. The first association is Freud's recollection of the first novel which he read at the age of thirteen, the age at which "the young Jew is received into the religious community of men through the ritual of the Jewish confirmation."[88] Freud reports that the hero of the novel went mad and kept calling out the names of the three women who had brought both the greatest happiness and the deepest sorrow into his life. In going mad, the novel's hero suffered "a *delusional psychosis,* then, the malignant expression of hopelessness."[89] The fact that there were three women in the novel reminds the dreamer, in turn, of the three Fates, who "spin the destiny of man," and it becomes quite clear to him that "one of the three women, namely, the inn-hostess in the dream, 'was' his mother. Love and hunger, he reflects, meet at a woman's breast; thus preparing (we add) the great alternative of basic psychosocial attitudes, trust and mistrust, which the maternal environment must balance in favor of trust and thus of lifelong *hope* in a benevolent fate."[90] The dream, in this case, exemplifies mistrust and thus a sense of hopelessness.

Freud's second association "also goes back to infancy when fate can cheat you before you know it." This is Freud's recollection of the remark of the man, who, "on seeing the good-looking woman introduced to him as his erstwhile wet-nurse, regrets the fact that he did not make better use of his opportunities."[91] Erikson notes but does not comment on this association.

The third association goes back to a childhood memory that Freud "now recognizes as most decisive for the dream."[92] He reports that "at the age of six (the age of going to school) his mother tried to convince him of the biblical claim that we are all made of earth and must return to earth by rubbing the palms of her hands together (like the hostess in the dream) and showing the child 'the blackish scales of epidermis' as a proof of her own composition of an earthy substance." Erikson suggests that this association relates to the element of the *cosmic order* in that "the very *origin of man,* and, in fact, the origin of living matter is at stake," and "the mother, the source of life-giving food and of hope-giving love, herself demonstrates the fact that her very body is created of dead matter, of earth and of dirt." Thus, the

88. Ibid.
89. Ibid. (italics original).
90. Ibid. (italics original).
91. Ibid.
92. Ibid., 182.

dreamer "associates to this what he believes to be the saying 'you owe *nature* a death,' whereas Shakespeare really says, 'Thou owest God a death,'" and therefore "puts nature, that is, a maternal figure, in the place of God, implying that a pact with maternal women is a pact—with death."[93]

From this observation that, for the dreamer, a pact with maternal women is a pact with death, Erikson moves to the second part of the dream where "one lone man appears, and no women." After some altercations, the stranger and the dreamer become "quite friendly with each other," and this "ends the dream." Erikson proposes that when all of Freud's hints are taken into account, the second part of the dream suggests "an investiture theme"; that is, the stranger bestows on the dreamer the legitimacy that he did not heretofore possess. Or, if this overstates the stranger's significance, the manifest content and the associations at least suggest that the dream's meaning is "that the dreamer turns from the women who have disappointed him to a man with whom he becomes friendly."[94]

Erikson notes that Freud's associations to the stranger "picture father figures who gave young Freud more substantial hope primarily by taking the intelligent boy into their community of learning."[95] Thus, "if the first part of this dream, evoked by hunger, goes back to the actuality of the first stage of life, the second part leads (as I think all successful dreams do) forward again: for it obviously promises to the sulky dreamer autonomy from women and participation in the world of intellectual skills."[96]

Erikson next observes that the names that Freud plays with in his associations are all male, and that most have names reminiscent of food (for example, *Knödel*, which means "dumpling," and *Fleischl*, which means "flesh"). He also notes that Freud recalled a witticism perpetrated on Goethe by his friend Herder, who asked him in a poem whether his name reflected

---

93. Ibid. (italics original) Freud's article "The Theme of the Three Caskets," to which I referred in a footnote in chapter 4, has direct bearing on this modification of Shakespeare's original wording, for the same threesome appears in Freud's article. In his commentary in the article on Shakespeare's *The Merchant of Venice,* in which suitors choose from among three caskets, Freud discusses the Greek myth of the three sisters who are the Fates: Clotho, "the fateful tendencies each one of us brings into the world"; Lachesis, "the accidental within the decrees of destiny"; and Atrophos, "the inevitable"—or death. In the concluding paragraph Freud suggests that the Fates are "the three forms taken on by the figure of the mother as life proceeds: the mother herself, the beloved who is chosen after her pattern, and finally the Mother Earth who receives him again" (Freud, "The Theme of the Three Caskets," 75). This conclusion directly supports Erikson's point that, for the dreamer, a pact with maternal women is a pact with death.

94. Erikson, *Insight and Responsibility,* 182.

95. Ibid.

96. Ibid., 182–83.

a descent from Gods—the Goths—or from *vom Kote,* which means "earth," "mud," or even "feces." From these associations the dreamer moves to his own name, a name that "has given people the opportunity for more or less witty remarks." He points out that anyone conversant with German will know that "the most obvious kind of low wit which could misuse Freud's name would be a reference to *Freudenhaus* and *Freudenmaedchen* ('house of joy' and 'girl of joy'), which mean whorehouse and whore: a reflection, then, on women of his name."[97]

Erikson concludes that this play with the meaning of surnames adds up to the equivalent to a dream oath: "If your own mother is made of earth or dirt, or worse, and if your own name is like a curse, you cannot trust mother, origin, or fate: you must create your own greatness." And, indeed, "all of the dreamer's associations concerning men converge on the great Vienna Institute of Physiology" where Freud spent the happiest hours of his student days, a happiness characterized "by the spirit of Goethe's poem" which asserts that "the 'breasts of Wisdom' promise an eternal pleasure ever renewed and ever increasing, for the thirst after knowledge is not only sublimated desire, it is also related to the actuality of the predictable world, and thus gives man the autonomous power to change the world."[98]

In short, this part of the dream and its associations express "the sublimation of all that oral desire which in the dream appears with such immediate needfulness," and "its displacement and application to the Alma Mater, the Mother of Wisdom who gives you more than perishable gifts, and provides you with the means to make something of yourself, *to change your fate.*"[99]

But here too the dreamer's associations warn of the second psychopathology of the oral stage, that of *addiction,* which seeks supplies of intense but short-lived hope in toxic substances. As frequently happens in Freud's dreams, he remembers cocaine, "which he once helped to introduce into local anesthesia, before its addictive qualities were known."[100] Erikson notes that the very function of *basic mistrust* is "to prevent the all too trustful incorporation of bad substances," but he also points out that "the danger of *too much mistrust* is the inhibition of the wish to take." Thus, "the dreamer feels that the dream warns him never to neglect an opportunity, but always to take what one can even if it involves doing a small wrong." The second part of the dream, therefore, "emphasizes the turn from dependence to self-help,

97. Ibid., 183.
98. Ibid., 183–84.
99. Ibid., 184 (italics original).
100. Ibid.

from women to men, from perishable to eternal substances, and ends with a friendly affiliation with a man with a pointed beard—a paternal teacher figure."[101]

Although Erikson does not specifically mention the third psychopathology of the first stage of the life cycle—a paralyzing *depression* in which hope is abandoned altogether—his interpretation of the second part of the dream and its associations suggests that this was precisely what the dream associations, with their caution never to neglect an opportunity, were a protection against. Thus, the dream consists of two movements: one back and the other forward. Because it consists of two movements, this "is not an 'oral' dream in a regressed dependent, hopeless, or foolishly hopeful sense," for, after all, it "successfully graduates from orality to turn resolutely away from the mother and to transfer all trust to more autonomous situations."[102] The dreamer's ego, then, is not regressed, "a term often thoughtlessly used when speaking of a dream's return to infantile wishes and frustrations." On the contrary, "the dreamer returns to his earliest dealings with (and subsequent reiterations of) one of life's major themes," and "he thinks himself forward again, through a number of stages, convincing himself that each mournful loss and each frightening graduation brings with it an increased autonomy and an enhanced ability to find in adult actuality the resources of competence and tradition."[103]

In effect, the first part of the dream centers on the psychodynamics of the first stage of life while the second part takes a decisive step toward the psychodynamics of the second stage (the psychosocial stage of *autonomy vs. shame and doubt,* with its corresponding ego strength of *will,* and the corresponding element of social order of *law and order*). In psychodynamic terms, this movement forward was effected through the sublimation of the oral desire of the first stage—as represented by the maternal figure who tells the dreamer that he must wait until *she* is ready—and its displacement onto the Mother of Wisdom, the one who provides the means to make something of oneself, to *change one's fate.* This Mother of Wisdom is made available through the agency of "the stranger" who at first claims the overcoat (a symbol of investiture?) as his own, but then relents, and becomes friendly toward the dreamer.

101. Ibid.

102. Ibid.

103. Ibid., 184–85. It is noteworthy that *competence* is the human strength of the fourth stage of the life cycle.

THE MOTHER OF WISDOM

Erikson's reflections on Freud's dream of the three Fates suggest that, if the dream is genuinely hopeful, this is because it displaces the dreamer's desires from his immediate needfulness onto the Mother of Wisdom herself. She is the Mother who gives life in the face of death, and she is the basis for the belief that one *can* change one's fate. Thus, the dream points beyond itself—through the dreamer's associations—to a *fourth* woman, the Mother of Wisdom, who, unlike the other women, and especially unlike the woman who represents the dreamer's own mother, legitimates the desire to be otherwise than one was originally fated to be.

In the earliest period of life, mothers, "the comprehensible world," are necessarily the very personification of fate. They possess the power to give and withhold life. Only the Mother of Wisdom is able to legitimate the belief that one's life can be other than it was fated to be. Only she is able to give warrant for this belief and to infuse it with conviction. The fathers play the important role of "taking the intelligent boy into their community of learning."[104] But it is the Mother of Wisdom who personifies the ability to change one's personal fate, to lift the curse of his origins so that he may become more than he was fated to be, and believe in himself despite his unpromising origins. Thus, she invites him to trust in himself, in his own ability to create his own greatness. This, however, entails the sublimation of desire for the mother and all that she represents through incorporation of the maternal so that the agency for changing one's fate is within the dreamer's own, autonomous control. This very incorporation is what the Mother of Wisdom represents and signifies.

But who *is* this Mother of Wisdom? If the Mother of Wisdom is the one who is incorporated, so that the maternal is no longer experienced in her original form of an externalized fate, I would suggest that she is the dream itself. Erikson's 1954 article, "The Dream Specimen of Psychoanalysis," based on two lectures in the Seminar on Dream Interpretation of the San Francisco Psychoanalytic Institute, supports this suggestion.[105] It begins with an extensive discussion of Freud's "Irma Dream."[106] This dream occurred on July 23–24, 1895, and was the dream that he credited with revealing to him the fact that "a dream is the fulfillment of a wish."[107] As proof of the significance Freud attached to this dream, James Strachey, the editor of

---

104. Ibid., 182.

105. Erikson, *A Way of Looking at Things*, 237–79.

106. Freud, *The Interpretation of Dreams*, 138–54.

107. Ibid., 154.

Freud's *The Interpretation of Dreams*, added a footnote reference to a letter Freud wrote to Wilhelm Fliess on June 12, 1900, several months after the publication of *The Interpretation of Dreams*, in which Freud described a later visit to the house where he had the dream five years earlier, then asked: "Do you suppose that some day a marble tablet will be placed on the house, inscribed with these words?—'In This House, on July 24th, 1895, the Secret of Dreams was Revealed to Dr. Sigm. Freud.'—At the moment there seems little prospect of it."[108]

In light of the foregoing discussion of the dream of the three Fates, it is worth noting that Freud compares Irma in the dream with two other women "who would be recalcitrant to treatment."[109] In the section of his dream-specimen article headed "Transference in the Irma Dream," Erikson suggests that a dream from a doctor about a patient is very likely to contain "references to counter-transference, i.e., the therapist's unconscious difficulties arising out of the fact that the patient may occupy a strategic position on the chessboard of his fate."[110] In fact,

> Freud tells us something of how Irma came to usurp such a role, and the intimate *du* in the dream betrays the fact that the patient was close to (or associated with somebody close to) the doctor's family either by blood relationship or intimate friendship. Whatever her personal identity, Irma obviously had become some kind of key figure in the dreamer's professional life. The doctor was in the process of learning the fact that this made her, by definition, a poor therapeutic risk for him.[111]

Erikson notes, however, that there was "another kind of 'counter transference'" in the Irma dream. This concerns the fact that "the dreamer's activities (and those of his colleagues) are all professional and directed toward a woman," but "they are a researcher's approaches: the dreamer takes aside, throws light on the matter, looks, localizes, thinks, finds."[112] This being the case, Erikson asks, "May it not be that it was the Mystery of the Dream which was itself the anxious prize of his persistence?"[113] After all, "Freud's dreams during those years of intensive dream study carry the special weight of having to reveal something while being dreamed."[114]

108. Ibid.
109. Ibid., 143.
110. Erikson, *A Way of Looking at Things*, 269.
111. Ibid.
112. Ibid.
113. Ibid., 269–70.
114. Ibid., 270.

Erikson goes on to observe that "in our unconscious and mythological imagery, tasks and ideals are women, often big and forbidding ones, to judge by the statues we erect for Wisdom, Industry, Truth, Justice, and other great ladies." This being so, a

> hint that the Dream as a mystery had become to our dreamer one of those forbidding maternal figures which smile only on the most favored among young heroes (and yield, of course, only to sublimated, to 'clean' approach) can, maybe, be spotted in a footnote where Freud writes, "If I were to continue the comparison of the three women I should go far afield. Every dream has at least one point at which it is unfathomable; a *central point*, as it were, connecting it with the unknown."[115]

Erikson points out that in the original German text the English translation's "central point" is a *Nabel;* thus, in English, "navel." Actually, though, the authorized English translation of this footnote *does* translate *Nabel* as "navel." It reads: "There is at least one point in every dream at which it is unplumbable—a navel, as it were, that is its point of contact with the unknown." Moreover, the editor, James Strachey, refers the reader to a much later passage in *The Interpretation of Dreams* where Freud writes: "There is often a passage in even the most thoroughly interpreted dream which has to be left obscure; this is because we become aware during the work of interpretation that at that point there is a tangle of dream-thoughts which cannot be unraveled and which moreover adds nothing to our knowledge of the content of the dream. *This is the dream's navel, the spot where it reaches down into the unknown.*"[116]

In any event, for Erikson, Freud's rather unusual use of the word *navel* "in such intimate proximity to allusions concerning the resistance of Victorian ladies (including the dreamer's wife, now pregnant) to being undressed and examined, suggests an element of transference to the Dream Problem as such."[117] That is, it invites us to view the Dream itself as

> just another haughty woman, wrapped in too many mystifying covers and "putting on airs" like a Victorian lady. Freud's letter to [Wilhelm] Fliess spoke of an "unveiling" of the mystery of the dream, which was accomplished when he subjected the Irma Dream to an "exhaustive analysis." In the last analysis, then, the

---

115. Ibid. (italics added)

116. Freud, *The Interpretation of Dreams,* 143.

117. Ibid., 270.

dream itself may be a mother image; she is the one, as the Bible would say, to be "known."[118]

The quotation marks around "known" testify that a sublimation of desire has occurred, and to the truth of Erikson's statement that the Dream Mother will "yield" only to "a clean approach" (i.e., a psycho*analytic* one). Continuing his allusions to the Bible, Erikson suggests that "the first dream analyst [Freud] stands in a unique relationship to the Dream as a 'Promised Land.'"[119]

Thus, the first act of the dream of the three Fates begins with the frustration of the dreamer's desires for food and sex, while the second act involves the dreamer's sublimation of these desires and their displacement in the form of a hunger and lust for knowledge. While this displacement places the dreamer in the company of men, the object of his hunger and lust after knowledge is the dream herself. Because his original desires take this sublimated form, his desire is not frustrated but fulfilled. The dream—as the Mother of Wisdom—"smiles" on the dreamer and "yields" her mysteries to him. To enter the "Promised Land," the dreamer did not go far but deep, entering the place where the conscious mind yields its life to the unconscious.

MOURNING, MELANCHOLIA, AND WISDOM

In chapter 5 we saw that the game that Jean played, which consisted of a single act, reflected a melancholic condition relating to her mother; but the game that Ernest played, which consisted of two acts, prepared him for the event of his mother's death, thus turning a potentially melancholy-producing situation into a situation of ego mastery (an expression, that is, of the resourceful self). The same may be said of Freud's dream of the three Fates. As Erikson points out, the dreamer "returns to his earliest dealings with (and subsequent reiterations of) one of life's major themes," and "he thinks himself forward again, through a number of stages, convincing himself that each mournful loss and each frightening graduation brings with it an increased autonomy and an enhanced ability to find in adult actuality the resources of competence and tradition."[120]

Thus, the first part of the dream reminds the dreamer of the time, in his sixth year, when his mother associated herself with death. But in the second part of the dream, he "hears" a different maternal voice, one that

118. Ibid.
119. Ibid., 271.
120. Erikson, *Insight and Responsibility,* 184–85.

"warns him never to neglect an opportunity, but always to take what one can even if it involves doing a small wrong."[121] Thus, the second part of the dream "emphasizes the turn from dependence to self-help" and the very real possibility that he can, in fact, *change* his fate. The "small wrong" in this case is perhaps the dreamer's demand that the Dream Mother reveal herself to him, a demand that may have residual vestiges of his original desires. As the biblical word *know* recognizes, the relationship between sexual desire and the desire for knowledge is an ambiguous one.

Because the one-act dream is associated with the dreamer's melancholic condition, we might say that the Dream Mother herself presents "a split image." As I pointed out in chapter 1, Erikson notes in "Human Strength and the Cycle of Generations" that as the child moves from the first to the second stage of life, the self-image of the child will prove to have been split and to remain so throughout life even as the ideal image of the loving mother has also been split, so that "the ambivalently loved image of the controlling parent" corresponds "to an ambivalently loved self, or selves."[122] Like the mother herself, the Dream Mother may, on some occasions, give the dreamer a "one-act" dream, and thereby cause him to feel injured and resentful (melancholic). On other occasions, she may give the dreamer a "two-act" dream, causing him to feel grateful and empowered. In this regard, Erikson's suggestion that the splitting of the maternal image and that of the self occur in unison brings us to a final consideration: the issue of the identity of the stranger in Freud's dream of the three Fates.

WHO IS THE STRANGER?

As we have seen, Freud believes that there is often a passage "in even the most thoroughly interpreted dream which has to be left obscure." He calls it "the dream's navel, the spot where it reaches down into the unknown."[123] I would suggest that the passage of Freud's dream of the three Fates that best qualifies as "the spot where it reaches down into the unknown" is the appearance of the stranger. After all, the stranger represents the unknown.

In his analysis of the dream, Freud indicates that the stranger "with the long face and pointed beard . . . bore the features of a shop-keeper at Spalato from whom my wife had purchased a quantity of *Turkish* stuffs."[124] Thus, unlike the first part of the dream, where nothing came of the encounter

---

121. Ibid., 184.

122. Ibid., 169–70.

123. Freud, *The Interpretation of Dreams*, 564.

124. Ibid., 240 (italics original).

between a man (Freud himself) and a woman (the inn-hostess), and unlike the occasion when Freud, overly cautious, did not make a purchase that would have been desirable, here a transaction between a man and a woman occurred while Freud, the woman's husband, looked on. I suggest, therefore, that the stranger represents the very shift from dependence to self-help that Erikson ascribes to the second part of the dream.

We may recall in this regard Erikson's comments on the ego strength of the second life-cycle stage (autonomy vs. shame and doubt), namely, *will;* and specifically Erikson's observation that to will "does not mean to be willful, but rather to gain gradually the power of increased judgment and decision in the application of desire."[125] He adds that although no ego can remain intact without *hope* and *will,* the formation of the will demands a heavy price; for, from here on, "the able and the impotent, the loving and the angry, the unified and the self-contradictory selves will be part of one's equipment."[126] Perhaps, then, the stranger in the guise of the shop-keeper at Spalato points to another stranger, to the dreamer's encounter with the "stranger" in himself. The dream's second act is restorative because the dreamer, heretofore "impotent," meets his "able" self. After some altercations between them, they find that they can be friendly to one another. Thus, the dreamer, who, in the first act, experienced the frustration of his desires, impotently leaving the kitchen feeling insulted, now encounters his able self, who calms him and counsels a hopefulness not based on the fulfillment of his immediate needs but on the exercise of will, which means gaining "gradually the power of increased judgment and decision in the application of desire."[127]

Because the encounter with the stranger occurs immediately after the dreamer's mistrustful flight from the kitchen, this encounter warns against the dangers of too much *mistrust*, which causes one to neglect the opportunities that are set before one, reflected in the dreamer's earlier failure to make the purchase at Cattaro. The "stranger" side of himself, the one he professes not to know very well, is the self who will *trust* enough—have *hope* in the future—so that he does not neglect the opportunities placed before him. As Erikson says of *will,*

> it survives, as hope does, the evidences of its limited potency ...
> Often defeated, one nevertheless learns to accept the existential
> paradox of making decisions which he knows "deep down" will

125. Erikson, *Insight and Responsibility,* 118.
126. Ibid., 120.
127. Ibid., 118.

be predetermined by events, because making decisions is part of the evaluative quality inherent in being alive.[128]

One cannot nullify fate, but one can incorporate her, in her guise as the Mother of Wisdom, and work in partnership with her. As Erikson describes the maturing hope of the child, "he learns to discern what is imaginable and to train his expectations on what promises to prove possible. All in all, then, maturing hope not only matures itself in the face of changed facts—it proves itself able to change facts, even as faith is said to move mountains."[129]

We may wonder why Freud did not "recognize" that the stranger in the dream was, in effect, his other self, and in so doing, discover "the dream's navel, the spot where it reaches down into the unknown."[130] Conceivably, the matter of the overcoat with its Turkish design was the Dream Mother's way—and symbolic—of the concealment of her deeper mysteries. Or perhaps Freud was overly influenced by the manifest content of the dream, with the physical similarity between the stranger in the dream and the shopkeeper in Spalato, and did not realize that the dream held the deeper truth that the conflict and its friendly resolution was an internal one.

It occurred to me, as I am sure it has occurred to readers, that Freud's description of the stranger with a long face and a short pointed beard seems to bear a striking resemblance to Freud, popularly referred to as "the bearded doctor." But a careful scrutiny of the photographs in Peter Gay's biography of Freud shows that Freud's face, unlike that of his father, was not especially long; and that his beard, in contrast to that of his youngest sibling, Alexander, was not pointed.[131] This pictorial evidence may suggest that there were unconscious familial associations—paternal and fraternal— with the stranger, but this would not be evidence against the view I have presented here, as these associations would point the dreamer to an identity for the stranger closer to home than that of the shop-keeper in Spalato.

JACOB AND THE STRANGER

The psychodynamics of Freud's encounter with the stranger—an initial conflict evolving into a friendly exchange—recalls another story that could well have been a dream, as it happened in the night, a story with which Freud would have been very familiar. This is the biblical story of Jacob at Jabbok

128. Ibid., 119.
129. Ibid., 117.
130. Freud, *The Interpretation of Dreams*, 564.
131. Gay, *Freud: A Life for Our Times*, 234–35.

where he wrestled with a stranger who would not reveal his name (Gen 32:22–32). (Although Jacob was Freud's father's name, this fact is only incidental to my proposal that the biblical story is relevant to Freud's encounter with the stranger.)

Jacob concluded that he had wrestled with God that night. This conclusion would not, however, rule out the possibility, even likelihood, that he had wrestled with his other self. In fact, it would support this interpretation. After all, the wrestling occurred the night before he was to meet his twin brother Esau, with whom he had "struggled" in their mother's womb, causing her to wonder why she even lived (Gen 25:22). He would be meeting his twin brother for the first time since he, with his mother's connivance, had tricked his brother out of his paternal inheritance (an investiture theme). This episode, then, was comparable to a dream composed of two acts: the wrestling itself and the stranger's refusal to reveal his identity. Jacob's conclusion that he had wrestled with God was also comparable to a dream association that brought him a great sense of peace—"I have seen God face to face, and yet my life has been preserved" (Gen 32:30, NRSV)—but the encounter, nonetheless, left him wounded (Gen 32:31–32).

In my view, the deeper meaning of the encounter with the stranger— its navel, as it were—was that Jacob's struggle was an internal one, and that he had wrestled with the self who had been capable of treachery against his own brother. If, then, it was his natural mother who had put him up to this treachery, it was the Dream Mother who enabled his able and honorable self to defeat (though not without injury) his treacherous and impotent self, and thus to prepare him for the morning, when he would meet his brother "face to face." As he went, limping, to the encounter with his brother, Esau, the wisdom of the Dream Mother was confirmed as Esau "ran to meet him, and embraced him, and fell on his neck and kissed him, and they wept" (Gen 33:4, NRSV). Jacob's internal healing was accompanied by a fraternal reconciliation. Thus, as Erikson's lecture title suggests, "psychological reality and historical actuality" converged on the field where the two brothers met and embraced each other.

CONCLUSION

We have considered two dreams in this chapter: the dream of a young theological student who had begun to manifest "border-line psychotic features in an inhibited obsessive-compulsive character," and the dream of the founder of psychoanalysis who had gone to bed hungry after a full day's travel. We concluded that in the case of the former, the patient, aided by the dream, journeyed back into his past—but he did not journey alone, for he was accompanied by his therapist, a *new person* in his life, and this fact made a world of difference, as it enabled him to see *himself* as a new person in the stage of life that was even then unfolding. To all appearances, the patient was a melancholy person, one who manifested the symptoms of melancholia described by Freud in "Mourning and Melancholia." But there was also a resourceful self living in the shadows of his melancholy existence, and it was this self that brought to his session with Erikson a dream remarkable for what it did *not* depict: a readily identifiable face.

It was much the same with Freud's dream of the three Fates, as it included a stranger with whom Freud has a brief altercation over who is the rightful owner of the coat that Freud is putting on. But then, when Freud provides evidence that the coat is his, the two men become friendly. Thus, here, too, Freud has an encounter with a *new person*, but, as we have seen, this new person is actually himself. In this sense, both claimants to be the owners of the coat are right, and the coat symbolizes the reconciliation of Freud's conflicting selves. And perhaps it is not too much for us to claim that the "lost object" against whom the melancholy self has much to complain about has revealed herself here as the Mother of Wisdom, for how else could she reveal herself—and prove that she has not abandoned him—except through the agency of a dream?

7

The Promise of Hope

promise:

(1) to give a basis for expectation;

(2) to declare emphatically, assure.

In chapter 3, we saw that Erikson considered *hope* to be the first human strength or virtue, and that all the other strengths or virtues are dependent on its development. If the infant does not develop some sense or degree of hope but instead forms an all-encompassing sense of hopelessness, the development of will, purpose, competence, fidelity, love, care, and wisdom is jeopardized as well. Of course, as Erikson notes, an "exclusive condition of hopefulness" would reflect and express a "maladaptive optimism," but without at least some modicum of hope, a viable human existence is impossible to imagine. As Erikson points out in his lecture on human strength and the cycle of generations:

> Hope is both the earliest and the most indispensable virtue inherent in the state of being alive. Others have called this deepest quality *confidence,* and I have referred to *trust* as the earliest positive psychosocial attitude, but if life is to be sustained hope must remain, even where confidence is wounded, trust impaired. Clinicians know that an adult who has lost all hope, regresses into as lifeless a state as a living organism can sustain. But there is something in the anatomy even of mature hope which suggests that it is the most childlike of all ego-qualities,

157

and the most dependent for its verification on the charity of fate; thus religious sentiment induces adults to restore their hopefulness in periodic petitionary prayer, assuming a measure of childlikeness toward unseen, omnipotent powers.[1]

It seems appropriate, therefore, that we return to the issue of hope and identify hopefulness as one of the primary constituents of the resourceful self.

As I have been concerned in this book with the melancholy self, and have been suggesting that the melancholy and resourceful selves have a binary relationship to one another, it is noteworthy that even as I have contended that the mother is central to the development of the melancholy self, Erikson contends that the mother is central to the development of the resourceful self. He points out that although religious sentiment encourages adults to restore their hopefulness through prayer to unseen, omnipotent powers, nothing in human life

> is secured in its origin unless it is verified in the intimate meeting of partners in favorable social settings. The infant's smile inspires hope in the adult and, in making him smile, makes him wish to give hope; but this is, of course, only one physiognomic detail which indicates that the infant by his trustful search for experience and assurance, awakens in the giver a strength which he, in turn, is ready and needful to have awakened and to have consolidated by the experience of mutuality.[2]

He goes on to note that

> Hope relies for its beginnings on the new being's first encounter with *trustworthy maternal persons*, who respond to his need for *intake* and *contact* with warm and calming envelopment and provide food both pleasurable to ingest and easy to digest, and who prevent experience of the kind which may regularly bring too little too late. This is far from being a merely instinctive, or a merely instinctual matter. Biological motherhood needs at least three links with social experience: the mother's past experience of being mothered; a conception of motherhood shared with trustworthy contemporary surroundings; and an all-enveloping world-image tying past, present, and future into a convincing pattern of providence. Only thus can mothers provide.[3]

1. Erikson, *Insight and Responsibility,* 115–16.
2. Ibid., 116.
3. Ibid.

Thus, Erikson makes clear that although hope is born in the infant-mother relationship, it is not an isolated affair. The conditions for hope are generational, societal, and ideological, with religion playing the central ideological role because it provides images and symbols of providence, of the existence of transcendent sources of provision. In effect, the mother is the human manifestation of the conditions for hope and of divine providence.

However, if Erikson recognized the decisive role that religion plays in the ideological undergirding of human hope, his personal identification with art played an especially influential role in his understanding of hope, including the role that religion plays in sustaining hope. As he noted in the preface to *Childhood and Society*: "I came to psychology from art, which may explain, if not justify, the fact that at times the reader will find me painting contexts and backgrounds where he would rather have me point to facts and concepts. I have had to make a virtue out of constitutional necessity by basing what I have to say on representative description rather than on theoretical argument."[4] Erikson followed this confession or explanation with the observation that he "first came face to face with children in a small American school in Vienna," and that he began his "clinical career as what is commonly called a child analyst, which does not mean that I psychoanalyzed while still a child but that I first psychoanalyzed children."[5]

One could perhaps argue that he *did* engage in amateur psychoanalysis as a child, and that his melancholic condition was the stimulus behind this engagement. But as this comment was meant to be a humorous observation on the ambiguities of linguistic conventions, it underscores the very fact that Erikson was more comfortable with visual than verbal media. In fact, he returns to the subject in the concluding chapter of *Childhood and Society* and notes:

> Feeling under his right thumb the thin sheaf of pages left of this book, the reader may wonder what kind of short conclusion could do justice to the matters of immediate concern illustrated in the last [i.e., preceding] chapter. Here I must concede that whatever message has not been conveyed by my description and discourse has but a slim chance of being furthered by a formal conclusion. I have nothing to offer except a way of looking at things.[6]

4. Erikson, *Childhood and Society,* orig. ed., 13.

5. Ibid.

6. Erikson, *Childhood and Society,* rev. ed., 403. Erikson derived the phrase "a way of looking at things" from Freud's *New Introductory Lectures on Psychoanalysis.* In lecture 31 titled "The Dissection of the Physical Personality," Freud indicated that he was going to discuss conscience as a special agency in the ego and name it the "super-ego," then

A Way of Looking at Things became the title of the collection of his articles, war memoranda, lectures, memorials, and other writings published in 1987.[7]

In this chapter, I will be drawing especially on Erikson's book *Toys and Reasons*.[8] Based on his 1972 Godkin Lectures at Harvard University, it was published in 1977. The title recalls his chapter in *Childhood and Society* on children's play, thus it signaled Erikson's return, a quarter of a century later, to a topic with which he was concerned in *Childhood and Society*. If we think of the fact that he named the eighth and concluding stage of the life cycle *Integrity vs. Despair*, then these two books—*Childhood and Society* and *Toys and Reasons*—represent the essential integrity of his work, for in the earlier book he portrayed integrity as a state of mind that reflects "the ego's accrued assurance of its proclivity for order and meaning."[9] Circling back around to the topics and themes that captured his attention in the beginning of his career is compelling evidence—and assurance—of his proclivity for order and meaning. It is also an indication that even as he began his clinical career as a child analyst, so he ended his career as a child analyst. As this chapter unfolds, it will also become clear that even as he originally came to psychoanalysis from art, so he has become accustomed to coming to art from psychoanalysis.

Toys and Reasons consists of three parts: "Play and Vision," "Life Cycle and Ritualization," and "Shared Visions." In this chapter I will be focusing on the section in part 1 titled "Seeing Is Hoping," the section in part 2 titled "Infancy and the Numinous," and the section of part 3 titled "Visions on the Wall." When viewed together, they enable us to see Erikson's deep professional and personal interest in the resource of *hope*.

---

added: "I am now prepared to hear you ask me scornfully whether our ego-psychology comes down to nothing more than taking commonly used abstractions literally and in a crude sense, and transforming them from concepts into things—by which not much would be gained. To this I would reply that in ego-psychology it will be difficult to escape what is universally known; it will rather be a question of *new ways of looking at things* and new ways of arranging them than of new discoveries" (Freud, *New Introductory Lectures on Psychoanalysis*, 75; italics added).

7. Erikson, *A Way of Looking at Things*.

8. Erikson, *Toys and Reasons*. As I noted in chapter 5, footnote 53, the phrase "toys and reasons" is derived from these lines in a poem by William Blake: "The Child's Toys and the Old Man's Reason / Are the Fruits of the Two Seasons."

9. Erikson, *Childhood and Society*, orig. ed., 232.

SEEING IS HOPING

In the section of part 1 titled "Seeing Is Hoping," Erikson notes that child-hood play depends "on a strong visual element" and is also dominated "by an almost visionary fascination with the temporal fate of figures meaning-fully arranged in a circumscribed 'world.'"[10] This being the case, play com-bines "the two meanings of vision, namely, the capacity to see what is before us, here and now, and the power to foresee what, if one can only believe it, might yet prove to be true in the future."[11]

This observation about the role of both seeing and foreseeing in play leads him to comment on Rene Spitz and his colleagues' work on the role of vision in the establishment of a rudimentary sense of reality in the in-fant.[12] He cites their observation that it is the gift of vision that first serves to integrate the messages received from the other senses (hearing, smelling, tasting and feeling); and that vision initially involves contact perception, but as time goes on, the infant develops distance perception, and by means of distance perception begins to understand continuity in time and coherence in space. By the third month, the infant's visual discrimination has matured sufficiently to enable him or her to remember a total gestalt.[13]

Erikson infers from Spitz's studies that the visual perceptions, now in-tegrated and retained, are associated with the pleasures of oral and sensory satisfactions: of being fed and held, touched, cleaned, and tucked into bed—and that through all of these administrations

> the motherly person lets her face "shine upon" the newborn's searching eyes; she thus lets herself be verified as the first com-prehensible image. And, indeed, once infants can nurse with open eyes, they are apt to stare at the mother's face even as they suck on her breast. Thus vision becomes the leading perceptual as well as emotional modality for the organization of a sensory and sensual space as marked by the infant's interplay with the *primal person.*[14]

In the infant's interplay with the primal person, vision confirms "simultane-ity in time as well as continuity in space, permanence of objects as well as coherence of the perceived field, the foreground figure and the fusion of the background, the motion of some items against the stationary position of

10. Erikson, *Toys and Reasons,* 46.
11. Ibid.
12. Piers, ed., *Play and Development,* 43–63.
13. Ibid., 54.
14. Erikson, *Toys and Reasons,* 47 (italics original).

others—and all of this held together by the desired presence of the provid-ing person."[15]

In Erikson's view, this vision of the motherly person is "the model of what later is felt to be the 'really real' enveloping the mere factual."[16] In time, of course, hearing will prove both useful and essential because it enables one to hear what is not in the visual field, and thus "reinforces the hope that the voice heard will come 'around the corner' and be confirmed as the familiar face," and this "double perception of the primary parent as both seen and heard is further verified as that person ever again vocally 'recognizes' the in-fant by some appellation which becomes a name even as the naming person is pleased to be recognized as the recognizer."[17] Through this joint domain of cognitive and affective growth, the power of vision in the two meanings mentioned earlier emerges: "that of comprehending what can be verified as factual with the maturing senses, but also that of foreseeing as attainable what is recognized as reliable enough to be repeated—ever again."[18]

Erikson concludes that the power of vision in these two meanings—of seeing and of foreseeing—"remain basic for man's spiritual needs." It is basic

> not only for a sense of reality endowing with meaning what we are learning to see and "grasp," but also for that visionary propensity by which man in all subsequent stages restores a measure of feeling reasonably at home in a predictable world, and that is: to be central in his sphere of living rather than pe-ripheral and ignored; active and effective rather than inactivated and helpless; selectively aware rather than overwhelmed by or deprived of sensations; and, above all, chosen and confirmed rather than bypassed and abandoned.[19]

Noting that he has postulated "that the rudiments of hope—the first psycho-social strength essential for ego development—arise out of a fundamental struggle between basic trust and basic mistrust in infancy," Erikson suggests that these two meanings of the power of vision—of seeing what is right there before one's eyes and immediately verifiable, and of foreseeing what or rather who is coming around the corner—are central to the establishment of an enduring sense of hopefulness.

What challenges or even undermines this sense of hopefulness is "the dread of the maternal face turned away, the fear of and the rage over an

15. Ibid.
16. Ibid.
17. Ibid.
18. Ibid., 47–48.
19. Ibid., 49.

image of the primal Other that becomes elusive or distorted—and thus the threatening loss of a reassuring reality."[20] Erikson notes in this connection Spitz's postulation of a specific "eight-month anxiety" in which an infant reacts to strangers with apprehensive frowns or a tearful outburst to which we laugh, say "Silly Baby," and reassure. Yet, in Erikson's view,

> that silly fear of the unfamiliar is only the first experience of alienation, a mixture of anxiety and rage which also persists into all later phases of life and can pervade a widening range of relations: the anxiety, just when and because one grows up to be a person, of being abandoned by what has become familiar and of being left a victim to crushing forces; the terror of the evil eye and the dread of being alone in a universe without a supreme counter-player, without charity.[21]

In other words, the baby's anxiety when seeing a stranger is the forerunner of the more devastating experience of witnessing the mother's familiar face taking on a threatening guise, an experience that generates a mixture of anxiety and rage that can become more and more pervasive as one grows up to become a person.

In short, the infant's first experience of a total gestalt—the face of the mother and all that it represents—is absolutely crucial to the formation of the two meanings of vision, namely, "the capacity to see what is before us, here and now, and the power to foresee what, if one can only believe it, might yet be true in the future."[22] The development and maintenance of a disposition toward hopefulness depends on these two meanings of vision, and this is why Erikson titles this section of the book "Seeing Is Hoping," which is, of course, a play on the saying that "seeing is believing." If the saying "seeing is believing" refers to the first of these two meanings of vision (of seeing what is directly before us), then the saying "seeing is hoping" refers to the second of these two meanings (of foreseeing what may be true in the future). Although the capacity to believe is also involved in the act of foreseeing, Erikson emphasizes here the development and maintenance of a hopeful disposition, and does so in part because the importance of a

20. Ibid., 50.

21. Ibid. Erikson's reference to a "widening range of relations" recalls what he had earlier identified in *Identity and the Life Cycle* as the "widening radius of significant relations" with which one interacts as one moves through the eight stages of life, beginning with the maternal person and concluding with the sense of being a member of the human species (humankind) while retaining the sense of connection with a subspecies ("my kind"). Erikson, *Identity and the Life Cycle*, rev. ed. 178.

22. Erikson, *Toys and Reasons*, 46.

hopeful disposition is so easily overlooked. Without it, one is unlikely to envision a promising future.

Finally, in light of the fact that Erikson emphasizes the infant's experience of seeing the face of the mother, and that despite his decision to abandon a career in art, he continued to make charcoal portraits of children and adults throughout his life (*A Way of Looking at Things* includes eleven of his portraits), it is noteworthy that Richard Brilliant, an art historian, believes that we are drawn to the face of the subject in a portrait because the first image we experienced as infants was that of our mother's face. Brilliant writes:

> The dynamic nature of portraits and the "occasionality" that anchors their imagery in life seem ultimately to depend on the primary experience of the infant in arms. That child, gazing up at its mother, imprints her vitally important image so firmly on its mind that soon enough she can be recognized almost instantaneously and without conscious thought; spontaneous face recognition remains an important instrument of survival, separating friend from foe, that persists into adult life.[23]

A little later "a name, 'Mama' or some other, will be attached to the now familiar face and body," and this name will be "soon followed by a more conscious acknowledgment of her role vis-à-vis the infant as 'mother' or 'provider,' and finally by an understanding of her character, being loving and warmly protective towards the infant (in an ideal world, of course!)." Then, eventually, "the infant will acquire a sense of its own independent existence, of itself as a sentient being, responding to others, and possessing, as well, its own given name."[24]

Brilliant goes on to identify "the essential constituents of a person's identity," suggesting that these include "a recognized or recognizable appearance; a given name that refers to no one else; a social interactive function that can be defined; in context, a pertinent characterization; and a consciousness of the distinction between one's own person and another's, and of the possible relationship between them."[25] Of these constituents of a person's identity, only "physical appearance is naturally visible, and even that is unstable." The others are conceptual and need to be expressed symbolically. This means that portrait artists are confronted with a set of complex demands which pose real challenges for their "artistic ingenuity and empathetic insight."[26]

23. Brilliant, *Portraiture*, 9.
24. Ibid.
25. Ibid.
26. Ibid.

If the impetus for portraiture begins with the infant's perception of the face of the mother, and with the desire to put a name to this familiar face, portraiture is inherently relational. As Brilliant goes on to note:

> Making portraits is a response to the natural human tendency to think about oneself, of oneself in relation to others, and of others in apparent relation to themselves and to others. To put a face on the world catches the essence of ordinary behavior in the social context; to do the same in a work of art catches the essence of the human relationship and consolidates it in the portrait through the creation of a visible identity sign by which someone can be known, possibly forever.[27]

These quotations from Brilliant's book on portraiture could well have been written by Erikson himself, as they emphasize the relationship between image and identity and the infant's desire to "put a face on the world." They also draw our attention to the portraits included in Erikson's *A Way of Looking at Things*. As the subtitle says that this is a collection of "selected papers," it would be easy to overlook the portraits, or even to assume that they do not belong were it not for fact that one section of the text is headed "Portrait Sketches."[28] This section is largely composed of verbal testimonials to various friends, but it also contains several visual portraits, one of which is that of his mother, whom he had sketched when she visited Erikson and his family in California in 1948.

Erikson does not identify her by name. He refers to her in a memorial tribute to Ruth Benedict, the well-known anthropologist, as one of several persons who that year "had evoked in me—a dealer in words—this irresistible urge to document a face by drawing it."[29] If her name had not appeared under her portrait, we may not have known that this "old Jewish woman from Mt. Carmel in the State of Israel," who "impressed us all with the new sense of dignity and identity which her work had given her" was, in fact, his own mother.

One wonders, of course, what he was thinking and feeling as he drew her face. As Brilliant notes, the physical appearance of the subject is unstable, and Erikson comments on the fact that the persons he sketched that year were old persons, and this very fact led Erikson to ask himself why he wanted to sketch these people: "Was it easier to draw old people because of the depth and finality of their facial lines? Or was I getting old, and looking

---

27. Ibid., 14.
28. Erikson, *A Way of Looking at Things*, 709–38.
29. Ibid., 717.

for people who seemed to make aging worthwhile?"[30] He concluded, how-ever, that he had seen "the common good" of these four old people: "some of the beauty and simplicity, some of the faith and serenity, announcing clearly and indestructibly the near fulfillment of a life cycle which has found accord with the moral and esthetic realization of its community."[31] They were, in other words, progenitors of hope for those who are younger and who have much of their lives ahead of them. Their faces revealed to him the foresee-able future, and his own mother was numbered among them.

INFANCY AND THE NUMINOUS

In chapter 3 on the resourceful self I discussed the fact that Erikson ascribed specific ego strengths or virtues to each of the eight stages of the life cycle. In a similar fashion in *Toys and Reasons*, he relates specific forms of ritual-ization to the stages of the life cycle. Noting that the word *ritual* is used in psychopathology in reference to behaviors like hand washing, and in an-thropology to refer to communal ceremonies, Erikson wants to make a case for studying the nonneurotic and nonceremonial rituals of everyday life.[32] He links these everyday forms of ritual behavior to the eight stages of the life cycle, identifies the form of psychosocial encounter each exemplifies, the disorienting experience that ritualized behavior counters or inhibits, and the excess—or ritualism—to which each is prone. His earlier reflections on the infant's recognition of the motherly person's face in the section titled "Seeing Is Hoping" are taken up and expanded in his discussion here of the first stage of the life cycle. In Erikson's ritualization schema, the first psycho-social stage—basic trust vs. basic mistrust—concerns the ritual element of the *numinous*: the ritual encounter involves the mutual recognition between infant and mother, the disorientation that the infant experiences is the sense of separation and abandonment, and the ritual excess is that of idolism.

Erikson titles his discussion in *Toys and Reasons* of the ritual element of the numinous "Infancy and the Numinous: The Light, the Face, and the Name."[33] This presentation is a revised and expanded version of the "In-fancy and the Numinous" section of his earlier, 1966 article "The Ontogeny of Ritualization in Man."[34] In the earlier article, he focused on the "greet-ing ceremonial" that occurs between the mother and her infant upon the

30. Ibid.

31. Ibid., 722.

32. Erikson, *Toys and Reasons*, 78.

33. Ibid., 85.

34. Erikson, *A Way of Looking at Things*, 575–94.

infant's awakening in the morning. He noted that this ceremonial marks the beginning of the infant's day and is a special form of everyday behavior. It is found throughout the world, has been an aspect of human life for ages, and has analogies with the behaviors of other species. (He specifically mentions birds.) Among humans, it takes the following form:

> The awakening infant conveys to his mother the fact that he is awake and (as if with the signal of an alarm clock) awakens in her a whole repertoire of emotive, verbal, and manipulative behavior. She approaches him with smiling or worried concern, brightly or anxiously rendering a name, and goes into action: looking, feeling, sniffing, she ascertains possible causes of discomfort and initiates services to be rendered by rearranging the infant's condition, by picking him up, etc. If it is observed for several days it becomes clear that this daily event is highly ritualized, in that the mother seems to feel obliged and not a little pleased, to repeat a performance which arouses in the infant predictable responses, encouraging her, in turn, to proceed.[35]

Although it is ritualized, this behavior is difficult to describe: "It is at the same time highly *individual* ('typical for the mother' and also tuned to the particular infant) and yet also *stereotyped* along traditional lines." One feature that is both individualized and stereotypical is the mother calling her infant by name. However the name was chosen and whatever may have been the reasons for the choice, "that meaning now exerts a certain effect on the way in which the name is repeated during the morning procedure." But this is just one of many acts of "caring attention" which "have a very special meaning for the mother and eventually for the child." Daily observations, "confirmed by the special aura of Madonna-and-Child images," suggest that "this mutual assignment of very special meaning is the ontogenetic source of one pervasive element in human ritualization, which is based on a *mutuality of recognition*."[36]

Erikson points out that a human being "is born with the need for such regular and mutual affirmation and certification," and, therefore, "its absence can harm an infant radically, by diminishing or extinguishing his search for impressions which will verify his senses."[37] Once aroused, "this need will reassert itself in every stage of life as a hunger for ever new, ever more formalized and more widely shared ritualizations and rituals which

35. Ibid., 577.
36. Ibid.
37. Ibid.

repeat such face-to-face 'recognition' of the hoped-for."[38] These ritualizations range from "the regular exchange of greetings affirming a strong emotional bond" to "singular encounters of mutual fusion in love or inspiration,
or in a leader's 'charisma.'" Thus, "this first and dimmest affirmation, this
sense of a *hallowed presence*, contributes to man's ritual-making a pervasive
element which we will call the 'Numinous.'"[39]

Erikson indicates that his use of the word "Numinous" for the greeting ceremonial that occurs between mother and infant reflects his judgment that this human ritual is a precursor of various religious observances
in which there is a mutual encounter and affirmation. He also notes that
the "Numinous" itself occurs at the beginning of life, continues through the
intervening stages of life, and reveals itself, once more, at life's conclusion:

> We vaguely recognize the numinous as an indispensable aspect
> of periodical *religious observances*, where the believer, by ap-
> propriate gestures, confesses his dependence and childlike faith,
> and seeks, by appropriate offerings, to secure a sense of being
> lifted up to the very bosom of the supernatural which in the
> visible form of an image may graciously respond, with the faint
> smile of an inclined face. The result is a sense of *separateness
> transcended*, and yet also of *distinctiveness confirmed*.[40]

Thus, at life's beginning, so, at the end, we are lifted into the bosom of the
One whose face inclines toward us, and we glow, as it were, in the "hallowed
presence" of the Other. Eyes meet in a mutuality of recognition, and the
separation that preceded this fulfilled moment is transcended, thus con-
firming the distinctiveness of each of us, whom the Other calls by name.
The condition that all such encounters address is the "sense of separation
by abandonment" which, if not "prevented by the periodical reassurance
of familiarity and mutuality," leaves "a sense of dread, estrangement, or
impoverishment."[41] Therefore, these mutual encounters make that which is
unfamiliar "*familiar* through repetition," even as they continue to sustain
"the *surprise* of recognition."[42]

38. Ibid., 577–78.

39. Ibid., 578. In *The Idea of the Holy*, 7, originally published in 1917, Rudolf Otto
proposed that the *numinous* is the state of mind that prevails in an encounter with the
holy or the sacred. The dictionary indicates that a *numen* in Roman mythology is "an
indwelling, guiding force or spirit" and that the *numinous* is "of or characteristic of a
numen" and "as having a deeply spiritual or mystical effect" (Agnes, *New World College
Dictionary*, 990–91).

40. Erikson, *A Way of Looking at Things*, 578.

41. Ibid., 579.

42. Ibid., 578.

Erikson concludes these reflections on the greeting ceremonial with a brief allusion to hope, the ego strength ascribed to the first stage of life, noting that hope is "grounded and fortified in the first stage of life, and subsequently nourished, as it were, by all those ritualizations and rituals which combat a sense of abandonment and hopelessness and promise instead a mutuality of recognition, face to face, all through life—until 'we shall know even as also we are known.'"[43]

In this portrayal of the greeting ceremonial, Erikson emphasizes the behaviors involved: those of the mother calling the infant by name and of the one gazing into the face of the other. In this sense, the greeting ceremonial is a ritual. However, it is also a spectacle, one which is basked in light. Because the word *numinous* is akin to *luminous*, we intuitively assume that the association is intended. The "hallowed" in "hallowed presence" also evokes the sense of the *holy* (as in "awe") but is also suggestive of the *halo*, the light that surrounds the face of the one who is benevolently inclined and the face of the one who expectantly returns her gaze. Even the "mutual recognition" that occurs between them has a certain luminousness about it, for Erikson says that of all the psychological disturbances we connect with the early stages of life, "the deepest and most devastating are those in which *the light of mutual recognition* and of hope are forfeited in psychotic withdrawal and regression."[44]

This association of light with the greeting ceremonial suggests that the mutual recognition that occurs has its own unique interiority. As Erikson pointed out in his discussion of hope in "Human Strength and the Cycle of Generations," the mother to the infant is "the original verification" that, later on, will come from other and wider segments of reality. This means that all "self-verifications" begin "in that inner light of the mother-child-world, which Madonna images have conveyed as so exclusive and so secure: and, indeed, such light must continue to shine through the chaos of many crises, maturational and accidental."[45] The internal radiance is the core, as it were, of the mutual recognition between mother and infant. Clearly, the greeting ceremonial plays a central role in the formation of a sense of hope.

In the preface of *Toys and Reasons* he notes that one of the readings for the seminar that accompanied the lectures on which the book itself is based was this earlier lecture on the ontogeny of ritualization. The section of *Toys and Reasons* on "Infancy and the Numinous: The Light, the Face, and the Name" consists largely of what he had written earlier on the greeting

43. Ibid., 579. This is a reference to 1 Cor 13:12 (KJV).
44. Ibid. (italics added)
45. Erikson, *Insight and Responsibility,* 117.

ceremonial between mother and infant. However, in this revised version he makes several changes in wording. More significantly, he deletes the allusions to hope with which he had concluded his earlier discussion of infancy and the numinous, and adds a paragraph on the mother's postpartum state and the infant's response to this state. This paragraph had been located in the section of the original article on "pseudo-speciation," his term for the tendency of humans to behave as though they are composed of many subspecies, each of which claims "a distinct sense of identity."[46]

Subtle changes have also been made in this particular paragraph. These changes may seem merely editorial and stylistic, but I believe that they give the mother-infant relationship, even in the greeting ceremonial itself, a more attenuated, less joyful and hopeful tone. In effect, the new version replaces the luminous aura of the original version of the greeting ceremonial with a distinctly melancholy tonality. After identifying the changes, I will explore the implications of this change in tone.

The most obvious change in wording occurs in the very first sentence. In the original, Erikson writes: "Let me begin with the 'greeting ceremonial' marking the beginning of an infant's day."[47] In the *Toys and Reasons* version, the "greeting ceremonial" has been eliminated, and the sentence reads: "Let us begin, then, with the way the maternal person and the infant greet each other in the morning."[48] The deletion of the phrase "greeting ceremonial" may seem rather inconsequential, but the revision replaces the idea that the mother and infant are engaged in a familiar interaction characterized by predictable features with the suggestion of a more informal interchange.

To his earlier statement that the greeting ceremonial is both "highly individual" and "stereotyped along some traditional lines subject to anthropological description,"[49] Erikson adds that "it is more or less freely given and responded to, and more or less coerced by duty."[50] In the paragraph where he mentions that the mother calls her infant by name and includes "other emphases of caring attention which have a very special meaning for the mother and eventually for the child,"[51] he replaces his earlier reference to "the special aura of Madonna-and-Child images" with the mother's reference to herself "with a special designation."[52] Also, the original text stated

46. Erikson, *A Way of Looking at Things*, 580.

47. Ibid., 576.

48. Erikson, *Toys and Reasons*, 85.

49. Erikson, *A Way of Looking at Things*, 577.

50. Erikson, *Toys and Reasons*, 86.

51. Erikson, *A Way of Looking at Things*, 577.

52. Erikson, *Toys and Reasons*, 87.

that the "hunger for ever new, ever more formalized and widely shared ritualizations and rituals which repeat such face-to-face 'recognition' of the hoped-for" range from "the regular exchange of greetings affirming a strong emotional bond to singular encounters of mutual fusion in love or inspiration, or in a leader's charisma."[53] The new version omits "of mutual fusion" and adds that the leader's charisma is "confirmed by (more or less) exquisite statues and paintings, or by mere multiplied banners and televised appearances."[54] Finally, the earlier observation that although "we love our children, we also find them unbearably demanding, even as they will soon find us arbitrary and possessive," has been rewritten to read, "For as we love our children, and children in general, they can arouse hate and murderous disdain, even as at best they will find us arbitrary in rejection and possessive in acceptance, if not potentially dangerous and witchlike."[55]

These changes in the original version of the greeting ceremonial may not seem very significant, but the idea that the behaviors involved in the greeting ceremonial are "more or less" freely given and responded to, and that they are "more or less" coerced by duty has a rather deflating effect, one that qualifies the earlier observation (present in both versions) that the mother approaches her baby "with smiling and worried concern, brightly or anxiously voicing some appellation, and goes into action." Similarly, the removal of the reference to "the special aura of Madonna-and-Child" and suggestion, instead, that the mother refers to herself with "a special self-designation" ("Mommy"?) removes the implication that this mother-infant interaction is analogous to a central theme of Christianity. Also, the elimination of the phrase "mutual fusion" removes some of the sense that mother and baby are one, and the added commentary on "the leader's charisma" seems to suggest or at least imply that this recognition of the leader's charisma is perhaps undeserved or, even if deserved, is subject to trivialization. Although this may appear to be an accurate assessment of many political and religious leaders, the suggestion that the interaction between mother and infant prefigures the encounter with such a charismatic leader seems to degrade not only the original ritualization but also the person—the mother—who is largely responsible for its performance.

Finally, although the earlier version recognized that the relationship between parents and children may have its tensions, the new version presents a much more mistrustful rendition of this relationship: The "unbearably demanding" child now arouses "hate and murderous disdain," and the

53. Erikson, *A Way of Looking at Things*, 577–78.

54. Erikson, *Toys and Reasons*, 88.

55. Ibid.

child's perception of the parent as "arbitrary and possessive" now finds the parent's *rejection* arbitrary, the parent's *acceptance* a disguised form of possessiveness, and the parent herself as "potentially dangerous and witchlike." This is a rather ominous portrayal of the mother-infant relationship, one that may seem out of place in a portrayal of "the greeting ceremonial."

There is also the fact that a paragraph on a mother's postpartum state has been inserted between the paragraph that introduces the greeting ceremonial itself and the paragraph that focuses on the mother's calling the infant by name. The intervening paragraph seems almost to interrupt the greeting ceremonial itself and to introduce a consideration that reinforces the suspicion that the mother's engagement in the ceremony is perhaps more "coerced by duty" than "freely given." In their original location, Erikson's observations about the mother's postpartum state were designed to show that her engagement with her infant reflects how such "pseudo-speciation" is deeply embedded in the ritualizations of a society's everyday life. Thus, he had noted that, like the infant,

> The mother in her postpartum state is also needful in a complex manner, for whatever instinctual gratification she may seek in being a mother, she needs to be a *mother of a special kind* and *in a special way*. This she becomes by no means without an anxious avoidance (sometimes outright phobic, often deeply superstitious) of "other" kinds and ways typical for persons or groups whom she (sometimes unconsciously) dislikes, or despises, hates, or fears as godless or evil, unhygienic or immoral.[56]

On the other hand, Erikson had also noted a positive side to this need to be a mother of a special kind, for in fulfilling this need, the mother "is reaffirmed in her identification with those who mothered her well; while her own motherhood is reaffirmed as benevolent by the increasing responsiveness of the infant." In turn, the infant "develops a benevolent self-image (a certified narcissism, we may say) grounded in the recognition of an all-powerful and mostly benevolent (if sometimes strangely malevolent) 'Other.'"[57]

Erikson's observations about the mother's need to be a mother "of a special kind" are carried over into the new version, but he has added that, besides "an anxious avoidance," she may also experience "some more or less subdued anger over the coerciveness of routine and role."[58] Also, the statement about the reaffirmation she receives in the mother-infant interaction has been expanded to include a reference to the negative examples of moth-

56. Erikson, *A Way of Looking at Things*, 581.
57. Ibid.
58. Erikson, *Toys and Reasons*, 86–87.

ering that she is expected to avoid; and to her perception of these other ways of mothering as "godless or evil, unhygienic or immoral," Erikson adds that she may be "guided by images of womanhood protested by her."[59]

These additions, along with his earlier reference to the "maternal person," may have been prompted by a desire to give his reflections on the greeting ceremonial a more contemporary tone. The idea that the mother protests certain "images of womanhood" is especially relevant in this regard. Even so, his insertion of the *pseudo-speciation* issue into these reflections tends to draw readers' attention away from the desire of the mother to come when her baby awakens in her "a whole repertoire of emotive, verbal, and manipulative behavior."[60] The eager responsiveness of the mother to indications that her infant has awakened has given way to a degree of resentfulness of the fact that she has a duty to perform.

Because the central point of Erikson's earlier interpretation of the greeting ceremonial was that mother and infant activate one another, the new version implies that the infant may be insufficiently attractive to the mother, and therefore less able to evoke the simple, loving, maternal response that counteracts whatever resentment (or sense of superiority over other mothers) she may feel about the cultural role assigned to her. The infant's failure to evoke the mother's own deep sense of motherhood as benevolence incarnate leads, in turn, to the infant's own greater demandingness, if not to fantasies of the mother's dangerous, even witchlike qualities. A seemingly benign and gracious greeting ceremonial, reminiscent of traditional images of the Madonna-and-Child, has become the locus of guerilla warfare in which the infant fights for life and recognition.

Nevertheless, Erikson does make reference to the *numinous* in these reflections. These references occur toward the end of this section in his discussion of how the infant's daily awakening introduces a need for "ritualized affirmation" that "becomes indispensable as a periodical experience and must in changing times find new and meaningful forms."[61] He points out that the need for such affirmation is confirmed by what happens to an infant when such affirmation is not forthcoming, when "the light of mutual recognition and of hope is early forfeited in autistic and psychotic withdrawal."[62]

He adds that such early affirmation soon develops into a "much needed reaffirmation in the face of the fact that the very experiences which through ritualization give a measure of security also expose the growing being to a

59. Ibid., 87.
60. Ibid., 85.
61. Ibid., 88–89.
62. Ibid., 89.

series of estrangements." Thus, with each successive stage of the life cycle, one encounters a new form of such estrangement. In the first stage, it is the "sense of *separation* and *abandonment* which is never quite overcome by periodical reassurance of familiarity and mutuality."[63]

To this cautionary note, however, Erikson adds that "this first and dimmest affirmation, this sense of a hallowed presence, contributes to mankind's ritual-making a pervasive element which is best called the *numinous.*"[64] He goes on to suggest that "organized religion has the strongest claim to being in charge of the *numinous,*" and he notes certain similarities between the mother-infant and the human-divine encounter: "The believer, by appropriate gestures, confesses his dependence and his childlike faith and seeks, by appropriate offerings, to secure the privilege of being lifted up to the very bosom of the divine which, indeed, may be seen to graciously respond, with the faint smile of an inclined face."[65] Thus, even as the mother lifts up and calls her infant by name, the *numinous* "assures us of *separateness transcended* and yet also a *distinctiveness confirmed.*"[66] And even as the infant, in addition to the fulfillment of oral and sensory needs, wants "to be gazed upon by the primal parent and to respond to the gaze," it is "clear that the religious element in any collective vision responds to this stage."[67] For example, "in the Visconti Hours, where Barbello depicts Maria's death, God in heaven is shown holding in his arms her spirit in the form of a swaddled baby, and 'returning the gaze of Mary's soul.'"[68]

Here, Erikson's reflections on the mother-infant encounter appear to end on a promising note, but only, it would seem, because he introduces the theme of the *numinous,* and observes the potential similarities between this

63. Ibid. (italics original).

64. Ibid., 89.

65. Ibid., 89–90.

66. Ibid., 90.

67. Ibid., 91.

68. Ibid. Erikson misidentifies the painter here as Barbello. He was Belbello da Pavia. *Books of Hours,* popular in the later Middle Ages and the Renaissance, owe their names to the Hours (or Little Office) of the Virgin Mary, which consisted of a sequence of eight short services to be recited in private at intervals during the day. The eight divisions of the Hours of the Virgin were most frequently introduced by scenes from the Christmas story and would end with the Assumption or Coronation of the Virgin. One of the first major Italian *Books of Hours* was the *Visconti Hours,* begun around 1388–1395 for Giangaleazzo Visconti, duke of Milan from 1378–1402, and completed for his second son, Filippo Maria Visconti, duke of Milan from 1412–1447. Belbello contributed to the *Visconti Hours* in the latter period. See Backhouse, *Illumination from Books of Hours;* de Hamel, *A History of Illuminated Manuscripts;* and Walther and Wolf, *The World's Most Famous Illuminated Manuscripts.*

very human encounter and the divine-human encounter as represented in a work of art. Moreover, this very work of art does not depict the mother-infant relationship. Instead, it portrays the *death* of the mother, and the transformation of *her* spirit into the form of a baby. This, then, is a painting not about the beginning of a life, but about its termination. As Erikson himself notes, this painting *"closes* the cycle of the first stage as projected on the whole of existence."[69]

We need to look elsewhere, then, for an artistic expression that offers the sense of hope portrayed in the earlier version of the "greeting ceremonial" but that was eliminated from this new version. We find it, I believe, in the section of *Toys and Reasons* titled "Visions on the Wall."

THE ANNUNCIATION AS PATERNAL BLESSING

Erikson begins "Visions on the Wall," the first section of the third part of the book—the part called "Shared Visions"—by commenting that he began the volume with a discussion of children's play and came to the conclusion that he had no reason to revise the suggestion he made in *Childhood and Society* that play "is only one model of the human proclivity to project onto a circumscribed 'microsphere' an arrangement of figures which dramatizes a moment of fate."[70] Thus, play is a model for the creative vision that later uses a circumscribed field, stage, or blueprint "to gain mastery over what [one] is in the process of becoming by means of evolutionary and historical, technical and personal developments."[71] It was necessary for him to point, however, to "the fear, the anxiety, and the dread which overwhelm man, small or big, when he finds his hoped-for leeway checkmated by inner inhibitions or by blind circumstances."[72]

With this allusion to children's play and the conclusions he drew from it, Erikson says that he will be concerned in this part of the book with examples of such creative vision in a number of fields, but that he will begin with "those closest to me by avocation and vocation, namely, art and psychoanalysis."[73] He refers to a recent paper by Hellmut Wohl in which Wohl "related the formal perspective of Renaissance painting to the

69. Erikson, *Toys and Reasons*, 91 (italics added).

70. Ibid., 111.

71. Ibid.

72. Ibid., 111–12.

73. Ibid., 122.

Christian faith it was to propagate, and both perspective and faith to the need for a vision of hope."[74]

This reference to the need for a vision of hope brings Erikson the central focus of "Visions on the Wall," a painting that he viewed in the De Young Museum in San Francisco. He identifies it as a painting of the annunciation ascribed to an early sixteenth-century Flemish master (whose identity is unknown). It caught his attention because in "all its anonymity and simplicity" it immediately seemed "to unite many of the basic elements of man's playful vision, from its ontogenetic origins in what can be seen to its most existential visionary meaning."[75] Thus, an annunciation "is a visitation announcing the Eternal Prospect, the expectation that the child to be born will be the Child who will forever save in man some portion of what childhood promises: The 'Kingdom.'"[76] He describes the painting:

> There is Mary, then, the to-be-elect. Becoming aware of the angel's presence and glance, she lowers an open book, and we can see that the page she had studied (and a page, too, is a framed visual field) is "illuminated": it shows the biblical theme of a kneeling figure before an apparition of light—is it Moses, the prophet of the old law, as Christ will be of the new? But Mary is almost overshadowed by the presence of the angelic messenger with the commanding glance, who brings the word that within her will be the Child, the guarantor of a New Man. And, indeed, the Holy Spirit, the agent, can be seen floating down on a golden and piercing ray of light.[77]

This painting, then, is notable for its luminosity—the page that Mary had been studying is illuminated, the figure is kneeling before an apparition of light, and the Holy Spirit is floating down on a golden and piercing ray of light.

Behind Mary and the angel, however, there is a "stage" with two door frames opening up on two rooms in the background: "The one behind Mary reveals her bed; the other leads our eyes straight to two further frames: a window opening on the town; and, beside it, an open triptych with rounded panels."[78] Given its brightness, the triptych could easily be mistaken for another window. And it too "shows a kneeling figure before an apparition of light, and we are reminded that to face the east means to be 'oriented' in a

---

74. Ibid.; Wohl, "On Point of View."

75. Erikson, *Toys and Reasons*, 122–23.

76. Ibid., 123.

77. Ibid.

78. Ibid.

world in which the darkness of night always opens up on the dawn."[79] At the center of the painting, as though it were also the center of the universe, is Mary's womb, and this, he suggests, is true of "any woman pregnant with child, and every child newly born: new eyes to be set on the world, a new face to be recognized, a new name becoming the mark of a new 'I,' and (who knows) a new person full of grace, not yet betrayed by the 'human condition.'"[80]

This observation that the painting centers on the expectation of a new birth leads Erikson to suggest that in order to "encompass the total world-view of which this small picture portrays only the promising beginning . . . we would have to include such other paintings as those that might surround an *Annunciation* on the walls of any studio, any church, or any museum."[81] These might include a picture of this very child "as the grown Son of Man, his hand raised in the persuasive gesture of blessing," or a picture of him "crying his last cry, his hands nailed to a cross, in the dreadful night of Golgotha." Another picture might portray "the Son of God benevolently saluting the saved and elect in Heaven" while a companion painting might show him "majestically discarding those to be damned in Hell." Other pictures might "depict one of the crowned heads who with ceremonial splendor have represented the crucified carpenter's son through history," or a "battlefield, hallowed 'in hoc signo,' with the felled infidels piled up in wounded and dying agony."[82]

This presentation of the whole story would locate the original *annunciation* within the much larger panoply of history, and although these additions might seem to decrease the significance of that original vision in Mary's room, the opposite is, in fact the case, for that quiet *annunciation*, "in which the light and spirit, the face and the word come together, derives its persuasiveness from the recurrent cataclysmic dread of total darkness and spiritual death, of facelessness and meaninglessness."[83] Thus, a review of the total worldview of which the *annunciation* may seem a small part brings the viewer back to the small picture with its portrayal of the promising beginning. The recurrent cataclysm portrayed in the larger panoply of scenes recedes behind another recurrence, equally predictable but more persuasive in its essential meaning: the recurrence of the appearance of a child newly born.

79. Ibid.
80. Ibid., 124.
81. Ibid.
82. Ibid.
83. Ibid., 125.

Still, there is more to the small picture of the *annunciation* than a celebrative witness to the birth of every child; for this painting concerns a special child, one who will "forever save in man some portion of what childhood promises."[84] This is the blessing that this painting envisions, the "protection" it promises "against the doom of some primal curse."[85] Thus, it is especially appropriate that this special child declared that the kingdom is of, by, and for the children, and that one may become a certified insider within this kingdom only by giving recognition to the child in oneself and embracing this child as one's very own.

As indicated, Erikson says that he was attracted to this *Annunciation*, ascribed to a Flemish master of the early sixteenth century because it seemed "to unite many of the basic elements of man's playful vision, from its ontogenetic origins in what can be seen to its most existential vision-ary meaning."[86] But could there have been a more personal reason why this painting, "in all its anonymity and simplicity," attracted Erikson's attention? I believe so, and here is why: In noting that this quiet *Annunciation* "de-rives its persuasiveness from the recurrent cataclysmic dread of total dark-ness and spiritual death, of facelessness and meaningless," a dread that it effectively counters with its portrayal of a new and promising beginning, Erikson also points out that

> to be magically convincing, the painter must be in technical command of an art providing a living style for the play with forms. Only then will his work appeal *to the deepest needs of the viewer and confirm faith with demonstrated truth.*[87]

Here, Erikson implies that this anonymous Flemish painter *did* possess the technical skills that enabled this work to have this very appeal for him per-sonally, namely, to address his own deepest needs and to confirm his own faith with demonstrated truth. This painting, then, admirably reflects what art can do for us:

> In gloriously affirming a visible world order as well as the order-liness of vision, art can give an aesthetic glow even to subjects of damnation and despair. It can illuminate the grandest illusions and outshine with realism itself the very lowness of daily life. We

84. Ibid., 123.
85. Ibid., 125.
86. Ibid., 123.
87. Ibid., 125 (italics added).

treasure Rembrandt for illuminating so grandly and so simply the transcendence of everyday hereness.[88]

Specifically, then, the painting appealed to Erikson's deepest needs because it gave "an aesthetic glow" to a subject that could—and perhaps had—evoked personal feelings of "damnation and despair," and it "confirmed faith with demonstrated truth" by illuminating "so simply the transcendence of everyday hereness."

The situation that it portrays is that of a young woman who is pregnant, but her husband (if she has one) is nowhere to be seen. Yet, the painting assures the viewer that this enigma is capable of being placed in a new frame. There is no place or need for a human father if the "agent" of Mary's conception is the Holy Spirit, seen "floating down on a golden and piercing ray of light."[89] Indeed, the very claim that she is pregnant by the Holy Spirit gives credence to the view that her child is "the guarantor of a New Man," a new form of humanity, one more truly reflective of the assurance that we are created in the very image of the divine. Erikson suggests that the figure kneeling before the apparition of light in Mary's book may be Moses, but does not hazard a guess as to the identity of the other kneeling figure in the open triptych. He might be the artist's patron, or even the artist himself.

However, Erikson's observation that by facing east, one may become "oriented in a world in which the darkness of night always opens up to the dawn," suggests that he personally identifies with this kneeling figure, and that he has "faith" in a world that consists of two ever recurring events: the darkness of the night followed by the lightness of the day. Observers of paintings often see themselves in a painting, especially if they are able to identify with one of the figures in the painting. But Erikson has a particular reason for doing so for, as I noted in chapter 1, he was not the son of his mother's estranged husband, and, just as a father is missing in the painting, his biological father's identity remained a mystery.

A textual clue to the fact that Erikson identifies with this painting in a more than casual way is that the painter depicts Mary engaged in studying an open book. As noted in chapter 2, he wrote the following in his autobiographical essay about his mother: "Even as I remember the mother of my early years as pervasively sad, I also visualize her as deeply involved in reading what I later found to have been such authors as Brandes, Kierkegaard, and Emerson, and I could never doubt that her ambitions for me transcended the conventions which she, nevertheless, faithfully served."[90] The scene

88. Ibid., 126.
89. Ibid., 123.
90. Erikson, "'Identity Crisis' in Autobiographic Perspective," 31.

in which Mary has been reading a book may have prompted for Erikson the association of his having watched his mother reading books, and may have evoked the recollection that the sight of her reading had inspired in him a sense of his own promise: that, like Mary's son, he too would "transcend" the conventional life that his mother felt constrained to serve.

These recollections may also explain Erikson's identification of the kneeling figure in Mary's book as Moses, for Moses was the infant who was abandoned by his birth mother so that his life would be spared (Exod 2:1–11). Long before the birth of Jesus, Moses was also a special child of promise. Also significant is Erikson's observation that Mary's book in the painting was an "open book." This suggests that there is no need to protect her "secret," that there is nothing to hide. As Erikson had noted in his earlier reflections on the painting in the *Visconti Hours*, "In religion, vision becomes Revelation."[91] However, this movement in religion from vision to revelation contrasts with Erikson's own situation. As we have seen, his mother sought to pass off his stepfather (whom he saw and lived with) as his natural father (whose identity was never revealed to him), and Erikson's efforts to establish the identity of his biological father were unsuccessful.

In other words, the painting places a potential story of damnation and despair in a new light, for, if one faces east, "the darkness of night always opens up on the dawn."[92] The "stage" on which "all this takes place" has "two doorframes opening up on two rooms in the background." The one directly behind Mary "reveals her bed." The other "*leads our eyes* straight to two further frames": the "window *opening* on the town" and the "*open* triptych."[93] In effect, the viewer's eyes are drawn *away* from the room that contains Mary's bed—the presumed setting where the conception (humanly speaking) occurred—and *toward* the window that opens on the world outside and toward the triptych that could easily be mistaken for another window. Thus, the one room (her bedroom) symbolizes "the darkness of night" and the associated sense of doom, while the other room (with its window opening on the town) signifies the dawn of new life manifested in the birth of a special child of promise. It is to this room of promise and hope that the artist directs our gaze.

Here, especially, is where the artist's technical skill is all-important. Without such "technical command," he may not have succeeded in leading the viewer's gaze toward the room with the open window and open triptych. He may instead have allowed the viewer's eyes to drift to the room that

91. Erikson, *Toys and Reasons*, 91.
92. Ibid., 123.
93. Ibid. (italics added).

reveals Mary's bed, or, alternatively, to shift, ambivalently, back and forth between the two rooms. Instead, the painting appeals "to the deepest needs of the viewer and confirms faith *with demonstrated truth.*"[94]

As a person who had ambitions to become an artist as a young man, and as one whose interest in art continued throughout his life, Erikson had undoubtedly viewed many *Annunciations* before viewing this one.[95] We have seen why this particular *Annunciation* caught his eye, but it is also worth noting that the painter was anonymous, as was Erikson's own biological father. Perhaps, then, this painting served as a kind of paternal blessing that was powerful precisely because the identity of the painter *is* unknown.

In chapters 5 and 6, I noted that the games and dreams that were restorative consisted of two acts. A one-act game or dream leaves the player or the dreamer feeling demoralized and dispirited, but a two-act game or dream manifests a significant sense of ego mastery. In effect, I have made a similar argument here, for the painting of the *Annunciation* presents two doorframes: one of which evokes a sense of damnation and despair, the other of which evokes a sense of promise and hopefulness. Erikson's emphasis in "Seeing Is Hoping" on the two meanings of vision is especially relevant here. As he points out, vision involves not only "the capacity to see what is before us, here and now" but also "the power to foresee what, if one can only believe it, might yet prove to be true in the future."[96] What is seen cannot be denied, but what is foreseen is truly believable.

THE PROMISE OF HOPE

To underscore this sense of promise and hopefulness presented in the *Annunciation*, I will conclude this chapter with a brief discussion of a memorial ceremonial at which Erikson spoke. If the greeting ceremonial occurs at life's beginning, a memorial service often marks its ending. In 1972, the same year that Erikson presented the lectures that eventuated in his book *Toys and Reasons*, he spoke "a few words of testimony" at the memorial service for Mary Sarvis at the United Church of Berkeley in Oakland, California.[97] A social worker and clinician, Mary Sarvis, was a close friend of

---

94. Ibid., 125 (italics added).

95. A collection published by Phaidon Press contains 121 *Anunciations* ranging from a Roman mosaic painted in 432–440 to a 1984 Andy Warhol painting.

96. Erikson, *Toys and Reasons,* 46.

97. Erikson, *A Way of Looking at Things,* 731–32; see also Capps, "The Verbal Portrait."

his. The cause of death is not disclosed, although readers sense from what he says that it was self-inflicted.

The testimonial begins with the observation that he is the oldest speaker at this memorial service, and therefore he feels "doubly the tragic paradox of speaking in memory of a young person who had still so much to give. *So may I be the one who expresses our deepest sympathy to her mother.*"[98] Then he confesses that he cannot help remembering on this occasion how much Mary Sarvis's early memories concerned death: "the death to which newborn Chinese girls were abandoned as too great an economic burden, and her own separation from her Chinese nurse—these are matters which, whatever the facts, we in our work learn to know as the determinants of psychological life and death."[99]

Thus, like Erikson himself, Mary had entered life under "the doom of some primal curse."[100] Both, though for different reasons, were misbegotten children. But, he continued, she "made life" out of these determinants "as vigorously as she could; she *translated her melancholy* into the *passionate wish* to help others and to make deprived and homeless people feel close and at home."[101]

Next, Erikson alludes to the decisiveness with which Mary would say yes and no. When she said yes, "it was with a laughter that shook her and us," and when she said no, "it was not infrequently with four-letter words which shocked some, but even they knew that here was a person who said no affirmatively."[102] When she said no to herself, "we knew it was when she felt that the powers of affirmation were failing her or, for that matter, *us*. Now we can only hope that a power greater than she and we will give her peace in the company of the most humorous of angels—and that He will let her help Him with the melancholy ones."[103] Erikson's testimonial concluded with this expression of eternal hope.

This brief testimony to the life of Mary Sarvis gives a very human touch to his concluding paragraph of the section of *Toys and Reasons* on "Infancy and the Numinous," in which he mentions the painting of God in heaven holding in his arms Mary's spirit in the form of a swaddled baby. The fact that Mary Sarvis bears the same name as the Mary of the *Visconti Hours* is perhaps no more than coincidental. At the same time, one is struck by

98. Erikson, *A Way of Looking at Things*, 732 (italics added).

99. Ibid., 732.

100. Erikson, *Toys and Reasons*, 125.

101. Erikson, *A Way of Looking at Things*, 732.

102. Ibid., 731–32.

103. Ibid., 732.

Erikson's concern in his testimony to Mary Sarvis to link matters of "life and death," and thus, as he says in the *Toys and Reasons* paragraph, to view the act of God in heaven—holding her spirit in his arms as a mother holds her swaddled baby—as one that "closes the cycle of the first stage as projected on the whole of existence."[104]

There is also his reference to Mary Sarvis's experience of being separated from her primary caretaker, apparently after her own parents had abandoned her—experiences that predisposed her to melancholy. Yet, as he notes, "she *translated her melancholy* into the passionate wish to help others," to make them "feel close and at home."[105] Thus, if melancholy is the condition that results from separation and abandonment, one way to counter its effects is to *translate* it into a *passionate wish*; in her case, a passionate wish to help others experience what it means to be "at home" in the world.[106] He also suggests that in spite of her melancholy, or precisely because of it, Mary was given to a laughter "that shook her and us." Additionally, her approach to life was overwhelmingly affirmative, though at times her "powers of affirmation" failed her.

Thus, in these few brief sentences, Erikson has deftly portrayed the melancholic condition not as one of chronic depression and low spirits but as one in which the desire to be "affirmative" is unusually strong, in which the ability to laugh is a "symptom" of the condition, and in which on rare occasions, one's powers of affirmation cannot be summoned forth. In those moments, the melancholy one says no with surprising intensity of feeling. The Mary Sarvis presented in his memorial, then, is the very personification of the resourceful self.

Erikson's desire to create an atmosphere of reconciliation is also evident here. As the oldest one to speak at the memorial service, he was the one who expresses "our deepest sympathy to her mother." We can imagine that he mother felt considerable pain over the circumstances of Mary's childhood, "whatever the facts" may have been. But this is not the time for covert accusations, or for patronizing observations that who among us can claim that we have *not* mistreated our children in one way or another? Rather, as Mary Sarvis lived *her* life, so Erikson's approach is affirmative. In fact, his brief remarks conclude with a benediction: "Now we can only hope that a power greater than she or we will give her peace in the company of the most humorous of angels—and that He will let her help Him with the melancholy ones." This concluding sentence affirms a hope based on "a power" that no

---

104. Erikson, *Toys and Reasons*, 91.
105. Erikson, *A Way of Looking at Things*, 731.
106. See Capps, *At Home in the World*.

human possesses. *He* will lift her up, return the gaze of her soul, and welcome her to the home that was prepared for her ever since she came into
being.

In recognition of the fact that laughter is a "symptom" of melancholy,
the benediction concludes on a note of humor, expressing Erikson's own
passionate wish that when Mary enters her new home, she will live in the
company of "the most humorous of angels and that He will let her help
Him with the melancholy ones." This humorous note contains a playful bit
of irony, that where God is the acknowledged head of the household, there
are some among his brood who are not entirely happy or secure. Erikson
implies that Mary Sarvis, like the Mother of Jesus, will not be without a
vocation in heaven. In fact, her work is just beginning.

Through his testimonial, Erikson has conveyed a message of hope.
That it occurred as a memorial service underscores the fact that the greatest
threat to hope is death. In one sense, there is nothing very remarkable about
this testimonial, for this is what religious leaders have always conveyed when
death has translated a living, sensate human being into a lifeless corpse. But
Erikson's testimony here has particular bearing on his conception of the
whole of life, for it gives particularity to his contention that the first ceremonial encounter—between mother and infant—not only repeats itself in
different forms through all subsequent stages of life, but is also recapitulated
at the last. Thus, the whole conception of life is truly cyclical, as life at the
end returns to its beginnings. Erikson's faith in the circularity of life enables
him to envision not a despairing but a hopeful scenario at life's conclusion.

If Erikson's testimonial for Mary Sarvis was ostensibly a message for
the others in the congregation, and especially a word of sympathy for her
mother, it was also a message for himself. When an older adult is confronted
with the reality of the death of someone much younger than himself, he
is likely to reflect on the fact that fate has mercifully spared him from an
early death. Thus, he finds *himself* confronted by the "tragic paradox" that
an older person is witnessing, and witnessing to, the death of one much
younger than himself. This "tragic paradox," together with the fact that he
shares Mary's melancholic temperament, enables him to identify with her,
and thereby to address himself to the hurt and bewildered child who exists
within himself. In effect, he reassures this child that *his* early sufferings have
proven useful, for he too has managed to translate his own melancholy into
a passionate wish to help others find a way to be at home in the world. His
conception of the life cycle is itself a reflection of this passionate wish.

Epilogue

Erikson's article "The Galilean Sayings and the Sense of 'I'" was published when he was eighty years old.[1] While he lived eleven years after the article was published, it was his last significant writing. An expanded version of *The Life Cycle Completed* was published the following year,[2] but the expansion was entirely the work of his wife Joan, who added three chapters on older adulthood.

Erikson's original plan was to write a book on Jesus. This plan had been stimulated by Thomas Jefferson's interest in the life and sayings of Jesus when Erikson was preparing his 1973 Jefferson Lectures in the Humanities.[3] Erikson was interested in the fact that Jefferson wrote a small book that he called *The Philosophy of Jesus*, which was intended, as Jefferson put it, to introduce American Indians to the "pure and unsophisticated doctrines such as were professed and acted on by the *unlettered* Apostles, the Apostolic Fathers, and the Christians of the first century."[4] Jefferson selected verses from the Gospels that he was convinced were the actual sayings of Jesus—that are

1. Erikson, "The Galilean Sayings and the Sense of 'I.'"

2. Erikson, *The Life Cycle Completed,* expanded version.

3. The lectures were published in 1977 under the title *Dimensions of a New Identity.* If Erikson was reasonably confident that he could write a book on Jesus, his son, Kai, a professor of sociology at Yale University, felt that his father might never complete the book. Having just become editor of the *Yale Review* in 1979, Kai encouraged his father to prepare an essay on Jesus for the journal, as a finished article would be preferable to an incomplete book. Erik was receptive to this idea, and he began to review old notes on Jesus and related subjects for the article, feeling as he did so that "he was working over a concern that interested him since his *Wanderschaft* years, when he made a woodcut of Mary holding the Christ child in her arms" (Friedman, *Identity's Architect,* 449). As he worked on the article, it became clear to him that the theme was that the "presence" of Jesus could enable one to become "present" to oneself. A much shortened version of the essay was published and because it bore the marks of Kai's editing skills, Erikson referred to it as "Kai's version" (ibid., 451).

4. Erikson, *Dimensions of a New Identity,* 45.

"as easily distinguishable as diamonds in a dunghill"—and presented Jesus as Jefferson understood him to be: "his parentage was obscure; his condition poor; his education null; his natural endowments great; his life correct and innocent"; this was a man who "was meek, benevolent, patient, firm, disinterested, and of the sublimest eloquence."[5]

Noting that Jefferson selected the entire Sermon on the Mount from Matthew's gospel but omitted every single miracle, Erikson says that if he might be permitted his own selectivity, there is a story that he would draw attention to even if Jefferson had not included it in his gospel. This is the story in Mark 9:33–38, which tells of how Jesus asked his disciples what they had been disputing about when they were on their way to Capernaum, and they were reluctant to tell him, because they had been discussing the question of who should have the highest rank among them. Jesus proceeded to tell them that whoever wants to be first will be counted as the last of all, as the servant of the others: "Then he took a little child and put it among them and taking it in his arms, he said to them: 'Whoever welcomes one such child in my name welcomes me, and whoever welcomes me welcomes not me but the one who sent me'" (vv. 36–37). Erikson observes:

> A child, not a boy or a girl; a child in its sensory, sensual, and cognitive wholeness, not yet defined in sexual roles and not yet over-defined by economic ones. Such a one has that childlikeness, which to regain in the complexities of adult life, is the beginning of the kingdom. All else is history.[6]

But if Erikson agrees with Jefferson's inclusion of this story, Erikson regrets that Jefferson omitted "all references to Jesus' healing mission."[7] Although "Jesus' own diffidence in regard to his very success in the traditional healer's role" may explain why Jefferson would want to omit all such references in a book intended to present a faithful portrait of Jesus, Erikson "cannot forgive him for omitting the story which we need dearly so as to remain oriented in the history of healing concepts which . . . change with any new identity."[8] To him, "the decisive therapeutic event" in the Gospels is the story in Mark 5:25–35 "of a woman who had lost not only blood for twelve years but also all her money on physicians who had not helped her at all."[9] What especially impresses Erikson about this story is that Jesus felt her

5. Ibid., 45.

6. Ibid., 46.

7. Ibid., 47.

8. Ibid., 48.

9. Ibid.

touch despite the crowd that surrounded him, "and this solely because her faith thus magnetically attracted some of his strength before he quite knew it."[10] Thus, the story is inherently therapeutic, because it conveys the truth that the resources of the supplicant activated the resources of the healer. As Erikson puts it, "There could be no doubt, then, that it was her faith in his mission that had made her whole."[11]

Erikson returned to these themes of the child and the healing process in "The Galilean Sayings and the Sense of 'I.'" He draws attention to the story of the hemorrhaging woman as illustrative of Jesus's "extensive capacity to address the wide variety of groups found in Galilee, and yet to be, potentially, in contact with each individual considered."[12] He also makes reference to Jesus's sayings that focus on childhood, and takes special note of the episode (Mark 10:14–16) in which "the disciples rebuked some people who brought their children ('even infants,' according to Luke) to Jesus so that they might be touched by him."[13] But Jesus indignantly rebuked his disciples, saying, "Let the children come to me, do not hinder them; for to such belongs the kingdom of God. Truly, I say to you, whoever does not receive the kingdom of God like a child shall not enter it." Mark adds, "And he took them in his arms and blessed them, laying his hands upon them." Erikson cites this story "as the first of a series of intergenerational expositions, the most fully carried through being the parable of the Prodigal Son."[14] Of this parable, Erikson notes that it portrays a father greeting "his delinquent young son's repentance as a return from death," and thus as a reminder to us "of all the maladjustments that can blight childhood."[15]

Thus, the saying "Unless you turn and become like children, you will never enter the kingdom of heaven" (Matt 18:3) is "a total affirmation of the radiant potentials of childhood," and it "is the more astonishing as today we consider ourselves the discoverers of childhood, its defenders against all those history-wide negative attitudes which permitted proud and righteous as well as thoughtless adults to treat children as essentially weak or bad and in dire need of being corrected by stringent methods, or as expendable even to the point of being killed."[16] Erikson adds that a "detrimental counterpart of

10. Ibid., 49.

11. Ibid.

12. Erikson, "The Galilean Sayings and the Sense of 'I,'" 327.

13. Ibid., 348. The quotations from Mark that follow in this paragraph are quoted by Erikson from the RSV.

14. Ibid., 348–49.

15. Ibid., 349.

16. Ibid.

these attitudes is, of course, a more modern sentimentalization of childhood as an utterly innocent condition to be left pampered and unguided." In light of these and other trends, "Jesus' saying seems simply revolutionary," not only because of its "affirmation of the radiant potentials of childhood," but also because "he refers to an adult condition in which childlikeness has not been destroyed, and in which a potential return to childlike trust has not been forestalled."[17]

Before taking up the parable of the Prodigal Son, Erikson mentions several other "intergenerational sayings" in the Gospels, and suggests that they confirm the *continuity* of the stages of development, thus communicating to the adult that "the step of faith expected of him" does not demand "his leaving the child, or, indeed, his youth behind him: on the contrary, only the continuation into maturity of true childlikeness guarantees his faith," a faith that, as he has emphasized in his own writings, "developed in the interaction of the budding *I* with the 'Primal Other,' namely, the maternal person (or persons)."[18]

In his reflections on the parable of the Prodigal Son Erikson notes that the two distinct parts of the parable "make us alternately sympathize with the lost son and with the older son who was so concerned over all the excessive attention to his younger brother."[19] But then he adds, "Yet the parable is so evenly constructed that we can end up only realizing that both brothers are at odds within us, too." This observation, which recalls our earlier discussion (in chapter 6) of the biblical story of Jacob wrestling with the stranger, has particular relevance to the emphasis of this book on the melancholy and resourceful selves as mirror images of one another.

Also, Erikson's observations about the father's role in the story has an unexpected bearing on our consideration throughout the book of the role of the mother in the formation of the melancholy self. Expanding on his observation that the parable is so evenly divided between the two brothers, Erikson notes that

> the Abba was steadfast in loving both these sons—so different in familial status and in personality. Almost like a mother, some readers may be tempted to say, and, indeed, as one reviews this parable's theme of the healing of the generational process, one cannot help asking: was there, in this earthly vision of the

17. Ibid.
18. Ibid.
19. Ibid., 354.

comparison, no mother, either dead or alive? And if alive, was she not called to say hello, too?[20]

Still, "a parable is not a case history or even history," and as for the implied comparison of the father with God, we need to remember "that in all the masculinity dictated by the patriarchal 'system' and the rules of language, the dominating quality of the deity was that of a pervasive spirit, out of bounds for any personal characterization: 'I am that I am.'"[21] We also, of course, need to keep in mind that Jesus himself identified the deity as his Father.[22] In any event, Erikson suggests that

> the parable's meaning, in its patriarchal and monotheistic set-
> ting, is the father's overall parental care and above all his forgive-
> ness which permits him to take chances with the lost ones—that
> is, to take chances with those who took chances—so as to let
> them find both themselves and him. The story of the Prodigal
> Son thus reaffirms generational and existential continuity, con-
> firmed by the joy of table fellowship.[23]

Noting that this finding of themselves and of the father involves "gain-ing their own identity in the very fulfillment of their intergenerational tasks within their cultural and economic matrix," Erikson asks, parenthetically, whether this "matrix" is "the missing mother?" This "matrix/mother" as-sociation recalls his citation in *Young Man Luther* of Luther's view that one's rebirth involves "surrender to God the Father; but it also means to be reborn *ex matrice scripturae nati*, out of the matrix of the scriptures," which prompts Erikson to suggest that "'Matrix' is as close as such a man's man will come to saying 'mater.'"[24] Erikson notes that when Luther was explicitly teaching on the merits of passivity—of surrendering oneself to God—he concluded that "a lecturer should feed his audience as a mother suckles her child";

20. Ibid., 355.

21. Ibid., 355–56. It is noteworthy that in his initial discussion of the sense of "I" in *Identity, Youth, and Crisis,* Erikson suggested that inasmuch as the "'I' means noth-ing less than that I am alive, that I *am* life, [the] counterplayer of the 'I' therefore can be, strictly speaking, only the deity who has lent this halo to a mortal and is Himself endowed with an eternal numinous certified by all 'I's' who acknowledge this gift. That is why God, when Moses asked Him who should he say had called him, answered: 'I AM THAT I AM.'" Erikson, "The Galilean Sayings and the Sense of 'I,'" 220.

22. In Capps, *Jesus: A Psychological Biography,* I suggest that Jesus's identification of the deity as his father was due, at least in part, to the fact that he, like Erikson, did not know the identity of his biological father. See especially ch. 6, "The Hidden Years," 129–63.

23. Erikson, "The Galilean Sayings and the Sense of 'I,'" 356.

24. Erikson, *Young Man Luther,* 208.

and Erikson adds, "I think that in the Bible Luther at last found a mother whom he could acknowledge: he could attribute to the Bible a generosity to which he could open himself, and which he could pass on to others, at last a mother's son."[25]

Erikson's suggestion—that the cultural and economic matrix in which the sons (and brothers) of the Prodigal Son parable fulfill their generational tasks is the "missing mother"—points to the fact that the infant-mother relationship is the primary context in which the newborn comes to be a participant in the world. But the "missing mother" may also be understood, in light of Freud's "Mourning and Melancholia" essay, as the mother that the growing boy loses as the mother helps him to separate from her so that he may identify with his father and the patriarchal society that he will inhabit in the subsequent stages of his life.

Yet if we take seriously Erikson's cautionary note that "a parable is not a case history or even history," then we will not be content with these more extraneous theories concerning the "missing mother," and will focus our attention on the fact that the parable of the Prodigal Son was a story that Jesus told to a group of listeners, and this may prompt us to ask: "Is Jesus himself the missing mother?" After all, Erikson suggests earlier in his essay that "one cannot help noticing, on Jesus' part, an unobtrusive integration of maternal and paternal tenderness."[26] Who better to tell a story of the tenderness of the father than the one who also possessed and exemplified the tenderness of the mother?

Thus, even as we saw in chapter 6 that the dream is the Mother, so we see in the parable of the Prodigal Son that the mother is fully present. She is not missing, therefore, for she is the one who has brought this intergenerational group together—like a mother who nurtures her hungry and anxious infant—and tells them a story of how they can find themselves and one another. As we listen to the story—a story about "the paternal voice of guiding conscience"—our eyes are on the storyteller, whose "affirmative face" reassures his listeners of their "unconditional acceptance." But as they gaze upon his face, they see something more: They see in him the mirror image of their own "pure self," the self "no longer sick with a conflict between right and wrong, not dependent on providers, and not dependent on guides to reason and reality."[27] He is the self-reconciled one, the one who was able to heal others because he was not sick with a conflict between his various selves.

25. Ibid.
26. Erikson, "The Galilean Sayings and the Sense of 'I,'" 349.
27. Erikson, *Young Man Luther*, 264.

And this very image of Jesus brings us back to the stories he told about children and the need to become as children again. So in light of the discussion in this book, our reference to Jesus here in the epilogue draws our attention to the childhood origins of our resourceful selves, and specifically to the virtues or human strengths of hope, will, purpose, and competence. Perhaps Erikson's insistence on including in his essay on Jesus a healing story in which the resources of the supplicant activated the resources of the healer gives special meaning to Erikson's concluding observation in his lecture on the human strengths and the cycle of generations: that the attempt to describe the emergence of these human strengths is, in essence, "the study of [the] miracles of everyday life."[28]

28. Ibid., 157.

References

Agnes, Michael, ed. *Webster's New World College Dictionary.* Foster City, CA: IDG, 2001.

Backhouse, Janet. *Illumination from Books of Hours.* London: British Library, 2004.

Brilliant, Richard. *Portraiture.* Cambridge: Harvard University Press, 1991.

Bryson, Norman. *Looking at the Overlooked: Four Essays on Still Life Painting.* Cambridge: Harvard University Press, 1990.

Capps, Donald. *At Home in the World: A Study in Psychoanalysis, Religion, and Art.* Eugene, OR: Cascade Books, 2013.

———. *Jesus: A Psychological Biography.* 2000. Reprinted, Eugene, OR: Wipf & Stock, 2010.

———. *Men, Religion, and Melancholia.* New Haven: Yale University Press, 1997.

———. *Pastoral Care: A Thematic Approach.* 1979. Reprinted, Eugene, OR: Wipf & Stock, 2003.

———. "The Verbal Portrait: Erik H. Erikson's Contribution to Psychoanalytic Discourse." *Journal of Religion and Health* 50 (2011) 880–98.

Coles, Robert. *Erik H. Erikson: The Growth of His Work.* Boston: Little, Brown, 1970.

Collins, Bradley I. *Leonardo, Psychoanalysis & Art History: A Critical Study of Psychobiographical Approaches to Leonardo da Vinci.* Psychosocial Issues. Evanston, IL: Northwestern University Press, 1997.

De Hamel, Christopher. *A History of Illuminated Manuscripts.* London: Phaidon, 1997.

De Santillana, Giorgio. *The Age of Adventure: The Renaissance Philosophers.* Boston: Houghton Mifflin, 1957.

Erikson, Erik H. *A Way of Looking at Things: Selected Papers from 1930 to 1980.* Edited by Stephen Schlein. New York: Norton, 1987.

———. *Childhood and Society.* New York: Norton, 1950.

———. *Childhood and Society.* 2nd ed. New York: Norton, 1963.

———. *Gandhi's Truth: On the Origins of Militant Nonviolence.* New York: Norton, 1969.

———. "The Galilean Sayings and the Sense of 'I.'" *Yale Review* 70 (1981) 321–62.

———. *Identity and the Life Cycle.* Selected papers, with a historical introduction by David Rapaport. New York: International Universities Press, 1959.

———. *Identity and the Life Cycle.* Rev. ed. New York: Norton, 1980.

———. "'Identity Crisis' in Autobiographic Perspective." In *Life History and the Historical Moment,* 17–47. New York: Norton, 1975.

———. *Identity, Youth, and Crisis.* New York: Norton, 1968.

———. *Insight and Responsibility: Lectures on the Ethical Implications of Psychoanalytic Insight.* New York: Norton, 1964.

———. *The Life Cycle Completed: A Review.* New York: Norton, 1982.

———. *Toys and Reasons: Stages in the Ritualization of Experience.* New York: Norton, 1977.

———. *Young Man Luther: A Study in Psychoanalysis and History.* New York: Norton, 1958.

Erikson, Erik H., et al. *Vital Involvement in Old Age: The Experience of Old Age in Our Time.* New York: Norton, 1986.

Evans, Richard I. *Dialogue with Erik Erikson.* Dialogues with Notable Contributors to Personality Theory 3. New York: Harper & Row, 1967.

Freud, Sigmund. *Beyond the Pleasure Principle.* Translated by James Strachey. Bantam Classic. New York: Bantam, 1959.

———. "A Childhood Recollection from Goethe's *Dichtung und Wahrheit.*" In *On Creativity and the Unconscious,* edited by Benjamin Nelson, 111–21. Harper Torchbooks. New York: Harper, 1958.

———. *Dora: An Analysis of a Case of Hysteria.* Edited by Philip Rieff. The Collected Papers of Sigmund Freud 4. New York: Collier, 1963.

———. "The Dynamics of the Transference." In *Therapy and Technique,* edited by Philip Rieff, 105–15. The Collected Papers of Sigmund Freud 3. New York: Collier, 1963.

———. "Family Romances." In *The Sexual Enlightenment of Children,* edited by Philip Rieff, 41–45. The Collected Papers of Sigmund Freud 5. New York: Collier, 1963.

———. "Further Recommendations in the Technique of Psychoanalysis: Observations on Transference-love." In *Therapy and Technique,* edited by Philip Rieff, 167–79. The Collected Papers of Sigmund Freud 3. New York: Collier, 1963.

———. "Humor." In *Character and Culture,* edited by Philip Rieff, 263–69. The Collected Papers of Sigmund Freud 9. New York: Collier, 1963.

———. *The Interpretation of Dreams.* Translated by James Strachey. A Discus Book. New York: Avon, 1965.

———. *Introductory Lectures on Psychoanalysis.* Translated by James Strachey. New York: Norton, 1966.

———. *Jokes and Their Relation to the Unconscious.* Translated by Alan Tyson. New York: Norton, 1960.

———. *Leonardo da Vinci and a Memory of His Childhood.* Translated by Alan Tyson. New York: Norton, 1964.

———. *The Complete Letters of Sigmund Freud to Wilhelm Fliess, 1887–1904,* Translated and edited by Jeffrey Moussaieff Masson. Cambridge, MA: Belknap, 1985.

———. "Medusa's Head." In *Writings on Art and Literature,* edited by Werner Hamacher and David E. Welbery, 264–65. Meridian, Crossing Aesthetics. Stanford: Stanford University Press, 1997.

———. "Mourning and Melancholia." In *General Psychological Theory: Papers on Metapsychology,* editor by Philip Rieff, 164–79. The Collected Papers of Sigmund Freud 6. New York: Collier, 1963.

———. *New Introductory Lectures on Psycho-analysis.* Translated and edited by James Strachey. New York: Norton, 1989.

———. "The Sexual Enlightenment of Children." In *The Sexual Enlightenment of Children,* edited by Philip Rieff, 17–24. The Collected Papers of Sigmund Freud 5. New York: Collier, 1963.

———. "The Theme of the Three Caskets." In *On Creativity and the Unconscious*, edited by Benjamin Nelson, 63–75. Harper Torchbooks. New York: Harper, 1958.

———. *Three Essays on the Theory of Sexuality*. Edited and translated by James Strachey. New York: Basic Books, 2000.

———. "The 'Uncanny.'" In *On Creativity and the Unconscious*, edited by Benjamin Nelson, 122–61. Harper Torchbooks. New York: Harper, 1958.

Friedman, Lawrence J. *Identity's Architect: A Biography of Erik H. Erikson*. New York: Scribner, 1999.

Frost, Robert. *The Poetry of Robert Frost: The Collected Poems, Complete and Unabridged*. Edited by Edward Connery Lathem. New York: Holt, 1975.

Gay, Peter. *Freud: A Life for Our Time*. New York: Norton, 1988.

Hendrick, Ives. "Work and the Pleasure Principle." *Psychoanalytic Quarterly* 12 (1943) 311–29.

James, William. *The Varieties of Religious Experience: A Study in Human Nature*. Mineola, NY: Dover, 2002.

Jung, Carl Gustav. *Answer to Job*. Translated by R. F. C. Hull. The Collected Works of C. G. Jung. Bollingen Series. Princeton: Princeton University Press, 1969.

Kristeva, Julia. *Black Sun: Depression and Melancholia*. Translated by Leon S. Roudiez. New York: Columbia University Press, 1989.

Leonardo da Vinci. *Leonardo on Painting: An Anthology of Writings by Leonardo da Vinci with a Selection of Documents Relating to His Career as an Artist*. Edited by Martin Kemp and translated by Martin Kemp and Margaret Walker. New Haven: Yale University Press, 1989.

Maïdani-Gerard, Jean-Pierre. "Léonard de Vinci, Sigmund Freud: L'application de la Psychanalyse á Une Oeuvre du Passé." Diss. in the U.E.R. de Sciences Humaines Cliniques, Université de Paris VII, 1985.

Osterrieth, Paul Alexandre, et al. *Le Problème des Stades en Psychologie de L'enfant*. Symposium de l'Association de Psychologie Scientifique de Langue Francaise. Bibliothèque scientifique internationale. Sciences humaines. Section psychologie. Geneva: Presses Universitaires de France, 1955.

Otto, Rudolf. *The Idea of the Holy*. Translated by John W. Harvey. New York: Oxford University Press, 1958.

Phaidon Press. *Annunciation*. London: Phaidon, 2000.

Piers, Maria W., ed. *Play and Development: A Symposium*. New York: Norton, 1972.

Riley, Charles A., II. *Color Codes: Modern Theories of Color in Philosophy, Painting and Architecture, Literature, Music, and Psychology*. Hanover, NH: University Press of New England, 1995.

Smee, Sabastian. *Lucian Freud*. Basic Art Series. Cologne: Taschen, 2007.

Snow, Edward. *A Study of Vermeer*. Revised and enlarged ed. Berkeley: University of California Press, 1994.

Stockard, Charles S. *The Physical Basis of Personality*. New York: Norton, 1931.

Walther, Ingo F., and Norbert Wolf. *The World's Most Famous Illuminated Manuscripts*. Cologne: Taschen, 2001.

Wohl, Hellmut. "On Point of View." *Boston University Journal* 20 (1972) 16–21.

Wolfenstein, Martha. *Children's Humor: A Psychological Analysis*. Glencoe, IL: Free Press, 1954.

Index